SUPER MEDIA

COMMUNICATION AND HUMAN VALUES

In this series

Media and Politics in Latin America:
The Struggle for Democracy
edited by Elizabeth Fox

Mass Media Religion:
The Social Sources of the Electronic Church
by Stewart M. Hoover

World Families Watch Television
edited by James Lull

The Mass Media and Village Life: An Indian Study
by Paul Hartmann with B. R. Patil and Anita Dighe

Super Media: A Culture Studies Approach
by Michael R. Real

Television and Women's Culture
edited by Mary Ellen Brown

Redeeming Modernity: Contradictions in Media Criticism
by Joli Jensen

SUPER MEDIA

A Cultural Studies Approach

Michael R. Real

SAGE PUBLICATIONS
The International Professional Publishers
Newbury Park   London   New Delhi

For information address:

SAGE Publications, Inc.
2111 West Hillcrest Drive
Newbury Park, California 91320

SAGE Publications Ltd.
28 Banner Street
London EC1Y 8QE
England

SAGE Publications India Pvt. Ltd.
M-32 Market
Greater Kailash I
New Delhi 110 048 India

Printed in the United States of America

Library of Congress Cataloging-in-Publication Data

Real, Michael R., 1940—
    Super media.

    (Communication and human values)
    Bibliography: p.
    Includes index.
    1. Mass media. 2. Popular culture. 3. Mass media—
United States.   I. Title.   II. Series: Communication and
human values (Newbury Park, Calif.)
P91.R38   1989   302.2'34   88-35645
ISBN 0-8039-3313-4
ISBN 9-8039-3314-2 (pbk.)

THIRD PRINTING, 1990

Contents

Preface

Super media—a strange phrase, almost a compound word. *Super* has a comic-book sensationalism about it, evoking power and prominence. *Media* can be everyday familiar and yet elusively complex. Super media—something we all know and experience first-hand. But do we understand the experience? Can we control it? What does it mean, not just individually but culturally and globally?

Super media are sounds we wake to from a clock radio. They ride with us in the car. In office and classroom, they are the sources of information. They occupy our home as an electronic window and printed page. Super media bring us the news, scare us, relax us, and at times inspire us. We cannot live without them, and we sometimes fear we cannot live with them.

As the subtitle indicates, this book proposes a cultural studies approach. *Cultural studies* is another two-word phrase of immense complexity. Constructed with building blocks from a half-dozen disciplines and many countries, this ascending tower has in recent years attracted many disciples and generated unusual excitement. At one moment cultural studies stands transparent with immediacy and common sense; at another it seems to recede, dense and profound. This preface provides no naively brief one-sentence snapshot. It takes a book and more to characterize the approach. And, necessarily, these pages provide *a* cultural studies approach, not *the* approach. Unanimity is neither yet present nor finally desired by the constructors of cultural studies.

The central question is, What kind of culture are we creating? For the individual this means, What kind of personal values, lifestyle, and world view am I constructing through my communication? For the society it means, Are super media contributing everything they might to this task and celebration we call life? Cultural studies suggests tools for answering these questions.

We all, from the preschooler to the postdoctoral scholar, come to super media with our own ambivalent love/hate feelings toward them.

Why? What is there that creates such contradictions? We love, enjoy, and look forward to television, movies, music, reading, but we also become disappointed and disgusted with them. All too often, we find them boring, banal, violent, exploitive; we flip the dial or the pages despairingly. This ambivalence, these contradictions are genuine and provide a starting point for engaging the dialectic stitched into the very fabric of super media.

But these ambivalences are not toward something "out there." The loved and hated media become part of our very selves. The media tell us who we are; they give us identity. They tell us what we want to be; they give us aspirations. They tell us how to get that way; they give us technique. And they tell us how to feel that way even when we do not; they give us escape (see Mills, 1956). Our identity and centeredness evolve in interactions face-to-face and through media, and these inter-actions connect us with structures of power. Thus, super media qualita-tively change the way consciousness, identity, and centeredness emerge and operate today. Our love/hate ambivalence runs into the very core of our being.

This formidable influence is expressed not only in abstract concepts and theories but also in the immediate experience of media. The point of contact between person and media text creates a complex charge that leaps between the two. That immediate experience is a distillation, a compression containing every element of super media. Therefore, we cannot talk only of the literature *about* super media, the in-group debates of scholars—we must enter into and examine super media *as experienced*. Hence the immediate value of the case-study method.

The chapters of the book introduce different modes of analysis. Chapter One considers the phenomenological and historical experience of super media. Then the cultural studies approach is introduced as a metadiscipline (Chapter Two), together with subdisciplines of empiri-cism (Chapter Three), structuralism (Chapters Four and Five), criticism (Chapters Six and Seven), and ritual (Chapter Eight). Chapter Nine looks back at super media, draws conclusions, and offers suggestions.

For those new to the study of information and communication media, this work provides introductions, overviews, and concrete case studies. The case studies test and extend theories and concepts and give to theory a living quality, ideally making even complex and subtle con-cepts relatively accessible to any thoughtful individual. Those curious about popular culture, journalism, literature, sociology, history, and related disciplines, as well as mass communications, should find relevance and stimulation in these pages.

For those more expert in communication, these pages offer something of a reinterpretation and extension of what is known. The conceptual and theoretical information represents a wide range of research and criticism of media. Cultural studies is compared and contrasted with more conventional behavioral and pluralist insights, a blending of approaches that is almost as uncommon as it is obvious.

The examination of super media in these pages aims at both substance and accessibility. These aims dictate certain emphases.

First, in order to draw from the widest range of possible examples and previous research, *all* media of communication form the subject matter, not merely one medium such as television or film, or one class of media such as electronic or print, or one scale of media such as mass or specialized information sources. Second, in order to consider content as well as channels of super media, the *popular culture* expressed in media is examined together with the technical means of dissemination. Third, in order not to eliminate potential sources of knowledge and insight, the academic perspective employed here is *interdisciplinary,* ranging across the social sciences, the arts, and the humanities, rather than utilizing only one set of methods, concepts, and theories. This breadth, of course, characterizes cultural studies. Fourth, a media-*user* point of view dominates, occasionally with a policy emphasis, rather than the preprofessional training point of view common in many media texts for journalism or broadcasting majors. Everyone in modern culture uses media, whether he or she ever produces media or not, and the relationship between the person and super media deserves careful attention as an essential part of the individual's life in contemporary society. Media do not simply present cultural products for consumption; they provide much of the stuff of everyday life through which we construct meaning and organize our existence.

To maximize their accessibility, cases and examples have been selected for their familiarity to an extremely broad range of readers. They include the most widely available expressions of culture in history: the Olympics, superpower politics, Oscar-winning films, prime-time television, and other transnational cases.

The cases allow readers to draw upon self-knowledge but place it within an international context. The cases and examples have a United States bent, primarily because United States scholars have a responsibility first to come to terms with our own American culture and media.

But insofar as possible, this United States emphasis is placed in an international context with special attention to the experiences of the entire English-speaking world and beyond. It can be frustrating to read a careful dissection of a cultural product with which one is personally unfamiliar—a rare Indian film, a local British television program, a provincial Australian political debate—from an inaccessible place or time. Instead, the examples and cases examined here reflect more common and widely shared media experiences. Indeed, one of the most challenging qualities of super media is the extent to which a relatively consistent single transnational lifestyle has emerged, associated with transnational corporations, information flow, products, commercials, and media. It is from this vast wealth of illustrative data that the super media case studies here have been drawn. And the search for central tendencies, or "dominant ideology," in those cases and in super media as a whole has directed the exploration.

The brief "scenarios" introducing and concluding chapters also attempt to flesh out the meaning of those chapters. These scenarios engage the imagination of readers in order to stimulate their reasoning as they tackle questions of super media, a technique of grounding employed throughout the popular super media industries themselves.

What sets this book on super media apart? The subject matter is not unique. Tens of thousands of books and research reports have been written about media of communication. Stated briefly, what is original is the *perspective* and the *synthesis*. The perspective is achieved by scrambling up on top of the best that has been researched and thought about the media of communication that so inhabit our lives. From that vantage point, the more important can be separated from the less important and highlighted accordingly. The synthesis is sought by connecting this perspective with media experiences that touch people across national boundaries and invade their everyday lives.

Thanks are due to many persons and opportunities for assistance in the development of *Super Media*. Materials in these pages have been worked up under a variety of conditions.

The theoretical and research information on media is a thorough reworking of major review pieces for *American Quarterly,* the *Journal of Communication,* and *Critical Studies in Mass Communication,* whose editors, Michael Marsden, George Gerbner, Robert Avery, and Clifford Christians, deserve thanks for those opportunities. Likewise, different versions of some of the case studies first appeared in *Media*

Development (from London), *Newsday* (from Long Island), *Unilag Communication Review* (from Nigeria), and other scattered sources, whose editors also deserve thanks for inspiration and opportunity.

The Olympic media analysis is indebted to the international research project developed under a modest grant from UNESCO in Paris. The Academy Awards study took shape from access to members and staff of the Academy of Motion Picture Arts and Sciences in Los Angeles and from writings for the *San Diego Union* and the Ablex review *Popular Culture and Media Events.*

Earlier versions of these materials were presented in Prague, New Delhi, Rome, Barcelona, Calgary, Mexico City, Honolulu, Boston, New Orleans, and other stimulating locations. Information and feedback from colleagues on those and other occasions make this work more indebted to others than can ever be adequately acknowledged. Especially valuable has been participation in the International Association for Mass Communication Research, the International Communication Association, and other scholarly bodies with a transnational focus.

Not only editors, publishers, and colleagues but in some cases co-authors helped develop cases used in this book. Grateful thanks are due Robert Mechikoff, David Goldstein, Patsy Winsor, Jonathan Jerald, Carroll Parrot Blue, and Chris Hassett for their original research and drafts of materials modified for this book. In the past two decades, faculty colleagues at San Diego State University and the University of California at San Diego, such as Herbert Schiller and Ken Jones, have been helpful, stimulating, and delightful beyond all reasonable expectations. Thousands of students, both undergraduate and graduate, during that same time have also been appreciated as fellow intellectual laborers and friends. Robert White, director of the Centre for Communication and Culture in London and editor of this series, has been the special support and prod in putting this work together. If he were any more proactive in his role, he would have to be made a coauthor, for his contribution is substantial and is deeply appreciated. George and Sara Miller McCune, Ann West, and others at Sage also deserve thanks. My family members, especially my wife and daughter, Paula and Marisa, are treasured above all else in this, as in every, endeavor. And finally, all those whose work is so abundantly pillaged and referenced in these pages are herewith thanked for making this work both possible and, to the extent it is such, successful.

Super media, our constant companion. We know them and love them, and we do not know them and hate them. Super media shape us, and we shape them. Yet, whatever hard judgments may have to be rendered against aspects of super media, it still remains that life today would not be anywhere near as much fun without them. May your decoding of this exploration be a pleasurable, provocative, and productive experience.

1

Our Media, Ourselves:
Identity, Culture, and the Experience of Super Media

> Once upon a time there were the mass media, and they were wicked, of course, and there was a guilty party. Then there were the virtuous voices that accused the criminals. And Art (ah, what luck!) offered alternatives, for those who were not prisoners of the mass media.
>
> Well, it's all over. We have to start from the beginning, asking one another what's going on.
>
> —Umberto Eco (1986, p. 150)

Media today saturate our daily lives. Signs on every side remind us that contemporary life is inconceivable without modern means of communications. From Bangkok to Brussels, offices and factories burst with files, typewriters, computers, note pads, and other technologies old and new for creating, processing, storing, and transmitting information. Homes process data from cookbooks, junk mail, stereos, newsweeklies, video, telephones, and other "extensions of humans," as McLuhan (1964) called media. Cities and countries, individuals and groups, are defined and interconnected through their complex networks of voice, data, and image exchange.

Media serve as the central nervous system of modern society. The search to understand these media draws us into a search for the center of all that is life in the late 20th century.

Our media, ourselves.

Concern for our future raises the question: How can we, as human beings and members of communities, consciously understand and direct the systems of influence and information that hold us together in a mediated culture and express our collective identity?

The Prominence of Media in Daily Life

Media are everywhere. The working life of many depends on media. Estimates place 50 to 80 percent of the work force in advanced societies in the "information sector." Leisure relies on media. Americans spend more time watching television than in any other activity except work and sleeping. Whether urban or rural, wealthy or working class, we stay home and listen to the radio, read the newspaper, and watch television, or we go out to consume foods, cultural events, ball games, and entertainments publicized in the mass media.

Social trends rise and fall with super media. Fads initiated by a movie or a rock star sweep through regions and continents with little regard for race, ethnicity, or country of national origin. Those who resist one popular media-initiated fad often do so only by holding tight to another. News readers use their newspapers and magazines to resist the wasteland of prime-time television. And when elite fashion trends from Paris trickle down through expensive publications into mass advertising and popular consumption, would-be cowboys—urban and otherwise—avoid such Brie-and-Chablis tastes by keeping their truck radios tuned to the six-pack culture of country and western music.

Media provide personal as well as collective means of communication. The telephone and computer are prominent specialized media, operating alongside the mass media. Where the telephone is widely available, it becomes essential to maintaining friendships, conducting business or politics, and even engaging in criminal activities. Computers enable us to communicate with ourselves (a curious achievement) as well as with friends, colleagues, machines, and completely anonymous others. Telephones and computers also play crucial roles in monitoring and directing public agencies and public life. Even those with no personal access to computers nevertheless find their lives computer-recorded by schools, police, credit raters, employers, licensing agencies, and countless nameless others. The poor appear as a statistic in United Nations data on Third World migrants; the rich appear in the account sheets of Swiss banks.

Media events surround and affect us with a pervasiveness impossible to avoid. At the moment of a royal wedding or a presidential funeral, the majority of a national population follows exactly the same activity at exactly the same time, a small number by being there in person, a huge number via media. During Super Bowl halftimes, officials worry about local water systems as entire populations engage simultaneously in the same excretory biological activity. Olympic Games, World C football, superpower summits, large-scale disasters—the transnational "media events" of our time—extend the uniformity of audience behavior to an international scale. These events are the tribal campfire around which the human race celebrates its common heroes, triumphs, defeats, myths, values, and hopes. Popular media today operate on a scale of inclusiveness unimaginable in earlier generations. The earth's population is drawn ineluctably toward universal media dependency.

On a basic phenomenological level, we are surrounded by the existential experience of super media in daily life.

Our media, ourselves.

Media and the Development of Personal Identity and Consciousness

Media penetrate daily life, creating the environment where identities are formed. Personal experience combines with media experience as we construct our individual lives under the directing influence of powerful institutions. Media interconnect personal lives and public activities (Gumpert & Cathcart, 1986) and shape our consciousness.

From his or her earliest moments in the crib, a child begins to form a sense of personal identity, an emerging consciousness of existence, life, and self, through interactions on three levels. First, the child interacts with persons—parents, siblings, relatives, neighbors, eventually classmates, and a range of face-to-face acquaintances. Second, the child interacts with the environment—the crib, the room, the house or apartment, the neighborhood, grass and trees, pets, and nature in general. But third, the child also interacts with stories read to him or her, with pictures shown, with "Sesame Street" and Smurfs, with Disney characters and Fisher-Price toys, with E.T. and Wonder Woman—gradually and increasingly with all of that vast second-hand experience of television, books, advertisements, movie posters, magazines, fashion, popular music, newspapers, radio, cassettes, phones, computers, and the rest of contemporary super media.

These mediated experiences influence the child's developing sense of personal identity in the same ways in which interaction with other persons and the environment does. The mediated culture surrounds him or her as the larger frame of reference, just as a small town might have _of reference in 18th-century rural America or the _night have provided the frame in the Middle Ages. _ercise influence on the child, not only directly but also _playing a role in shaping those people with whom he or _—family, peers, and eventually fellow workers and politi- cal _ _cial leaders. Super media also play a role in shaping the physical environment with which the child interacts—its architecture and systems of transportation, surrounded by all the products created in the image and likeness of super media. Together with people and nature, the super-mediated culture becomes the individual's psychic and social context, from birth to death.

Media provide role models for behavior. Biographies in books and films move people to imitate Gandhi, Mozart, Patton, or Pee Wee Herman. Olympic heroes and sports celebrities are first motivated as children by media role models. On the negative side, John Lennon's assassin was motivated by the novel *Catcher in the Rye,* and President Reagan's was driven by his obsession with Jodie Foster and the movie *Taxi Driver.* And the modern terrorist would not exist without media exposure (Elliot, Murdock, & Schlesinger, 1986). More broadly, all of us find elements of our validity and connectedness in the media. Our individual identities blend into media identities. This is just as true when the urban professional plans and fantasizes according to what she reads in the *Times* as it is when a factory machinist moves with the rhythms of Rambo or reggae (Lull, 1987) or a homemaker sighs with the heroines of romantic fiction (Radway, 1984). Group identity, too, waxes or wanes with media confirmation. Consumer activism, gray power, Moslem unity, Olympic enthusiasm, postmodernist deconstruc- tion, dance fever, Black pride, student revolt—each peaks or declines in importance in the public agenda according to its rise or fall in the media agenda (McCombs & Shaw, 1972).

The developing child first experiences, in Piaget's view, a one-way dependence on a superior authority. He is "heteronomous," or other- directed. Media, at this stage, are another superior authority to be followed. Somewhat later the child achieves a bilateral relationship with peers and acquires the "autonomy" that this mutual support brings. The development of competence is directly related to this cooperation and consonant self-actualization. Once a level of competence has been attained, the media are used in a balanced way as one of many means of self-expression and growth. Unfortunately, this stage of "mastery" of media is delayed for many and never achieved by others. The cooperative, autonomous self with a healthy sense of personal identity and self-consciousness may be achieved, may be delayed, or may remain forever fugitive.

Consciousness refers to the internal cognitive and emotional awareness inherent in each person. It is consciousness that is most directly affected by media exposure, as when we walk out of a movie theater feeling and thinking very differently than when we entered. The media of communication have been labeled "the consciousness industries" (Enzensberger, 1974). They do not produce tangible goods; rather, the media produce signals that create a specific consciousness in the media user. Media impinge on our sensory apparatus—we see or hear them—and result in a particular consciousness. In the media process, the writer or director creating the media message first conceives it in his or her own consciousness. Then it is transferred through a medium, more or less successfully, to become an experience in the consciousness of the receiver. Behaviorism, or the study of measurable human behavior, sheds only indirect light on the essence of this media transfer of consciousness.

Our experience of others, of nature, and of media constructs our self. This continuous dialogic interaction between self and nonself creates our sense of personal identity and consciousness.

Defining *Super Media:*
Qualitative Change in Human Experience

The phrase *super media* is intended to convey a sense of the prominence of media in daily life and of their ambiguous quality. Theorists have sometimes understated or ignored this prominence; calling the phenomenon "*super* media" underscores the special force of these mediating instruments in human life.

As a neologism, *super media* may echo the stridency of its mass-merchandised counterparts. The mythical powers of Superman and Wonder Woman can never quite overcome the triteness of their names. As the early television hit "Super Circus" gave way over the decades to the Super Bowl on Super Sunday, who did not tire of "super" superlatives? Superstars turn out superhits; superpowers compete through their superheroes and megatonnage; supersavings are available at supersales from which one can take home a supercleanser. Things may even be supercalifragilisticexpialidocious. Like many superlatives in the age of super media, the term *super* has been used, abused, and overused. So why use *super* here?

The original meaning of *super* refers to the position of a thing physically above or on top of another. A second, more figurative meaning refers to a thing's higher rank, quality, amount, or degree—as when a supermarket outranks a mere market. A third and more absolute meaning of *super* refers to "the highest degree, in excess of a norm," as in *superabundant. (Compact Edition of the Oxford English Dictionary,* 1971, p. 3157).[1]

Super media are both higher in rank than non-technologically relayed communication and the highest in degree of known media, combining the second and third meanings. Plainly super media are higher in rank, quality, amount, and degree than nonmediated human speech and gesture, limited as those are to immediate time and space. Where the primitive media of stone tablets and talking drums extended somewhat the reach of communication, modern print and electronic media extend it much more widely through time and space. Super media today have achieved a state "in excess of a norm," when the combination of satellites, fiber optics, microchips, lenses, cables, and other encoders, relays, and decoders can create an advanced physical, multisensory experience. The experience is made no less amazing by its everyday familiarity and the possibility of its being shared simultaneously by millions of people scattered over the face of the earth. Modern means of communication are more "super" than their predecessors in quality, amount, and degree—although presumably our future technical capabilities will be even more super.

But the meaning of *super* in *super media* is primarily *qualitative*. The *manner* in which media now express and reflect human culture has changed. Although the growth of media has been gradual, the sum total brings with it a qualitatively different way of communicating, thinking, and existing humanly. This use of *super* assigns a meaning significantly different from either the "powerful effects" or "limited effects" conception of media. Behavioral researchers argue over whether media cause slight (McGuire, 1986) or great (Noelle-Neumann, 1973) behavior change in audiences. These two positions are based on the evidence of measured behavior only, ignoring consciousness, and assume that media act as a mechanical or instrumental stimulus. They also assume a distance between the media and the affected person. In the age of super media that distance has been collapsed. The human subject is integrally related to the media environment through continuous transmission-reception. Man and woman are expressive and conscious subjects in a determinant culture and not merely mechanical devices responding in measurable ways to singular stimuli. Together with other cultural practices and experiences, *super* media inform and infuse the consciousness, identity, and expressiveness of the subject in a way that is more qualitative than quantitative.

The term *media* is no less essential to the meaning of *super media*. The singular form, *medium,* refers to an intermediary agency, ranging from a fortuneteller to a painter's oils.[2] In general, a medium can be any intervening agent through which a force acts on objects at a distance or through which impressions are conveyed to the senses. For human communication, a medium may be seen, heard, touched, tasted, or smelled. A shrug or an epic poem can serve as a medium of human communication. A standard medium today may be a film, radio, magazine, book, telephone, computer, billboard, or any other message-relaying technology. A list of examples would be endless, because everything from a note on the refrigerator to a raised fist can be a medium of human communication.

The plural form, *media,* today refers to technological extensions of the human sensory apparatus. In their broadest definition, media can include all forms of technology. To Marshall McLuhan (1964), the wheel was an extension of the human foot, and clothes were a medium extending the human skin. In a narrower sense, media are established instruments of communication that transmit messages through controlled channels. Print media transmit written messages by duplicating and distributing the messages physically. Telecommunications media transmit electronic messages encoded as impulses sent over wires or airwaves. Super media include all forms of technologically relayed media as they serve us individually or collectively.

It is apparent that the *super* in *super media* implies a great deal. It connotes the culmination of a series of developments; correspondingly, super media can be seen as the apex of development of media and culture, the culmination that gives order and meaning to all mediated communication. They transform the meaning of earlier media and permeate cultural development. *Super* connotes an event or experience out of the ordinary, filled with emotion, even a kind of heightened "liminal" ecstatic state (Chapter Two); correspondingly, super media take us outside everyday routine and into the major expressive, emotional, cultural events of our culture. *Super* connotes the "hyperreal" that takes us beyond the shadows on the wall of the cave and into an

ultimate; correspondingly, super media become the measure and validation of politicians, presidents, athletes, news events, disasters, learning, success, love, and all that is or could be. *Super* connotes "outside
the limit," "beyond which there is no higher or further"; in this sense,
super media are science fiction come true, our final mythologies and
fantasies, our fondest hopes and our highest dreams.

Super media, then, serves as a useful shorthand label for the *technologically relayed communications,* whether large-scale or small-scale,
that are pervasive in everyday life.

Our super media, ourselves.

Media and Personal Identity:
Our Location in Space and Time

Nothing is more basic to personal consciousness than the sense of
positioning in time and place, the sense of centering and belonging.
Who I am as an individual, who I am as a member of a group, who we
are as a collective—these points of individual self-identity and awareness are intimately related to our sense of being in a particular place at
a particular time and being able to recognize that fact of positioning. At
each instant of our existence, we occupy a particular point in that
otherwise seamless web of successive moments and continuous locations that are time and place. On this level of self-perception, super
media can have a profound influence.

Perhaps the first famous victim of mass-media delusions was the Man
of La Mancha, Cervantes's amazing Don Quixote. Long before 20th-
century radio or television, the media were apparently influential and
were victimizing audiences. Miguel de Cervantes (1605/1937) appreciated and satirized their potential brainwashing effects centuries before
experimental scientists debated the "limited effects" hypothesis. The
origin of Don Quixote's condition was his undisciplined reading and
believing of books of romantic chivalry from the previous century,
works of exaggerated fantasy set in a medieval context no longer in
existence. Cervantes writes of Quixote,

> He plunged himself so deeply in his reading of these books . . . [that]
> through his little sleep and much reading, he dried up his brains in such
> sort as he lost wholly his judgment. His fantasy was filled with those things

that he read, of enchantments, quarrels, battles, challenges, wounds, wooings, loves, tempests, and other impossible follies [p. 19].

The effect on Quixote's behavior and consciousness was total:

> Finally, his wit being wholly extinguished, he fell into one of the strangest conceits that ever a madman stumbled on in this world . . . that he himself should become a knight-errant and go throughout the world, with his horse and armour, to seek adventures, and practice in person all that he had read was used by knights of yore [p. 19].

For Cervantes the influence of media in changing the perception of one's own time and place could be total: "Our knight-errant esteemed all which he thought, saw, or imagined, was done or did really pass in the very same form as he had read the like in his books." After the first of his high-minded but disastrous adventures, those around Quixote complained, "Those accursed books of knighthood, which he hath, and is wont to read ordinarily, have turned his judgment. . . . Let such books be recommended to Satan" (p. 45). But even the exorcism and burning of his library of "more than a hundred great volumes" came too late to save Quixote from his fantastic media-inspired quest. Whether we praise the grandeur of Quixote's impossible dream or condemn the illusions that doomed him, Cervantes clearly depicts a consciousness so distorted by undisciplined media saturation as to misconstrue entirely the hero's sense of time and place.

Four centuries later, as Quixote's heirs, we have all had our perception of time and place radically altered by modern media of communication and transportation. As media surround us with their great scale and penetration, they place us in a universe quite different from that inhabited by our ancestors. When Columbus discovered the New World in 1492, it was months before any Europeans knew about it and years before the impact of the event was appreciated. In contrast, a half millennium later, when astronauts walked on the moon for the first time in 1969, hundreds of millions of people viewed it as it happened; in fact, the value and impact of the moon landing were widely appreciated even before it happened. In previous centuries, news of events that occurred at great distances reached others only after great delays, if at all. In the age of super media, that information, which once took weeks and months to circulate widely throughout society, is now instantly available.

Our sense of space shifts radically with media's ability to overcome distance. When Alexander the Great conquered "the world" in the fourth century B.C., his Greek empire extended eastward over a section of what is now known as the Middle East, an important but nevertheless geographically narrow fraction of the earth's surface. When Soviet and American negotiators established an atmospheric nuclear test-ban treaty in the 1960s, they were debating arms that could annihilate all life on this planet. The scale on which we conceive of our life, within the context of contemporary media, arms, and international relations, is fundamentally different from that of the past.

Children today have no difficulty with the opening phrase of each of the *Star Wars* films: "Long, long ago in a galaxy far, far away . . ." Yet, it is only a few centuries since humans perceived the earth as a flat surface of which they knew only its relatively recent past. Five centuries ago, awareness of a distant country was difficult for all but the most learned, while now, in the world of modern media, imagining distant galaxies requires no effort from even a preschooler. This is not to say that the super media child necessarily "knows more" than his predecessors but only that he knows differently. Today's children may never learn to milk a cow, track a rabbit, or till a field, but they dream easily of distant millennia and galaxies. They locate themselves in time and space differently than those who went before.

Our sense of location in place and time, crucial to our self-identity, is inseparable from our media environment and experience.

Traditional Society Versus Super Media Culture

To appreciate the place of super media, it is helpful to recall the style of life and communication in a culture that is *not* mediated by modern means of communication.

In a traditional society, before the dawn of the age of super media, a person or group knew who was the source of a piece of information and how trustworthy that source was. Moreover, the information could be tested against personal experience. Communication was person-to-person, coming directly from a family member or local tribe member whose life history and relative authority were known. The messages concerned the immediate environment and experience and could be tested by touch, taste, hearing, seeing, and smelling. Lying and misrepresentation were not protected by anonymity or mobility, and a sense of collective identity dictated against violating community norms. Of course, folk tales, myths, and other fantasies abounded, but these were not individual misrepresentations but, rather, collective and imaginative constructions that figuratively explained aspects of living and delighted recipients. We should not overly romanticize primitive existence. It was not utopian; it could be harsh and brutal. But communication was an immediate and testable experience.

The form and content of consciousness and personal identity in preliterate cultures were also distinctive. The sense of belonging and positioning in time and space were narrowly bounded by the limits of historical and geographical knowledge. Only imagined linkages to mythically conceived aboriginal heroes, times, and places provided an extension of self-identity into past and future, local and distant. Informed understanding of other cultures and eras was inaccessible.

Thousands of years of media development and five hundred years of mass media development have changed all that. Today a person must constantly function with information that is from remote sources and not immediately testable. And he or she lives with a sense of personal location and history defined in terms of years and countries, centuries and galaxies, rather than village and kinship group. Table 1.1 summarizes this difference.

The changed consciousness between traditional and modern society occurs because, in the words of McLuhan (1964), we create our media and after that our media create us. Humans invent the technologies and content of mediated communication, but then the form and substance of the media gain ascendancy over the manner in which large numbers of humans believe, feel, think, act, and interact.

Media and Culture in Historical Perspective

In the long view, changes in dominant media technologies profoundly affect many dimensions of life. Changes in the dominant *medium* of communications—oral, print, electronic—are as important as the *content* of the media in determining the dominant definitions of personal and social reality in any given historic period. *Oral* communication favors more personalized and localized identities, with tribe and elders and handed down knowledge at the forefront. *Print,* because of its linear, sequential organization of information, fosters rational, disciplined reasoning and social organization, similar to that favored by the

TABLE 1.1 Traditional Versus Mass Communication

	Traditional	*Mass*
Source	Kin, neighbor	Institution
Channel	Face-to-face	Technological
Transmission time	Immediate	Immediate or delayed
Distance	Close	Remote
Receiver	Kin, neighbor	Anonymous, heterogeneous
Feedback	Direct	Indirect or none (delayed, filtered)
Accountability	Personal, identifiable	Fragmented, bureaucratic

far-flung British Empire (Eisenstein, 1979, 1983). *Electronic* media encourage recognition of gestalt fields of information with a less sequential, "all at once" form of thinking. Electronic culture resurrects certain tribal and nonrational modes suppressed by print culture. Media changes translate into differences between the eye and the ear, between visual and aural cultures, between print and electronic societies, between lineal and nonlineal codifications of reality, and between various other cultural dichotomies (Carpenter & McLuhan, 1960).

Changing media forms tend to change personal consciousness and social organization, according to Innis, McLuhan, and others (Havelock, 1963; Carey, 1967; Ong, 1967 and especially 1982; M. Mander, 1983; Postman, 1985). Each of the three eras of media (see Table 1.2) is associated with certain characteristics. *Space-bound* media are durable but difficult to transport, such as stone tablets, while *time-bound* media are light but less durable, such as human speech (Innis, 1950, 1951). Because spoken language carries only a short distance and disappears immediately, oral societies are time-bound and compensate with a heavy emphasis on tradition, religion, and morality. Societies reliant on print, in contrast, are space-bound and compensate with an emphasis on expanding the secular state and the technical order. The history of Europe and the modern West, to Innis, is founded on a monopoly of knowledge based in print.

The pace of change appears to increase in the modern era. With the first mass medium, the printing press, over time there emerged books, beginning with the Gutenberg Bible in 1456. More than a century later

TABLE 1.2 The Development of Oral, Print, and Electronic Media

PERIOD	Media	Beginning Date
I.	ORAL MEDIA	500,000 B.C.
	Speech and face-to-face communication beginning with *Homo erectus* and *Homo sapiens*	
II.	PRINT MEDIA	
	Three stages:	
	Ideographic writing	4000 B.C.
	Phonetic writing	2000 B.C.
	Printing press	A.D. 1456
	Books	1456
	Newspapers	1621
	Magazines	1731
	Penny Press	1833
III.	ELECTRONIC MEDIA	
	Telegraph	1844
	Telephone	1976
	Phonograph	1877
	Motion pictures	1894
	Radio broadcasting	1920
	Television	1923
	Computer	1946
	Satellite	1957

NOTE: Beginning dates are approximate for all events B.C.

newspapers originated, with the single sheet "corantos" of foreign news in 1621 and the regularly published *Oxford Gazette* in 1665. In the following century magazines began with *The Gentlemen's Magazine* in London in 1731. A century later still, the first cheap mass publications emerged with the "penny press" in 1833. Electronic innovations emerged more quickly, as Table 1.2 indicates, in conjunction with increasing industrialization, urbanization, and mass education. Because of intellectual limitations and the pace of change, American social analysis was only partially able to comprehend the impact of modern communications since the mid-19th century (Czitrom, 1982). The consequences of technological change are complex. Modern media have decreased for individuals the significance of physical presence, as Joshua Meyrowitz finds in his encyclopedic study, *No Sense of Place: The Impact of Electronic Media on Social Behavior* (1985). Television interacts with cultural groupings and attitudes, as David Marc shows in *Demographic Vistas: Television in American Culture* (1984). Oral, print, and electronic cultures each possess distinct characteristics that now combine and interact in complex and elusive ways in the era of super media.

Media and American National Identity

Media play a decisive role in expressing and reflecting the personal identification of an individual with the country to which he or she belongs. With the development of mass printing in the 15th century, popular books and maps gave the public the opportunity to "see" their country and to identify with its language and literature (Eisenstein, 1979, 1983). The founding of the United States of America with a written Mayflower Compact, Declaration of Independence, and Constitution illustrates the importance of print media in the colonial period. Postman (1985) called the country of that time "typographic America."

Visual reproduction has played a major role in establishing and modifying American national identity. Like painting before it and movies and television after it, photography has enabled Americans to see the people, places, and symbols that represent the national experience. Mathew Brady's meticulously detailed photographs of the American Civil War were little known during that war, were only gradually appreciated following the war, and, together with his other photographic achievements, were still not enough to prevent Brady from dying in poverty. But Brady and an immediate circle of contemporaries had a sense of the possible importance of what he was doing. Francis Carpenter, a Lincoln portrait painter, wrote at the time:

> My friend Brady, the photographer, insisted that his photograph of Mr. Lincoln taken the morning of the day he made his Cooper Institute speech in New York—much the best portrait, by the way, in circulation of him during the campaign—was the means of his election. That it helped largely to this end I do not doubt. The effect of such influences, though silent, is powerful [Illinois State Museum, 1987].

Few might agree that Brady's photo of Lincoln "was the means of his election," but today visual media are often assumed to have decisive historic influence. The impact of wartime photography has dramatically escalated since Brady's time. In contrast to Brady's experience, Eddie Duncan's single 1968 photo of a suspected Vietcong being shot in the head in Saigon by General Loan of the South Vietnamese secret police was seen the next day on the front pages of American newspapers, won Duncan a Pulitzer prize that year, and came at a crucial time in shifting American opinion against the United States' involvement in Southeast Asia. The improved technology, dissemination, and impact of photography as a medium made possible Duncan's good fortune and historic role in the 20th century even as it limited Brady's in the 19th century.

Americans such as Alexander Graham Bell and Thomas Edison helped invent media; then, in turn, those media over time created the American self. Writing in 1894, the same year Edison raced Lumière to invent moving pictures, two sociologists, Small and Vincent, commented on the press, books, and other technical devices: "In connection with all these technical devices for preserving and transporting symbols, we find functional arrangements of persons and property into social organs" and eventually "the many communicating channels are combined into a great system." They criticized the performance of newspapers and then employed a striking generalization that behaviorism later killed and cultural studies resurrects: "A communicating system penetrates the whole social organism . . . ramifying throughout society to its minutest subdivision, and, as a whole bringing into more or less complete physical contact all these parts of the organism" (Wright, 1986, p .23). Before the turn of the century, media were already being portrayed as a kind of central nervous system of society.

The first mass electronic medium, radio, illustrates how Americans created media and then media created America. World War I brought together the patented inventions that made the birth of radio broadcasting possible. Radio then let millions laugh together, be frightened together, and follow public affairs together, all at the same time and even in much the same way. America invented a new form of radio, and after that radio invented a new national experience.

Even as broadcasting was in its infancy, Walter Lippmann foresaw the power of such modern media in shaping "the pictures in our heads." His *Public Opinion* (1922) described the dependency of citizens on the media for their understanding of all public affairs. In a now famous passage, he describes how Miss Sherwin of Gopher Prairie imagines

World War I, then in progress in Europe. Never having been to Europe
or seen armies maneuvering, she reduces it in her mind to a personal
duel between a French general and the German Kaiser. Lippmann also
understood how a sense of membership in one's own country is equally
dependent on second-hand images. From the earliest pamphlets in the
American colonies, the American national experience, like that of other
countries, has been profoundly dependent on media of information and
communication.

Super Media and Expanded Human Potential

While historical influence may be difficult to measure, the vastly
expanded opportunity to reach the attention of many persons at one time
expands the potential for personal influence in the age of super media.
Twenty-three centuries ago Aristotle managed his profound effect on
Western intellectual history by teaching some dozens of peripatetic
pupils. In the 1970s Jacob Bronowski addressed millions on various
continents through his television series "The Ascent of Man," as did
Kenneth Clark before him in the "Civilisation" series and Carl Sagan
after him in the "Cosmos" series. The master teacher now speaks to a
global classroom rather than merely those few who can gain physical
proximity to him. Compared with Aristotle, is that better or worse?
Answers may vary, but no one can deny that it is certainly different in
scale. As David Manning White (1971, p. 18) enjoys pointing out, when
20 million viewers saw the Royal Shakespeare Company's *Midsummer
Night's Dream* on television, they constituted more persons than the
original Globe Theatre could seat in 10,000 performances.

The number of persons now involved in a communication act has
expanded geometrically from what was possible a short half millennium
ago. In the early 15th century, the most dedicated propagandist could
address only the number of persons he or she could gather together
physically, or those who could gain access to handwritten copies of
the message. Gutenberg's movable type began to change that, and
Marconi's wireless accelerated the process. The printing press, followed by electronic media, multiplied by exponential factors the potential receivers of a message.

More recently, computing and information technology have expanded opportunities. Jean Jacques Servan-Schreiber (1986, p. 1)
observes, "What the invention of the printing press did for mankind five

centuries ago, the computer is doing today. It has spurred a radical change in every aspect of our lives, moving with devastating speed and unleashing forces likely to be traumatic." This implies that "automation in factories, offices, and all sectors that must be modernized involves extending and organizing computer networks throughout the entire complex, from conception to manufacture" (p. 35). He summarizes the conclusion of a major Tokyo seminar in these words: "The only real source of power will, from now, be the creation of new knowledge" (p. 66) and "It demands that we put education at the very top of our national priorities" (p. 41). According to Servan-Schreiber, internationalism and competition are unavoidable:

> The invention of a new product in one country has immediate repercussions everywhere. This is the process of "creative destruction." . . . At the time of the invention of paper by the Chinese, it took centuries. Today, it is instantaneous.
>
> Borders can no longer stop competition. . . . Every people must play against the champions, whether it wants to or not, or become their slaves [pp. 76–77].

The accelerated movement of super media messages parallels the quickened movement of objects in our era as transportation improves. Humans can now circle the earth in hours in a satellite; messages circle the earth in seconds. Circling the earth had never been accomplished by any means before Magellan's circumnavigation in the 16th century, a time quite recent when viewed against the hundreds of thousands of years of human existence and culture. At the beginning of the 20th century, circling the earth still took months, even with the development of early electronic media and steam powered travel. Since then, acceleration in transportation and communication has reduced human perception of the once all-encompassing Mother Earth to a comparatively small object, conceived by Buckminster Fuller as Spaceship Earth, gliding among immensely vaster objects and forces. On a practical level, a major challenge now facing planners of modern transportation is to replace transportation with communication, to eliminate the physical movement of persons and objects and replace it with the electronic movement of symbols. Conducting work from a location in or near one's residence, rather than commuting, solves rush hours and traffic jams more profoundly than do expanded freeways.

Mediated communication interacts with all other dimensions of life. The examples above illustrate the integral connection between changes in media and changes in personal influence, national identity, transportation, and perceptions of location in space and time. We construct our personal identity within a different context than those who lived in earlier centuries.

Our media, ourselves.

Pessimists and Optimists:
The Love/Hate Relationship with Super Media

The fundamental love/hate ambivalence that most feel toward media can result in widely varying evaluations of their ultimate benefits. Is media's cup half empty or half full? Pessimists argue for the former, optimists for the latter.

Cultural pessimists come in many varieties. Moralists initiate periodic moral panics over the amount of violence on television (Rowland, 1983) or the presence of sex in films, television, local bookshops, student reading lists, or rock-and-roll music (Eysenck & Nias, 1978). An extreme example occurred in Tallahassee, Florida, when the Lakewood Baptist Church burned $2,200 worth of rock music records by such artists as Elton John and the Rolling Stones because of the music's "appeal to the flesh." The Reverend Charles Boykin, associate pastor and youth director, said he had seen statistics reporting that "of the 1,000 girls who became pregnant out of wedlock, 984 committed fornication while rock music was being played." He was vague about the source of his data but warned that the "jungle beat" was irresistible. He added that syncopation was the key and had led to "open sex" in the audiences of Benny Goodman concerts a generation earlier and had contributed to problems with classical music as well, evidenced by the 22 children of Bach.

Pessimists exist at sophisticated levels as well. Classicists of literature and art wring their hands over the deplorable state of the popular arts. They find the esthetic values of the media panderers sadly deficient and fear for the political, economic, religious, educational, and cultural future of the country and the world, as well as the artistic future. The mass-culture critiques of Tocqueville (1835, 1840/1944), Ortega y Gasset (1932), Dwight MacDonald (1983), Daniel Bell (1976), and many others elaborate endlessly on these themes. Garth Jowett (in press) finds distinct elitist, conservative, and humanitarian attacks on mass culture. Allan Bloom's *The Closing of the American Mind* (1987) and E. D. Hirsch's *Cultural Literacy: What Every American Needs to Know* (1987) continue this tradition by arguing that mass education and culture are to blame for a decaying American culture.

Television has been blamed for everything from the breakdown of the family to the rise in cancer rates (Winn, 1975; Mander, 1978). Postman (1985) and Meyrowitz (1985) note how childhood has been broken out of its isolation by television, a medium which requires no literacy for access and which exposes one and all to adult as well as adolescent concerns. The United States presidency has been severely affected by television, especially since John Kennedy (Pious, 1979; Schudson, 1982; Woodruff, 1982). Attacks on television sometimes tend toward "blaming the messenger," an ancient technique of Asian despots who are alleged to have slain the messenger who entered the royal court bearing the news of a major defeat.

Thoughtfully pessimistic critiques have also come from Christopher Lasch in *The Culture of Narcissism* (1978) and Noam Chomsky in *Towards a New Cold War* (1982). Critiques of technology by Jacques Ellul, Lewis Mumford, and other social philosophers argue the depersonalization, loss of control, and manipulative potential of modern media. Ellul argues that technology has become so pervasive that the mentality of *le technique,* or unrelenting efficiency, has come to dominate all dimensions of human life, losing the richness and variety of true human culture (Real & Christians, 1979).

The absolutely negative judgments are countered at the other extreme by absolutely positive judgments of super media. The view advocated by media managers is that the system works wonderfully if only we can keep government and regulators out of the way. More media and information of any kind, created in an unrestricted marketplace, support and defend democracy and protect the American way of life. Deficient cultural products will die a natural death as they compete against superior technical achievements and entertainment. Even regulators at the Federal Communications Commission, such as the zealous former chairman Mark Fowler, argue that the abundance of technologies ensures adequacy of communications without a need for regulation, except in limited technical specifications. Such new technology optimists reinforce the traditional free-marketplace optimists.

Rebuttals to attacks on mass culture feature many celebrators of the popular culture. David Manning White (1957), Edward Shils (1963), and Alvin Toffler (1970) offer variations on the theme that media only give the people what they want and increase access to cultural riches of all kinds. In the past two decades, it has become permissible for academics to study popular culture and admit they like it. This has created the combined scholar-fan whose affection for his or her subject is often charming. But a heavy dose of such works creates a sense of uncritical optimism. *The Popular Culture Reader* (Geist & Nachbar, 1983), *Superculture: American Popular Culture and Europe* (Bigsby, 1975), and other anthologies, as well as the *Journal of Popular Culture,* the *Journal of American Culture,* and books from the Bowling Green Popular Press, contain some examples.

Narrow behavioral research has sometimes supported the optimistic position. This has happened in two ways. First, the methodological stance of "objective science" has often translated into an excuse to avoid judgment. Super media are not criticized but only measured, implying that whatever exists must be okay. Second, the "limited effects" fallacy—the belief that media do not much matter—defeats the need for criticism. Social science research on media, as a consequence, has tended to permit, if not encourage, a relaxed comfortableness about the entire role of media in society.

The temptation to choose one side in the pro and con debate on super media produces colorful rhetoric. Arguing that the effect of media is all bad brings up grand-sounding humanism and can produce widespread guilt but usually little change in habits. Defending the virtues of the status quo, by comparison, calls up patriotism and commitment admired by all right-thinking citizens. But the resulting complacency and conformity are not the hallmarks of impressive culture.

A more challenging option is to retain a sense of the ambivalence of love and hate, optimism and pessimism, in the dominant culture. This can become motivational and explanatory through the emerging dialectic that it drives. Clearly, for most there remain positives and negatives throughout our systems of media and culture. Separating one from the other, understanding where each originates, assessing their respective consequences, and considering alternatives energize the work of cultural studies and reward the effort of coming to terms with super media in all their complexity.

Self-love and self-hatred are powerful emotions. To the extent that our media are ourselves, they deserve careful clarification.

Clarifying Concepts of Communication and Media

Super media operate within and around a constellation of other forces and concepts. Terms such as *communication, mass communication, specialized media,* and *culture* call for definition in their interaction with media.

Communication

Super media exist within the larger world of all forms of communication. Generically, communication can be defined as "social interaction through messages" (Gerbner, 1967). Communication can take place on the interpersonal level between face-to-face individuals, on the data level between information senders and receivers, and on the mass level between institutionalized media and audiences. On each level, senders transmit messages through channels to receivers to achieve effects and feedback. One unplugs the communication cord from personal friends and plugs it into the remote figures of mass media, or vice versa, continually throughout life.

Mass Communication

Super media are especially associated with the means of mass communication. The phrase *mass communication* refers to public, rapid, and transient communication through a complex corporate organization to a relatively large, heterogeneous and anonymous audience (Wright, 1959). The source is institutional, rather than individual as in interpersonal communication. The channel electronically or mechanically multiplies the message, rather than just carrying it as an interpersonal channel would. The receivers are diverse, rather than the face-to-face few of interpersonal communication. The feedback is restricted, unlike the interpersonal opportunities to agree, object, or amplify at will. In summary, mass communication transmits messages from an institutional source (such as the BBC) through mechanical or electronic multiplication and distribution (such as periodicals or telecommunications) to many heterogeneous receivers (the "mass" audience) with only limited and indirect opportunities for feedback. A television viewer cannot talk back to a news anchor in the same way that she can respond verbally or nonverbally in an interpersonal encounter.

So imperfect is "mass communication" that the two words have been called contradictory, in the argument that what is "mass" cannot be genuine "communication." In some languages, the phrase *public com-*

munication or *social communication* replaces the phrase *mass communication*. Since Max Weber, sociologists have debated whether *mass* is a useful term for describing any social groupings and phenomena. Despite these reservations, *mass communication* is the standard label in English and is often used interchangeably with the term *media*.

Media, as defined earlier, has come to be preferred by many to the problematic phrase *mass communication*. The journal *Media, Culture and Society*, for example, notes, "The rejection of the term 'mass communication' was a conscious one, designed to prevent an unnecessary narrowing" (Collins et al., 1986, p. 3).

Specialized Media

Whereas mass communication requires large group transmission or reception, the specialized media of nonmass communication are the channels of point-to-point voice, data, or image transmission. These channels of specialized media are especially prevalent today in the form of telephone systems, computer networks, and electronic data relays. Specialized media are central components of super media, as are mass communication media.

Figure 1.1 summarizes the relationship among concepts as described above.

Interaction Between Levels of Communication

There are also "mixed experiences." Mediated communication, both mass and specialized, intermingles with interpersonal communication in our daily lives and experiences. A television program is recorded and edited with specialized media before being mass communicated. The transmission of the television program entails computers and point-to-point signaling as well as mass distribution. Then, watching the resulting television program in a family setting while eating a meal blends mass and interpersonal communication. Likewise, a live concert today is mass mediated, featuring electronic sound systems and mass audiences, but also interpersonal, allowing a face-to-face encounter and direct feedback through cheers and jeers. Stereos provide mass-originated accompaniment to the broadest range of interpersonal communications.

An experience may be primarily mass media but partly interpersonal, or it may be primarily interpersonal and partly mediated, or it may lie somewhere in between. Effective distance-learning projects combine the personal experience of tutors and small-group discussions (at the

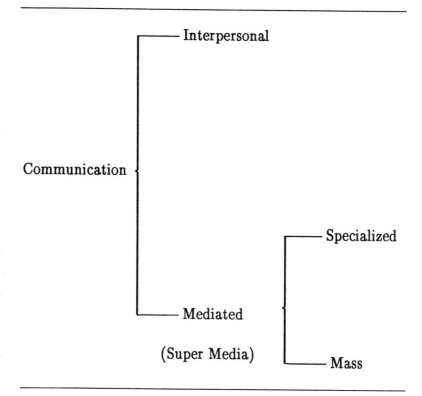

FIGURE 1.1 Categories of Communication

interpersonal end of the continuum) with televised lectures and demonstrations (at the mass-mediated end of the spectrum). There is a continuum that connects the extremes of mediated and interpersonal communication.

The interactions between levels of communication may extend and multiply the significance of super media in personal and social life. Two adolescents' telephone conversation may, for example, live and breathe with the technologies and contents of super media. Technologically, this person-to-person interaction once required only simple wires and transmitter-receiver pieces, not the "super" technologies of today. But now the conversation will normally involve complicated switching devices, channel load distributors, automated information, maybe even fiberoptic and satellite relays—technologies that would appear quite "super" to Alexander Graham Bell.

In its content, the telephone conversation between the adolescents will likely have been shaped and influenced by the larger context of super media. If teenagers talk of love, it will be in the context of love in popular songs and films. If they talk of idols and role models, they may include families and friends but also the popular celebrities of mass-mediated music, sports, fashion, and other "super culture" icons. The teenagers' word choice, phrasing, and inflection may be based on media models, as well as on their previous interpersonal experiences. Even their lifelong interpersonal experience—the face-to-face interactions with parents, siblings, neighbors, schoolmates, and others—has been shaped in the context of many decades of national experience of mediated popular culture. Their regional accents may have been leveled off by media, and their models of family, status, friends, and ideals subtly standardized by a century of increasing super media.

Our communications and media, ourselves.

Culture and Levels of Taste

Super media cannot be separated from culture, as they convey popular and mass cultural products for various levels of public taste.

Culture

Super media create, express, and reflect culture. *Culture* refers to those elements that set one human grouping apart from others. Culture is the systematic way of construing reality that a people acquires as a consequence of living in a group. Culture may apply to groups as large as Western culture or as small as the devotees of "cyberpunk culture," a high-tech subgenre of science fiction. Culture is expressed and reflected in art, dress, family relations, dance, and any other human activity.

The cultural levels of media products themselves have come to be classified roughly by social class. In fact, what a generation ago was considered the "great debate" between high, low, and middlebrow culture has now largely settled down into a relatively simple classificatory system.

Elite art serves mostly the upper classes by providing technically and thematically complex expression judged by a normative body of recognized classics, as in classical music, painting, literature, and the like. With a capital *C,* the word *culture* narrows to refer to only *elite art,* the esthetic expressions of the leisure class identified as classical art. With a small *c, culture* refers to all human expressions.

Folk art serves the localized, grass-roots, precommercial needs of traditional rural villages through blues and gospel songs, country ballads, ethnic dances, native carving, and similar expressions at the opposite extreme from classical elite art.

Mass art serves a large cross-section of the population through readily accessible and understandable products devoid of the sophistication of elite art and the traditionalism of folk art. Virtually all of television programming, popular music, the mass press, feature films, and other super media cultural products are at the popular/mass level.

Popular culture has come to refer to folk and mass art and, at times, to elite art as well. That is, "popular culture" is the generic label for study of any level of cultural expression, with the possible exclusion of elite art. The "great debate" in popular culture disputes whether the cultural content of mass culture either threatens the values of elite culture, as the conservative argues, or expresses the pluralism of liberal democracy, as the liberal contends. (See, for example, Bigsby, 1975.)

As popularity increases, so does the role of super media, and popularity is one measure of importance in social and cultural matters. Jack Nachbar (1978, p. 5) points this out: "There is, after all, a logical pattern established by assuming a kind of formula for the study of popular culture in which the more popular a thing is, the more culturally significant it is likely to be." Following this lead, Harold Hinds (1988, p. 210) would narrow the meaning of popular culture: "The definition of popular culture ought to be: those aspects of culture, whether ideological, social, or material, which are widely spread and believed in and/or consumed by significant numbers of people, i.e., those aspects which are popular." Adoption of a cultural product or expression "in more then one regional culture and by more than one narrow socioeconomic group" would constitute a minimum standard of popularity. In addition, numerical data should be sought to confirm popularity. This principle of popularity would delete the categories of folk, elite, and mass from popular culture. However, the more common use of *popular culture* remains the inclusive one.

Taste cultures is the label given by Herbert Gans (1974) to the gradations of taste associated with membership in certain strata of society. He identifies four such classes, drawn from the various levels of art above.

High Culture. A small, educated, and usually affluent segment of the public prefers the serious creator-oriented works of elite art as these shift from the formalism of the 1950s to the Pop Art of the 1960s, the conceptualism of the 1970s, the neoexpressionism of the 1980s, and the various postmodernisms.

Upper-Middle Culture. Many professionals, executives, and managers and their families prefer the less complex and abstract music, literature, theater, newspapers, and magazines that are considered "good" but not overly difficult.

Lower-Middle Culture. Increasingly the dominant force in super media taste, this vast group of white-collar, lower-professional, or technical workers favor traditional values, clear plots, fast action, and recognizable stars in the mainstream media they follow assiduously.

Low Culture. Blue-collar skilled and semiskilled workers and their families form the second most dominant group of super media tastes with their preference for the sensations of violent films, the escapism of tabloids and soaps, the predictability of laugh-track sitcoms, and the compensations of sports competition.

Quasi-folk culture is the term Gans uses to describe traditional expressions from poor and rural origins. *Ethnic culture* normally refers to the remnants of traditional folk culture from a particular country or people, now transplanted to a new location. However, George Lewis (in Lull, 1988) finds that musical tastes do not coincide clearly with the taste levels defined by Gans and questions any universal applications of the foregoing categories.

The relationships among these concepts are presented in graphic form in Figure 1.2. The proportionate number of products and people in each category is roughly represented in the right-hand column.

Super media play a role in all levels of culture today, from elite to folk, but they are most intrinsically associated with the levels from upper-middle down through low culture.

Media Event

In the past decade, the phrase *media event* has emerged alongside the terms just mentioned and refers to large-scale live events built around mass media and large audiences. Elihu Katz (1980) includes as necessary conditions the *live* transmission of a *preplanned* event especially framed in time and space, featuring a *heroic* personality or group and

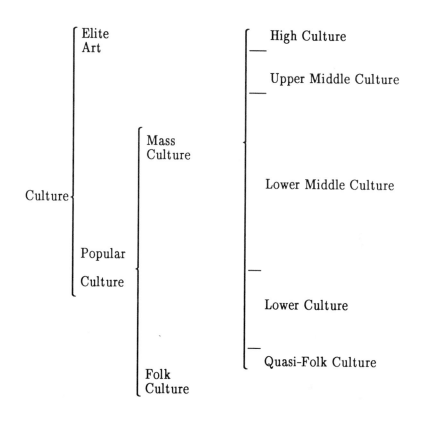

FIGURE 1.2 Levels of Culture, Taste, and Art

having high *dramatic or ritual* significance, all of which results in viewing seeming *mandatory* to members of that public. This narrow definition makes the phrase applicable to the Olympics, royal weddings, fund-raising televised rock concerts, major papal visits, and similar well-publicized international events. But *media event* can also apply to the smaller cases of a local press conference, a ball game, an election, or a conflict that is built around media, as in Daniel Boorstin's original and pejorative use of the term *media event* to refer to an essentially bogus promotional political or economic activity. The phrase *super media* likewise refers to large-scale dominant transnational communications or to smaller, more localized analogues. The sense of superness in *super media* especially evokes massive international media events but is by no means restricted to large-scale phenomena.

Communication and culture reciprocally cause each other in an endless cycle of mutual causality. Super media play a central role in contemporary communication and culture. Identities are built up, consciousness developed, ideology implanted, and face-to-face interactions conditioned by super media. We create our media and culture, and our media and culture create us.

Our media, our culture, ourselves.

Questions of Responsibility

Who is responsible for super media? Of course, we all are. The ultimate intent of many analyses of super media today is "consciousness raising." An informed citizenry must be aware of the nature, style, and techniques of super media in order to conduct a harmonious personal and group life. Only if we consciously see through the web of imagery and information overload by developing a sense of what super media do well and do poorly, how they inspire and how they distort—only then can we conduct our lives as fully self-conscious, self-directed human beings.

Eco asks who is responsible for the popularity of a polo shirt with an alligator on it: the designer? the manufacturer? the advertiser? the celebrity endorser? the TV director who, to characterize a generation, has a young actor wear the polo shirt? the consumer? Eco (1986, p. 149) warns against easy answers: "The media have multiplied, but some of them act as media of media, or in other words media squared." As a best-selling international author himself with *The Name of the Rose* (1983), Eco acknowledges that there are messages sent and an ideology behind them. But in searching for their origin and meaning, he concludes (1986, p. 149) somewhat disconsolingly yet all the more provocatively:

There is no longer Authority, all on its own (and how consoling it was!). . . .
All are in it, and all are outside it: Power is elusive, and there is no longer
any telling where the "plan" comes from. Because there is, of course, a
plan, but it is no longer intentional, and therefore it cannot be criticized
with the traditional criticism of intentions. All the professors of theory of
communications, trained by texts of twenty years ago (this includes me),
should be pensioned off.

Our media? Ourselves?

Questions

1. List examples from your own experience of how super media have provided role models and influenced your sense of group identity.

2. What proportions of your daily life are spent in interpersonal communication, in mass communication, and in communication using specialized media?

3. How do super media contribute to the development of personal identity, consciousness, and culture?

4. How does current super media culture differ from the pre-media culture of traditional societies?

5. How do changes in media relate to changes in our perceptions of time and space?

6. What role do media play in developing a sense of national identity?

7. What are the negative elements of super media that pessimists decry and the positive elements that optimists praise?

8. What meaning and significance are attached to the words *communication, mass communication, specialized media, culture, elite art, popular culture,* and *mass culture?*

9. In what ways do our media become ourselves and we become our media?

Notes

1. The English term *super* has a varied history and several meanings. It first appears about the mid-15th century and by the 19th century appeared in such words as *superhive, super-screwing,* and *superbody. Superhive* refers to the removable top section of a beehive and reflects the first meaning of *super* as literally above or on top of. *Super-screwing* refers not to what some may pantingly have hoped but to stealing pocket watches: "super" in the slang of British thieves meant a watch, and "screwing" was a method of theft by removing the watch knobs. To the same colorful 19th-century subculture, "banging a

super" also lacked sexual connotations and meant watch theft by breaking the watch ring between the thumb and forefinger. Likewise, *superbody* originally referred not to the results of aerobics and weight training but rather to the action of fitting a body upon something, as to "superbody" the frame onto the chassis of an automobile (*Compact Edition of the Oxford English Dictionary,* 1971, p. 3157).

2. A spiritualist medium intervenes between humans and spirits through fortunetelling, tarot cards, voodoo, and other magical processes. In 1643 the English word had much the meaning it has today, as in Ross's reference to "the air, which is the medium of music and of all sounds." The first magazine, *Gentleman's Magazine,* in 1795 was told, "Some useful information . . . may . . . be hoped for through the medium of your curious Publication." In painting, a medium is any liquid vehicle with which pigments can be mixed, such as oil, water, or albumen (*Compact Edition,* 1971, p. 1760).

2

Cultural Studies as Metadiscipline: Interpreting Presidential Assassinations

The president pauses before entering his car and waves to the small groups of well-wishers clustered nearby. Suddenly shots ring out. The president is hit! Pandemonium reigns as he is hustled into the car and rushed to the hospital. A pistol-waving youth is wrestled to the ground and removed into custody.

Super media flash to the world: Monday, March 30, 1981. President Ronald Reagan today received a chest wound from an assassin's bullet. His condition is uncertain as a medical team performs emergency procedures. . . .

A strange story emerges. The assassin is motivated to shoot the ex-actor president by a movie he has seen and his infatuation for one of its actresses. The assassin's role model was played by an actor who that night is scheduled to win the Best Actor Oscar, at a ceremony featuring a personal statement by the president.

The attempted assassination is, without question, a many-layered text.

In the age of super media, heads of state have become the personalized symbols of the relationship of individuals to the entire social order. For this reason, the assassination of a president or prime minister traumatizes a nation like nothing else. November 23, 1963, is a moment frozen in time. On that sunny day in Dallas, President John F. Kennedy was shot and killed while riding in a motorcade with his wife at his side. In the 1980s the assassinations of India's leader, Indira Gandhi, of Sweden's popular prime minister, Olof Palme, and of the heads of state in Pakistan, in Liberia, and elsewhere occasioned similar traumatic dislocations felt deeply by persons who may never have had direct personal contact with the victim. Murder is an overused plot device in super media, and audiences are vicariously conditioned to accept it unthinkingly, but despite that, the real-world experience of death can often be catastrophically unsettling in its finality and consequences. Even an unsuccessful near-miss, as in John Hinckley's wounding of

President Reagan in 1981, can create widespread excitement, fear, and debate.

How does research interpret these momentous messages and messengers? Fortunately, for all the apparent newness of super media, the forms of information and communication have been examined thoughtfully and scientifically for more than half a century, and many intellectual instruments have been brought to bear on our media environment and culture. While various empirical and theoretical strategies have had to be revised or discarded, as Eco warned, we are not starting from the zero point. It must be admitted that no single integrating theory coordinates our scientific understanding of super media. However, in recent decades *cultural studies* has emerged as a label for a broadly critical theory and method that is proving especially useful in diagnosing the nature and condition of media in society. This chapter outlines the cultural studies approach. The organization follows the organization of the book as a whole: Cultural studies as a metadiscipline is presented (1) in relation to the American mainstream tradition of empirical media-centered analysis and then (2) in relation to more recent culture-centered analysis in its subcategories of (a) structuralism, (b) critical theory, and (c) ritual analysis. Our media shaped identity possesses empirical, structural, critical, and ritual dimensions. Cultural studies examines these.

Competing Approaches: Criticism Versus Behaviorism

Despite the extreme variety of approaches to super media, it is possible to identify two fundamental groupings. *Behaviorism* broadly identifies the examination of media by social science, with an emphasis on measuring audiences and behavioral effects through controlled experiments and surveys. It is "media centered" in a restrictive sense, looking at direct media experience and outcomes individually, especially those that can be measured empirically. It seeks unambiguous scientific results that can predict subsequent similar behaviors. In contrast, *criticism* broadly identifies the examination of media through social and artistic theories, with an emphasis on understanding the creation, content, and implications of media as human expression and experience. It is "culture centered" in an expansive sense, looking at institutions, historical contexts, esthetic levels, and collective outcomes. It criticizes for the purpose of appreciation and improvement, seeking understanding rather than prediction. As we ask what kind of media culture we have inherited and are creating, behaviorism and criticism compete to give us answers.

Presidential assassinations receive differing treatments by behaviorism and criticism. Behaviorists look for measurable predictors of assassins. What personality profile, political background, clothing style, visible behavior pattern, or other social psychological variables identify a potential assassin? On the basis of measurable past experience and observation, what circumstances in Washington, New Delhi, Stockholm, or elsewhere are most dangerous for a head of state? How is word of an assassination attempt communicated through a society, and what behaviors result? The White House Secret Service consults such behavioral information, but it is of limited value to the general public. Working on a different level and with different tools, criticism seeks above all to comprehend the meaning and implications of an assassination or its attempt. What general public climate in the culture contributes to assassination attempts? What vested interests, historical forces, and social conflicts are at work beneath the surface in assassinations? In what ways does the public interpret the attempt? What explanations and rituals enable a country to come to terms with an accomplished assassination?

Both behaviorism and criticism serve to clarify our experience of super media, but in vastly different ways. The two approaches are associated with a long list of other descriptors that highlight the differences between them, differences reminiscent of the gulf between two separate cultures (see Snow, 1963). Behaviorism has emphasized micro levels of analysis, using quantitative methods in the social science tradition. Criticism stresses macro levels of analysis, often using qualitative methods from the humanities and liberal arts tradition. Behaviorism prefers experiments, behavioral measurements, and positivist social research methods. Criticism draws from political economy, history, literature, epistemology, and classics of political philosophy. Behaviorism has been especially centered in the United States, while critical media analysis has been centered in Western Europe, the United Kingdom, and Latin America.

In its analysis of super media, behaviorism is closely identified with pluralism (Curran, Gurevitch, & Woollacott, 1982) because of its contention that many and varied voices are heard through the media in a society comprising multiple cooperative segments. Behaviorism is also pluralist in using a variety of tools of method and research without a single, articulated perspective. Behaviorism's pluralism seeks to be value-free and has been associated with a commercial "free press" model of media organization.

Criticism's analysis of super media has been described as structuralist, denoting a critical emphasis on structure, whether anthropological, political-economic, semiotic, esthetic, or general. This emphasis on structure on different levels is captured in a widely cited and discussed statement by Stuart Hall (1973): "In the analysis of culture, the interconnection between societal structures and processes and formal or symbolic structures is absolutely pivotal" (p. 4). Criticism debates values as well as behavior and has been associated with arguments for democratic communication in a reorganized international communication order.

Behaviorism and criticism can be contrasted, in an admittedly exaggerated form, in their views of media production, content, and audiences (see McQuail, 1983). Behavioral pluralism sees media production as objective in news reporting and creative in entertainment programming, whereas criticism sees production as routinized and controlled. Pluralism sees in media content diverse and competing views responsive to audience demand, whereas criticism finds in the content representations of the dominant ideology. Pluralism sees the media audience as fragmented and selective, whereas criticism sees the audience as dominated in confirmation of the established social order. But one can find trends counter to McQuail's generalizations as well. For example, behavioral pluralism has established the notion that media audiences can be influenced at least in small choices, such as product selection, whereas criticism has emphasized the active audience which reads media texts in unpredictable and oppositional ways. Thus, both pluralism and behaviorism in different ways see the audience as being influenced by media toward standardization but also as capable of selective variation from the norm.

General contrasts between criticism and behaviorism are summarized in Table 2.1.

There are advantages and disadvantages in using the contrasts of Table 2.1 to approach super media. The disadvantages involve the table's oversimplifications, overgeneralizations, and dichotomous absoluteness. It exaggerates each side and presents extremes that are never that simple, that absolute, and as neatly contrasting. The table also omits crossovers. There are, for example, critical behaviorists in ethnomethodology and other traditions. There are both quantitative and

TABLE 2.1 Competing Approaches: Criticism and Behaviorism

	Criticism	*Behaviorism*
Level of analysis	Macro Culture-centered	Micro Media-centered
Technique	Qualitative	Quantitative
Academic orientation	Social theory Humanities Politics	Social behaviorism Sciences Psychology
Research methods	History Literature Esthetics Interpretation	Statistics Experimentation Positivism Causality
Research topics	Culture Ideology Institutions Processes	Mass communication Technology Individuals Effects
Media potential	Informative Esthetic Liberating	Informative Entertaining Diverting
Media production	Standardized Controlled	Creative Objective
Media content	Limited	Diverse
Media audiences	Dominated Reactive	Selective Active

NOTE: This table is a heuristic device and does not represent two actual paradigms. It and the discussion of the approaches are loosely based on schemata found in Curran, Gurevitch, and Woollacott (1982), Collins et al. (1986), Lodziak (1986), McQuail (1987), McQuail and Windahl (1981), Fejes (1984), Smythe (1981), Lazarsfeld (1941), Becker (1985), McAnany (1986), Schramm and Porter (1982), DeFleur and Ball-Rokeach (1982), and others.

qualitative methods in the work of a Pierre Bourdieu, who combines critical theory and large-scale data collection and analysis. But the primary advantage of the contrasting columns in the table is that they prohibit one from denying the existence of one side in favor of the other. On the right side, a media-centered experimental behaviorist cannot claim that no other approach exists. On the left, a culture-centered social critic cannot ignore the place of behaviorism in researching super media.

An advantage of the table is that it provides a context for presenting cultural studies in its relationship to other alternatives. The general approach taken in these pages is to employ cultural studies as a relatively inclusive approach that is primarily identified with the critical option but, on occasion, also draws from particular findings and insights developed within the behaviorist tradition. For some, particularly in Great Britain, "cultural studies" is a more restrictive label applied only to a specialized subcategory within the larger category of Marxist criticism (Curran, Gurevitch, & Woollacott, 1982; Collins et al., 1986). They eliminate structuralism and political economy from the definition and reduce cultural studies to a "culturalism" concerned with super media texts only; such culturalism does not directly examine the arrangement of social power that surrounds and informs these texts. However, in this examination of super media, cultural studies retains a broader and more flexible definition.

What is the meaning of *cultural studies,* and how has it attempted to clarify the nature of our media, our culture, and our lives?

"Culture" Expanded and the Origins of Cultural Studies

Relatively new but widely respected, cultural studies as a form of criticism both draws from and criticizes previous research on communication and media, as well as previous work in other academic disciplines. The unique emphasis of cultural studies on *interpreting the texts of everyday life and media* gives the approach an immediacy and clarity appropriate to super media in all their complexity. In communication, the approach is especially associated with the names Stuart Hall, James Carey, James Curran, Tony Bennett, Michael Gurevitch, Janet Woollacott, Raymond Williams, and others scattered throughout the United Kingdom and the English-speaking world.

Prior to World War II, the term *culture* generally referred to the high culture of classical literature and art or to the quaint customs of primitive peoples. The popular expressions and pastimes of the middle and lower classes were considered mere "entertainment." But in the middle 1950s, the widely used literary term *culture* was given a broader meaning.[1] In the British context, Richard Hoggart (1957) extended the category of culture by examining the culture of his own working-class origins as a lived experience. His attention was turned not to constructing an anthropology of a foreign culture nor to criticism of the literary culture of men of letters, but to developing introspectively a literary-anthropological appreciation of the "ordinary and homely" culture of

British row houses, club-signing, and threepence weekly fiction magazines. His sense of valued culture rejected the high/low distinction conventionally used to endorse classical culture and denigrate the nonelite culture of ordinary people.

At about the same time, but working with more artistic materials, Raymond Williams (1958) moved toward a similar sense of culture as he worked away from the traditionally narrow literary concern for history, society, and culture. Reflecting his Welsh working-class origins, Williams rejected the separateness of elite culture with a capital *C* and defined culture as "the sum of the available descriptions through which societies make sense of and reflect upon their common experiences" (Hall, 1980, p. 59). This democratized and socialized, made "ordinary," a word that in literary and artistic circles had been restricted to only "the best" that had been thought and said. In this redefinition, culture was no longer synonymous with high art. Rather, art and literature were considered only two among many vehicles involved in the general process of culture, a process that creates and structures meanings, conventions, and institutions. Williams (1981, p. 13) also identified culture as "the signifying system through which . . . a social order is communicated, reproduced, experienced, and explored."

The result of this redefinition was an inclusive sense of culture that somewhat defied definition at the same time as it stimulated a new integrative, critical mode of analysis. Ultimately, for Williams, "culture is *a whole way of life*" (Hall, 1980, p. 60). On one side, anthropology traditionally used the term *culture* in this inclusive sense but without specific attention to contemporary, industrialized culture and its creative products. On the other side, literature wrote of culture as modern, creative works but tended to exclude the popular arts and nonelite, lived culture. Williams combined the anthropological and the literary.

All social practices and spheres of human activity were included in this notion of culture and became the subject of interpretation. Folkways, science, politics, home life, art—everything is included, without being separated into independent spheres of activity. Cultural studies is, in the words of Williams, "the study of the relationships between elements in a whole way of life" (Hall, 1980, p. 60) The search is for those patterns of organization within or underlying *all* social practices. Rather than treating art, production, trading, politics, and the raising of families as separate activities, cultural studies seeks to discover characteristic patterns through studying a *general organization in a particular example.* The prize sought for is the *"structure of feeling"* characteristic of all the practices and patterns experienced as a whole in any particular period and place.

In the middle 1950s changes in the definition of culture were also taking place in the United States. For two decades a debate on mass culture had been underway, initiated in the United States by critical Marxists who had fled Hitler's Germany and who became known as the Frankfurt School. Conservative classicists joined in this debate, which culminated in the publication of a best-selling anthology, *Mass Culture: The Popular Arts in America* (Rosenberg & White, 1957). After that point, the emphasis began to shift from mass culture as an industrialized, manipulative culture to "popular culture" as a more complex mixture that defied simple pro-and-con judgments. Debate around questions of super media and the meaning of culture moved beyond the mass culture uniformities. The establishment of popular culture as an area of study in the 1960s brought with it critical appreciation of everything cultural from *A* to *Z*, from advertising and Afro-American culture to the Vietnam War, westerns, women's studies, youth culture, and zealotry.

The understanding of media and culture as popular expression offered a needed alternative at that time to mainstream American research on media from a narrowly behaviorist viewpoint. Research on mass communication, with its roots in the practical enterprises of journalism and speech, had joined the prestigious bandwagon of "hard" science following World War II and narrowed it methods and approaches (Carey, 1981a). Scientific media research then progressed without a vital relationship to social theory, ignoring European phenomenology, structuralism, hermeneutics, Marxism, and other critical movements. Behaviorist and media-centered, such American study expressed little interest in the complexities of culture that so eluded experimental methodology. Gradually, under the influence of British and popular culture currents, an alternative approach to media study emerged that was critical and culture-centered (Real, 1980, 1984, 1986). Not just media and media-related behavior, but the larger culture that media reflected, expressed, and shaped, became a focus of media research, and American critical theory and cultural studies gradually emerged alongside their British, European, and Latin American counterparts.

The label "cultural studies" is a compromise one. Generations ago Max Weber argued the need for a "cultural science" that was "interpretive" rather than reductionist in the form of causal or functional explanations. Weber's term *science* was softened by Hall and Carey to the less specific *studies* to avoid a possible slide toward more behaviorist "scientism," which appears scientific but lacks intellectual significance. The pivotal term remains *cultural,* because although Carey and Hall select communication and media as the dominant subject matter for their analyses, they each find the labels "communication," "mass communication," "media studies," "popular culture," and their many cognates too confining. They accept Raymond Williams's argument against confining attention to mass communication narrowly defined. Such narrow labels limit study to a few specialized areas such as broadcasting and film while excluding attention to the "forms, conventions, and practices of speech and writing as well as to the mass media" (Carey, 1979, p. 411). The term *mass* immediately biases toward conceptions of large, passive audiences best studied only by conventional effects research. In Carey's view, the label "mass communication," or even the broader "communication," directs us to the study of one isolated segment of existence, whereas the word *culture* directs us toward the study of an entire way of life.[2]

A presidential assassination attempt operates at levels that demand the broader definition of *culture* offered by cultural studies. Shots fired at a head of state do not constitute an elite literary event, nor does the event take place in a remote folk culture. Rather, such an act tears at the central fabric of current cultural constructs. An Oswald or a Hinckley is especially terrifying because he shares the common structure of feeling in American culture, however deviant his individual interpretation and application of that culture's norms. "Foreign" influences alone could not explain Oswald's act and played no role with Hinckley's. A uniform definition of *mass* culture cannot accommodate such variety among individuals as well as a more flexible notion of popular culture can. The role of super media in culture is complex; they play a subtle or direct part in each step of an assassination attempt and require an equally subtle interpretation.

Criticism of the cultural studies type offers certain advantages over behaviorism and classicism for explaining media culture because of certain characteristics of the media experience. The experience of super media is essentially collective and cultural, rather than merely individual and behavioral. Super media are not merely imposed by mass culture and received passively; they are also popular and expressive of persons and groups. They are not an inferior alternative to superior high art, but a meaningful range of expressions marked by a consistent structure of feeling across the experiences they present. As such, super media create a complex and wide-ranging expression of culture that finds in cultural studies an ideal tool for examining and understanding it.

Cultural Studies and Empirical Media-Centered Analysis

Cultural studies, with its expanded definitions of culture and media, has both a negative mission, critiquing and pruning the roots and branches of traditional media research, and a positive mission, nurturing its own soil and growth through a thoroughgoing intellectual examination of media, drawing from anthropology, literary criticism, philosophy, history, and other contemporary scholarship.

The negative mission of cultural studies in critiquing behaviorism is essential. Traditional mainstream research on media in the empirical behaviorist tradition not only is limited in its reach but also tends to be intellectually one-dimensional and, to that extent, theoretically sterile. The more interesting and important lessons of the attack by John Hinckley on President Reagan or by Lee Harvey Oswald on President Kennedy are largely inaccessible to behavioral research. For such purposes, behavioral research has not been "wrong" so much as it has been inadequate in the range and depth of its questions. Behaviorism restricts its attention to the measurable effects of experiments and surveys, seeking for the study of human behavior the same scientific precision that exists in the physical and biological sciences. This otherwise admirable goal can result in a narrowed attention that deals only with individual acts and quantifiable facts. A behaviorist study of media and violence, for example, often sets up a completely controlled laboratory setting. Experimental subjects are then randomly assigned to either a control group shown a nonviolent film or an experimental group shown a violent film. After the showings, aggressiveness is measured in both groups through observed behavior or test responses. The results have generally shown increased levels of aggressive tendencies in the experimental group and not the control group. These behavioral results are valuable but result only in limited probabilistic predictions about future behavior in similar conditions.

With its restricted methods, behaviorism can speculate on the behavioral conditioning and stimuli leading to an attempted presidential assassination, but scientific proof about such acts is impossible. Behaviorist data, however scientific, reveal little of the meaning, interpretation, and symbolic importance of the act to the perpetrator or to the members of the public. The widespread public anxiety over the shootings of John and Robert Kennedy appeared in popular songs such as the Rolling Stones' "Sympathy for the Devil" and even inspired the name of one punk rock band, The Dead Kennedys. Behavioristic measurement cannot provide even broad interpretations of such anguished questioning. Quantitative and behaviorist empiricism restricted to individual acts, facts, and data has served limited purposes well but has fallen short on difficult and important issues. Increased empirical specialization serves only to compound rather than solve this problem.

Behaviorism's emphasis on tangible data, its "empirical" thrust, however, is not inimical to cultural studies. Cultural studies uses empiricism insofar as it begins analysis and interpretation with verifiable facts; in this it is empirical. Cultural studies departs from behaviorism, however, in that it goes beyond individual facts to perceive general patterns and infer broad characteristics that may be inaccessible to behaviorist methods. Cultural studies accepts the limited findings of behaviorism about the probable human responses to specific stimuli, but it refuses to reduce human culture to nothing more than an accumulation of such individual stimuli and responses. Humans express and respond in complex and creative ways in and through culture; they are not automatons.

The positive mission of cultural studies is the interpretation of cultural phenomena, such as super media, as a text. Central to this effort, especially in the work of Hall, are the terms *text, interpretation, meaning, conflict, ideology,* and *hegemony.* Rejecting behaviorism and questioning the liberal pluralist image of a society unified by bland consensus, cultural studies attempts to interpret a society bound together by communication but containing profound conflicts and problematic maldistributions of power. The institutionalized structure of the society, a structure that influences all communication, is indirectly reflected in the ideology that justifies and idealizes that society's character. For Hall especially, institutions and ideology exercise dominance over members of the society in serving the vested interests of the prevalent power structure and its privileged beneficiaries. The dominance is not total, because the system is unavoidably leaky, but there is a subordination that creates positions of superior and inferior. Hegemony, as a mechanism of dominance, enables a culture or group to extend its influence and direct the consciousness of the public. Through hegemony powerful groups exercise dominance by incorporating others into the market relations of cultural consumption. Cultural studies examines these issues by reading media as texts that emerge from and reveal the society and culture.

A Hinckley or an Oswald is an aberrant offspring of these conflicts, pressures, and uncertainties examined by cultural studies. He confuses media fantasies with personal realities and compensates for private inadequacies with public destruction. The assassination act comes from individual maladjustment, but it also emerges from a culture marked by a climate of violence, accessibility of weapons, encouragement of individual adventurism, inattention of social agencies and personal acquaintances, lack of cohesive community membership, failure of traditional institutions, destructive role models, and many other cultural factors associated with the complex world of super media. The killing of John Kennedy, Indira Gandhi, John Lennon, Martin Luther King, Jr., Bobby Kennedy, Anwar Sadat, and President Zia of Pakistan and the attempt on Ronald Reagan are not just individual behaviors; they are also cultural events.

The assassination act also results in public anxiety or hysteria that might threaten established interests if not quieted. For this reason, when a public accounting is demanded, it is in the interest of dominant powers to offer an individualistic and psychological explanation of the assassination attempt, as was done by the Warren Commission for Kennedy's death; this minimizes public anxiety and avoids feeding into radical attempts to criticize organizations or systems. The hegemony of the dominant ideology favors such explanations, phrased in the simplified individualism of behaviorists. But cultural studies seeks to uncover special interests and motives and suppressed meanings. We find that even 25 years after John Kennedy's assassination, 58 percent of a sample of 450 registered voters believed his death was the result of a conspiracy (La Fee, 1988). The nagging doubts are widespread and refuse to go away, despite the official consensus about the lone assassin.

Interpretation and symbolic importance in a cultural context are a central concern of cultural studies. The "meaning" of the Kennedy assassination to the American people and the world, the unsettling and chilling force of the Kennedy and Oswald killings, the suspicion of vested interests possibly served by those killings, the significance of Oswald's weapon being a mail-order rifle in a gun-rich society, the ritual style and therapeutic function of the national funeral, the symbolism in the transition from Kennedy to Lyndon Johnson, the lingering effects on a generation—these are the kinds of issues accessible to cultural studies. These also happen to be areas of natural public interest and debate.

Cultural studies can be viewed as a metadiscipline in the Greek sense of *meta* as "coming after and going beyond," as Aristotle's *Metaphysics* came after his *Physics* and engaged questions more ultimate and subtle. In this sense, cultural studies attempts to take up where other approaches leave off and achieve a needed reintegration of understanding, criticism, and comprehension. It responds to the question of what kind of culture we are creating—our media, ourselves—by incorporating tools of structuralism, critical theory, and ritual analysis.

Structuralism and the Polysemic Text

Structuralism is concerned with how meaning is generated in social texts. Its variations examine the structures of language (Saussure), of signs in society (Peirce), of narrative sequences (Propp), of myths (Barthes), of binary oppositions (Levi-Strauss), of social dominance (Hall), of race (Snead), and of gender (Kaplan).

In a now-famous essay, "Deep Play: Notes on the Balinese Cockfight," Geertz (1973) observes that understanding the cockfight is less like diagnosing a behavior or dissecting an organism than like penetrating a literary text. The overarching question is: What is the meaning of the cockfight? A collectively sustained symbolic structure, present in Balinese cockfights and all popular expressions, offers to Geertz a problem of social semantics more than one of social mechanics. In the cockfight, the Balinese forms and discovers his own temperament and his society's temper at the same time—or, rather, a particular face of them, for each culture offers many faces at different times.

Treating the symbolic cultural form as a text enables one to seek that culture's own reading of the text, whereas functionalist and psychological interpretations of rites and pastimes tend to be reductionist. A popular expression or event may not be universal or typical in meaning but will provide a paradigm in which we can read and reread a culture's sensibility (Geertz, 1973). The interpretation of the Kennedy assassination takes on a more romantic Latin tenor in Mexico, for example, as Dan Dickey has shown in *The Kennedy Corridos: A Study of the Ballads of a Mexican American Hero* (1978). Geertz writes, "The culture of a people is an ensemble of texts, themselves ensembles which the anthropologist strains to read over the shoulders of those to whom they properly belong" (p. 452). The guiding principle is: "Societies, like lives, contain their own interpretations. One has only to learn how to gain access to them" (p. 453).

How does cultural studies approach super media? In the words of James Carey (1979a), "A cultural science of communication . . . views human behavior, or more accurately human action, as a text. Our task is to construct a "reading" of the text. The text itself is a sequence of symbols—speech, writing, gesture—that contain interpretations. Our task, like that of a literary critic, is to interpret the interpretations" (p. 421). Rejecting the search for causality, prediction, and formal theory, Carey suggests that cultural studies carries with it a more critically self-conscious and realistic set of purposes:

> Cultural studies also has far more modest objectives than other traditions. It does not seek to explain human behavior, but to understand it. It does not seek to reduce human action to underlying causes or structures but to interpret its significance. It does not attempt to predict human behavior, but to diagnose human meanings. It is, more positively, an attempt to bypass the rather discrete empiricism of behavior studies and the esoteric apparatus of formal theories and to descend deeper into the empirical world. The goals of communications-studies as a cultural science are therefore more modest, but also more human at least in the sense of attempting to be truer to human nature and experience as it ordinarily is encountered [p. 418].

A century ago older models of thought contrasted primitive and modern thinking: How could primitive thought be so riddled with error? With the discovery of commonalities in all thinking as well as differences, Carey observes,

> Human thought, on the new model, is seen more as interpretations men apply to experience, constructions of widely varying systems of meanings, which cannot be exhaustively verified by the methods of science. What men create is not just one reality, but multiple realities. Reality cannot be exhausted by any one symbolic form be it scientific, religious, or aesthetic [p. 423].

From the study of particular rituals, plays, conversations, songs, and myths, cultural studies can "gingerly reach out to the full relations within a culture or a total way of life" (p. 424).

The emphasis Carey (1985, p. 37) proposes replaces the narrow concern for measuring media effects with the broad question of "how it is through communication . . . that societies are created, maintained, and transformed?" This rejects neither research methods nor the field's past achievements but, rather, deconstructs and reinterprets what is known so that research questions arise within the most important intellectual and real-world issues of the present and past.

Polysemy and the struggle for meaning focus the cultural studies search for interpretation. Polesmy refers to the multiplicity of meanings or sign (*sema*) values inherent in a text, just as *polyphony* refers to two or more melodic lines sung simultaneously over one another. Polysemic readings vary according to each reader's social situation, being bounded and structured by the text but not to a single, universal interpretation (Hall, 1982; Fiske, 1987). A struggle for meaning occurs because ideologically favored groups in society have vested interests in a particular interpretation becoming dominant. The United States government during a presidential crisis, such as the Kennedy assassination or the Nixon resignation, moves quickly to emphasize to foreign publics the continuity and constitutionality of the transition in power from old to new president. That interpretation is imposed, with or without success, to reassure those reliant on American goods and institutions that they need not feel insecure and to head off those anticipating a revolution or breakdown in the American political order.

Super media become explainable, in their most immediate incarnation as text, through the interpretive methods of cultural studies. To explain a media text or event, a critic must at some point pitch his or her tent among the natives. This effort to interpret is not mere unbounded or one-dimensional message analysis, because text always includes *context*. Texts occur only within a culture, a system with subsystems and multiple layers of meaning. Textual interpretation takes "text" as the center of meaning but of a meaning that is social and historical as well as personal. In interpreting a communication act as text, cultural studies recognizes the importance of what previously happened within relevant social institutions as well as what subsequently results as human behavior. Yet, it focuses on the immediate text, the point of contact in which the participant encounters and lives the culture. In this methodology, the work of literary and historical criticism closely parallels the methods of interpretive anthropology.

Illustrating the polysemy of an assassination text, there are conflicting definitions of when death actually occurs. Different cultures have often had conflicting definitions of what constitutes death—the eyes going blank, the spirit departing, a grayness descending, the pulse disappearing, and others. And even within a single culture, definitions of death vary (Carey, 1979a). In Kennedy's case, to his widow his death was immediate at 1:30 P.M. EST as he slumped at her side and she cried, "My God, they've killed Jack." As the motorcade arrived at Parkland Hospital eight minutes later, the president appeared dead to observers, but the doctors led by surgeon Kemp Clark attempted various procedures before officially proclaiming him dead at 2 P.M. By that time, 68 percent of American adults knew of the shooting, but to the public he was not dead before 2:32 P.M., when UPI quoted Father Huber, who had administered the last rites, or 2:33 P.M., when presidential press aide Mac Kilduff officially announced it to the press. To a constitutional lawyer, his death became complete an hour later at 3:38 P.M., when Lyndon Johnson was sworn in to succeed him during the flight back to Washington with the body. Ritually and emotionally, however, the death became real and accepted by many only three days later, on Monday, with the funeral procession and burial. And to the president's small children, it is likely his death was weeks or months in being understood as final; his son celebrated his third birthday with a party on the same day as the funeral, Monday, November 25, with no clear sense of his father's permanent absence.

None of these definitions of death is "wrong," and attempts to explain the differences causally or functionally play a secondary and somewhat futile role compared with the immediate task of sympathetically interpreting the sense of death in each case. Reducing the difference in definitions to something else—a scientific law, a social function, a behavioral construct—in fact, takes us away from the primary task of cultural studies: untangling "the meanings placed on death and innumerable other phenomena" (Carey, 1979a, p. 421). If we cannot grasp the imaginative universe in which the acts of our actors are signs, we cannot claim to understand or explain them. Studies of communication must untangle, in the words of Geertz (1973, p. 10), "a multiplicity of complex conceptual structures, many of them superimposed upon or knotted into one another, which are at once strange, irregular, and inexplicit and which [the student] must contrive somehow to grasp and then to render."

Structuralism in linguistics, anthropology, and literature emphasizes the fundamental importance of sign structures, verbal structures, mental structures, and social structures in giving organization and meaning to human life. For example, fundamentally different social meanings are assigned in binary categories of man/woman, young/old, White/non-White, worker/employer, capitalist/communist, rich/poor, sick/healthy, and so on. These are "structured" categories built through interpersonal and mediated interaction. Semiotics, as the science of signs in society, and structuralism, as the study of the organization of meaning, suggest the complexity of super media's polysemic texts and stratified audiences. Interpretations vary with the many-layered meanings implicit in the text and with the many-layered classes of audience members reading those texts.

Both texts and audiences are many-layered, as Figure 2.1 indicates. The actual interpretation of a given text by a given audience member results from a negotiation of the many levels of meaning implicit in the text and the many levels of social group, class, and individuality embedded in the audience member. These layers lie over one another in great profusion even in the simplest soap opera, western, or situation comedy. Like tightly wound balls of yarn, they await unraveling.

Returning to the example of presidential assassinations, the attempt on President Reagan's life in 1981 presents an especially complex media text for interpretation. The assassin, John Hinckley, was motivated to create this media event by his previous exposure to a film, *Taxi Driver*, and by his self-deluding infatuation with movie star Jodie Foster, who played in it. In his own explanation, Hinckley was moved to assassinate a major politician in order to gain the attention of Foster, who by that time had temporarily left films to pursue an undergraduate degree at Princeton. His act was directly modeled after that of *Taxi Driver's* title character, played by Robert DeNiro, a violent and emotionally unstable loser who plans the assassination of a presidential candidate to gain the admiration of the pathetic character played by Jodie Foster.

Hinckley's attempt occurred, amazingly, on the very day of the scheduled Academy Awards telecast where DeNiro would win the Best Actor award for creating a similar intensely realistic character with a violent streak, Jake LaMotta in *Raging Bull.* That film was directed by Martin Scorcese, director of DeNiro as Hinckley's role model in *Taxi Driver.* Because of the assassination attempt, the Oscar telecast was delayed 24 hours and the prerecorded videotape greeting from President Reagan was omitted, since as a result of a movie interpretation, he now lay immobilized in a hospital.

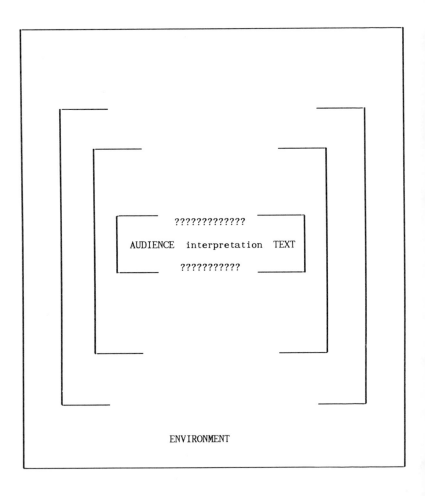

FIGURE 2.1 The Many Layers of Interpretation: Polysemic Texts and Stratified Audiences

On reflection, we can see in this one assassination text the many levels of layered meaning discernible in super media. The assassination attempt, widely replayed on television and described in the press, is the surface level. Beneath that is the motivational dream world of John Hinckley. Inhabiting that level is a bizarre text mingling Hinckley's actual life and his fantasy of Foster that includes *Taxi Driver.* He had seen all of Foster's films many times and had attempted to write and call her. The text of *Taxi Driver* itself exists beneath Hinckley's dream world, filling and distorting it.

In the Reagan assassination text, Hinckley carries the film text within himself and is motivated by it. The additional text of the Academy Awards and their telecast adds a special note of irony, as the culture officially rewards the creators of the deviant motivating text. The victim of the assassination attempt, Reagan, is himself a celebrity of the media—sports announcer, matinee idol, and "Great Communicator" politician. From his celebrity vantage point, he had taped a greeting to his friends in the film industry and the public, to be telecast during the very ceremony that would honor with its highest award the actor who inspired his assailant.

It is especially important to note that all these levels of textual significance are available to any member of the culture. These are "native" readings of the assassination text. They are not theoretically imposed from outside. They neither exaggerate nor reduce the meanings in the process of interpretation via cultural studies. The events of March 30, 1981, also illustrate Eco's designation of "media squared," a situation in which media feed on media that feed on media and in which real people live and deal with these layered texts of super media.

Critical Analysis: Political Economy, Ideology, and Hegemony

Critical analysis generally asks five main questions: How do dominant groups exercise control of the media? How are subordinate groups persuaded to give willing consent to this? How do media techniques and genres systematically cover up inequities? What are the institutionalized logic and relationships among economic forces, political decision making, and ideological formation? How can communication be made more democratic?

Super media not only serve but are vital parts of the dominant economic and political structures of the late 20th century. Mass production and sales of consumer goods are made possible by the mass advertising transmitted by super media. Advertising, in turn, provides the financial support for capitalist media, combining in varying degrees with income from direct sales. Entertainment and news reflect an economic world of private enterprise corporations and their political counterpart, expensive media-driven electoral politics. National and international super media are based in a political economy within capitalism that stresses investment and profit as the bottom line concern behind everything else. No television programming decisions are made, no Hollywood films are put in production, no daily newspapers are printed, no musical group is sent on a major album tie-in tour, no computer hardware or software is marketed without consideration of the financial imperatives. They must offer the promise of making money, or they cannot obtain money. And without money, super media do not happen.

The study of political economy adds a dimension of realism and criticism to media analysis that explains many of the internal dynamics of media operations. It also brings to the forefront the potentially biasing influence of economic and political structures and entrenched dominant groups. Anticommunism in popular film and television reflects the procapitalist base of American media. Racial and gender underrepresentation and stereotyping are also intimately related to the economic structure and incentives in the media. The battle for the largest audience, expressed in the highest ratings, is fought in order to attract more advertisers at higher rates and thus increase profits. Networks periodically admit, as in the 1972 Senate hearings on television violence, that there is more violence on television than one would wish, but they find it plays a role in attracting audiences and making money, so they consider themselves powerless to reduce it. If the largest segment of the audience is most comfortable with subtly sexist, racist, violent, and mindless entertainment, then media managers must work within that in the search for maximum audience and profit.

Three major ideological forms conceal domination, according to Anthony Giddens (1979, pp. 193–195): (1) "the representation of sectional interests as universal ones . . . ," (2) "the denial or transmutation of contradictions . . . ," and (3) "the naturalization of the present: reification." These forms work together to represent the present arrangement of society not as arbitrary but as natural, even necessary. Information and interpretations that conflict with this are denied, and the interests of the dominant group are presented as in the best interest of everyone. For example, social control by White male owners and managers is represented as rooted in universal history. Historically, in racist and sexist cultures, discrimination against women and minorities, including its ultimate manifestations in rapes and lynchings, was not defended but simply represented as a normal part of the social order. The examination of ethnicity and gender in super media in Chapters Four and Five presents current conflicts of dominant representation. Critical analysis examines and opposes the distortions resulting from the ideological forms described by Giddens.

The critical approach to super media employs a vocabulary unafraid of the terms "interaction, conflict, authority, domination, class, status, and power" (Carey, 1985, p. 30). Ideological study supplants behaviorism not only because of ideology's omnipresence and explanatory potential but also because, in the past, behaviorism was part of the "social process by which ideological forms masked and sustained the social order" (p. 31). In retreating from its previous alignment with the dominant social order, media research becomes free to critique its own moral and political commitments. In cultural studies the researcher does not pretend to stand objectively outside the subject of investigation as in behaviorism, but is subjectively engaged in it as a human and social being. Where behaviorism's claim of objectivity is epistemologically naive and in fact distances observers from subjects, cultural studies requires engagement: "to give up, in short, the pose of the observer and to undertake, explicitly, the task of using intelligence to change, modify, or reconstruct the social order" (Carey, 1985, p. 38). History and anthropology save us from relativism and identify the "durable features" of our condition as a way out of postmodernist despair (Carey, 1988).

Critical thinking about political economy provides the material backdrop for concerns about the more abstract notions of ideology and hegemony. If certain economic interests dominate media decisions, are all people's interests served positively and equally? Or are certain limited ways of thinking favored and made into a supposed "common sense" presented as always true in this or any culture? Hall has championed an interest in *hegemony* and *dominant ideology* as ever-present concerns for cultural studies. Hegemony he summarizes as the manipulation of consensus in the preservation of social dominance, a means of control of which Antonio Gramsci wrote from his prison cell in Mussolini's Italy.

The notion of ideology offers innumerable complications and competing definitions. Nichols (1981, p. 7) offers the simple notion of ideology as "the image society gives of itself in order to perpetuate itself." This self-image of society legitimizes the existing power structure and becomes indispensable for its reproduction. It encourages willing consent among members of the society. Whether an ideology is false or not, it provides an "explanation of the world which universalizes a partial social point of view" (Breen & Corcoran, 1986, p. 213). In classic Marxism, ideology was regarded as false consciousness that emanated from the direct relationship between base and superstructure, between material economic conditions and resultant consciousness. Louis Althusser's elaboration of the part played by ideological state apparatuses assigns a decisive role to be filled by public and private media as ideological influences. But it is primarily Gramsci's notion of ideology and hegemony that has energized more recent cultural studies debates about the role of media.

In contrast to earlier deterministic theories of direct manipulation by a dominant class, Gramsci distinguished between two forms of control: coercion and consent. Besides repressive external coercion, a social group can exercise supremacy internally by molding personal convictions into a replica of prevailing norms. One way of thinking becomes diffused throughout society by consensus. Raymond Williams (1977, p. 110) calls hegemony "saturation of the whole process of living—to such a depth that the pressures and limits of what can ultimately be seen as a specific economic, political and cultural system seem to most of us the pressures and limits of simple experience and common sense." In this way ideological hegemony *sets limits and exerts pressures,* whether the hegemony concerns gender, ethnicity, the Cold War, or other areas of social life. Mainstream media research has suffered by ignoring or underestimating such issues, as Hall (1982) has explained. The analysis of Cold War influence in Chapters Six and Seven illustrates and elaborates on the workings of ideology and hegemony in super media.

It is possible to distinguish three levels of ideology and meaning (see Parkin, 1972, pp. 79–102; & Fiske and Hartley, 1978, p. 104). The *dominant system* emerges from the structure of transnational power economically and politically. This powerful mainstream force, protective of elite favoritism, dominates the ideological climate of any given culture. In its early history, as an example, the dominant system of United States ideology accepted slavery and racial segregation. A *subordinate system* can operate within the dominant ideology in the manner of loyal opposition; this subordinate system accepts the structure of society as a whole but wishes to change a specific practice. For example, in the civil rights movement, led by Dr. Martin Luther King in the United States, allegiance was constantly reiterated for "America" as a whole, but specific segregationist practices were opposed. King preached, "I have a dream deeply rooted in the American dream." Against the dominant ideology, an *oppositional or radical subsystem* is one in which the social group rejects essential structural elements of the system that it is criticizing. The more revolutionary rhetoric of Malcolm X before his assassination in 1967 represents this oppositional position. His attacks on American racism were much more critical of the total American socioeconomic system than were those of Dr. King. These three levels reappear in Chapter Four in the examination of Bill Cosby and recoding ethnicity.

In terms of presidential assassinations, McAnany notes what might be called a struggle for cultural hegemony as a backdrop for the assassination of President Anwar Sadat of Egypt in 1981. At that time there was, as McAnany notes (1986, p. 3), "a strong backlash in the Middle East by religious leaders and their followers, specifically toward some of the 'western' images on television and toward the U.S. political and cultural presence in many Middle Eastern Muslim countries in general." Dallas, for example, was one of the most popular television shows in Egypt as well as the United States and many other countries. Although no direct relationship between the shootings of J.R. and Sadat is suggested, the tensions in Egypt leading to the assassination certainly included Sadat's American and Western alliances, which were opposed by many Muslim leaders who favored a stricter orthodoxy. Their subordinate ideology became fully oppositional. A similar hegemonic struggle provides the backdrop for the assassination of President Indira Gandhi, considered by opponents at the time to be the leading figure of Hindu hegemony against the Sikh separatists. Neither Sadat nor Gandhi had achieved complete hegemony over other domestic ideologies, but they were accused of trying to do so and fell victims to the backlash.

Critical analysis extends structural analysis into areas of political economy on the material side and areas of hegemony on the ideational side. Ritual analysis integrates the analysis of the workings of super media around the understanding of the powerful social role of myth and ritual in traditional and modern societies.

Myth and Ritual in Super Media Analysis:
Communal Celebration

Analysis of media as ritual opens up the communal dimension of super media as the center of contemporary mythic, ritual, liminal experiences. In news broadcasts, papal visits, space launchings, and summit meetings, and in the little dramas of our everyday mediated experience, we come together to share moments and motifs that bind us as a people.

The larger role of media as public ritual moves the field beyond behaviorism and draws together the concerns of semiotics, structuralism, and critical theory. Carey (1988) suggests, "To grasp hold of the popular arts with terms like *myth, ritual, pilgrimage, liminality, story, narrative, chronicle*—to state but a select portion of the list—is to see in a miraculously discontinuous world persistent practices by which that world is sedimented and held together" (p. 15). Myths and "consensus narratives," he finds, draw society together around the continuous reweaving of given patterns of action and signification.

A grasp of modern *myth and ritual* provides access to essential dimensions of the super media experience. Myths arise as community stories that celebrate collective heroes, origins, and identity through expressive rituals. All cultures have their grand narrative histories that explain the origins of a people and present their ultimate destinies and ideals. Universal evolution and continuous scientific progress are mythic ideals alongside those of the Garden of Eden, the Fall, and redemption. According to Silverstone (1981), police and action adventure shows on television celebrate the mythic hope that good will triumph over the criminal bestiality lurking in all of us. *Dallas* and *Dynasty* achieved worldwide popularity by celebrating widespread myths of family solidarity, personal loyalty, and the exercise of power.

Understood as ritual expressions, the media can be seen to provide essentially communitarian or collective experiences far beyond what traditional research examines as measurable effects on individual behavior. The media involve the whole community in the creation of culture—producers, investors, writers, actors, audiences, creators, and others (Newcomb & Alley, 1983). They provide a cultural forum for expression (Newcomb & Hirsch, 1985). The media also involve the whole community in the resulting experience, as in the Olympics, the Academy Awards, and other media ritual events (Katz, 1980). Cassirer's (1944) notion of myth, as one of six symbolic sets alongside art, science, religion, history, and language, opens up dimensions of media as they relate to emotions, social life, and symbolic activity in general. Mircea Eliade (1959) sees myths as providing the sacred poles of our identity that separate us from mere profane and pointless existence. Gregor Goethals (1981) has taken the notion of icons and rituals from Eliade and others to explain how viewers "worship at the video altar" in the television ritual.

There are multiple levels in the mythic narratives through which television and other media tell stories (Silverstone, 1981). There is, first, the thematic *content* taken from everyday life. "Thirtysomething" draws from the domestic, "Cheers" from the recreational, and "L.A. Law" from the professional content of everyday life. There is, second, the *chronological* ordering of events that moves action through a framed period of time to a satisfying resolution. A problem in search of a solution creates a sequence of action for "Magnum P.I.," "Cagney and Lacey," and "Hill Street Blues." There is, third, a cultural *logic* that makes the story by extension representative of problems experienced by audience members and solutions available to them. The dilemmas of "Taxi," "Newhart," and "I Love Lucy" strike responsive chords among viewers. There is, fourth, an *archetypal* formula of good over evil as compelling in modern television as it was in traditional fairy tales and legends. From "Star Trek" to "Championship Wrestling" we can identify with the good guys and enjoy our virtuous struggle and triumph. The discussion in Chapter Eight of the Olympic global ritual explains how media myths present (1) a perceptual system of common social understanding, (2) heroic models for imitation, (3) means of conflict mediation, and (4) vehicles for making history intelligible, as proposed by Breen and Corcoran (1986).

Myths are *analogue* structures placed over against the *digital* pragmatics of the rest of life. Applying this distinction, we can see that John Hinckley was able to function on the pragmatic "digital" level of information exchange and specific acts as he moved around the country seeking Jodie Foster's attention: he was able to check in and out of housing, order and eat meals, and perform other social functions. But he was finally overwhelmed when his movie fantasy world on the "analogue" level took hold of him with its in-depth myths and ritual models and led him to attack President Reagan.

Super media are communitarian and also have regenerative powers as "liminal experiences" (Turner, 1977). Liminal experiences are those that take one beyond a threshold. Rituals among Central African tribes reveal how social dramas and liminal experiences occur on all levels of social organization, from state to family. The rituals arise out of conflict situations, take participants through a "liminal" transition state, and achieve resolution through public ceremony. In the process, social structure, status, and transitions are marked and transitions achieved. The process is a sequential, dramatic one. During liminality, adolescents being initiated into adulthood, for example, may be isolated in a remote spot, stripped of childish accoutrements and made naked, scarred or painted, put through trials and tests, and made to exist for this liminal transition time as no longer children but not yet adults. Heightened awe, emotional intensity, and an uncertain outcome make such experiences decisive. Most of all, the meaning placed in these liminal transitions makes them the powerful texts that they are. The subject emerges changed forever, finally an adult. Somewhat similarly, the powerful novel or film that changes one's life, the epic competition that draws one out into something larger, the taut cathartic drama, the globally witnessed Olympic triumph—these media experiences have the potential for emotional involvement and liminal transition that Turner and others have found in traditional mythic rituals. But the liminal experience need not be life-changing; it may simply be the temporary experience of that transitional state between other activities, a state that offers respite and recreation in the tradition of classical notions of leisure.

Even otherwise repressive media, such as North American advertising and television invasions of Latin America, can be appropriated for their own ends by the popular classes through the mediating influence of the daily life of the family and the *barrio*. Jesus Martin-Barbero (1987) has suggested that daily life mediates between possible and actual effects of media. The wildly popular Spanish language soap operas, the *telenovelas,* despite their unrealistic romanticism and individualistic escapism, nevertheless suggest a sense of popular justice, an accentuation of conflict, a subtle ridicule of the powerful, and an active recognition of the life of the *barrio,* the extended family, and the city. For the great majority, political motivations have their first expression in comedy, satirical music, and melodramas of injustice. *Mediations,* Martin-Barbero suggests, are the crucial points of articulation between the presentations of media and the daily life of viewers. Mediations appropriate elements from the regressive media mythology of consumer capitalism and cultural domination in the service of still-living myths of tradition, productivity, and independence. As Fiske (1987) argues, the audience finds multiple meanings in media and develops oppositional readings of the media texts.

Returning again to our example of assassinations, the mythic ritual power of super media has never been more obvious than in the period following the nationally traumatic assassination of President Kennedy. Consider the scene.

> For three days regular television programming and commercials are suspended. A hundred million persons sit in shocked wonder staring at their television screens as the body of a vital young president is flown back to Washington and carried to its final rest.
>
> Only the solemn sound of paced drumbeats accompanies the riderless horse and casket as they parade slowly through the streets of Washington. The widow and two tiny children stand vigil. The fallen president's energetic, glamorous siblings and their families mourn at the center of national attention. Artists and poets struggle to help a nation comprehend the inexpressible.
>
> A nation and world momentarily unified in tragedy expresses its sorrow, fears, and dreams through the inadequate but necessary wonders of super media.

For the United States, this experience consolidated the role of television and supplemental media as ritual and liminal experiences. The sudden murder of the president left the public feeling individually isolated, stripped naked, scarred. Following the subsequent events from Friday to Monday through super media carried the audience through this trial and test and uncertainty with the appropriate heightened awe and emotional intensity. Finally the nation emerged from the liminal experience reconciled once again to life and the world, but a collective life and world different from what went before.

The Case-Study Method in Cultural Studies

The case-study method provides cultural studies with a particularly appropriate methodology for raising and answering questions about super media and culture. Without eliminating real-world contexts and communitarian dimensions as behaviorism does, the case-study method provides a series of structured steps built around central concepts and concerns of cultural studies. Chapters Three through Eight illustrate the case-study method.

Selection

The case-study method in cultural studies begins with a "problematic" that is situated historically and contextually in one or a series of related cases that raise cultural, ideological, economic, and/or political questions. The selection of the case or cases is crucial. The most productive cases are those which influence and represent many other aspects of culture and in which ideology and hegemony are especially operative. Any presidential assassination text is likely to meet these criteria. The problematic present in the case is pursued in a spirit of evaluation and critical self-awareness.

Text

The case study presents a specific point-of-impact text in which the culture expresses itself and the public creates interpretations. The text may be a media text in film, video, audio, or print, or it may be a set of social practices, such as the working routines of a newsroom. For example, an attempted assassination is a widely reported act; the reports become texts for analysis.

Ethnography

An exact account must be provided of the facts of the case, just as an anthropologist obtains the facts of an unknown rite and its uses within the group that practices it *before* he or she sets about interpreting the rite. The immediate characters, plots, practices, and interpretations of the text require careful definition. Here, questionnaires, surveys, in-depth interviews, experiments, quantitative content analysis, detailed logs, audience ratings, marketing analysis, and other empirical instruments may be employed as a step toward understanding the case. *The Kennedy Assassination and the American Public* (Greenberg & Parker, 1965) combined surveys and related instruments to trace ethnographically the dissemination of information about the Kennedy assassination and the emotional effects it had on people. Slightly more than half (51%) first heard the news of the shooting from interpersonal rather than media sources; the average home viewed approximately ten hours per day of assassination-related television from Friday till Monday; Blacks were more disturbed by the assassination than Whites; some 4 percent of the public felt Kennedy had brought it on himself; and the three stages of obtaining news, surviving the shock, and achieving social reintegration were shared by a huge majority of the American people.

Ethnography considers the immediate context; exegesis examines the larger context.

Exegesis

The traditional scriptural technique of textual exegesis goes beyond the immediate ethnography to identify precisely the literary genre of a work, the comparative life situation from which it emerged, and the intention of the original author. This it does by comparing the work with closely parallel works and placing it carefully in time, place, and purpose. Exegesis is not an arbitrary interpretation or the practical application of a text to another purpose, but a careful, expanded analysis of it. Comparison of the Hinckley attempt on Reagan with other attempts against heads of state clarifies both the commonalities, or "conventions of the genre," as they might be called, and the differences, or inventions of the particular assassin-author. Assassinations also parallel other disastrous events such as the fatal explosion of the *Challenger* space shuttle, the Chernobyl nuclear meltdown, the controversial downings of a Korean Airline flight by Soviet jets and of an Iranian passenger flight by an American warship, the shooting of the pope, the poison-gas deaths of thousands in Bhopal, India, the mass suicide in Jonestown, Guyana, and earthquakes, floods, fires, and accidents of all descriptions. From such direct parallels, more exact interpretations of a case are possible. In each situation, who owns what, whose interests are most served, and what alternatives were excluded may all enter into exegesis of a case study.

Criticism

Together with the foregoing sociological, historical, and analytic practices, the case-study method in cultural studies engages in direct criticism. Here the questions of esthetic judgment, of social power and conflict, of ideology and hegemony, of human values and bias, all enter explicitly into the case. Responsible research does not avoid but articulates this level. Official explanations of assassinations usually call for such criticism. The Warren Commission, as the official investigation of the Kennedy assassination, concluded that Oswald acted alone and unaided by anyone. Great evidence supported this, but other evidence did not. There were rumors that the assassination had originated either in Cuban revenge for Kennedy administration plans to assassinate Castro (Oswald's Soviet and Cuban connections) or in Mafia revenge for Kennedy administration attacks on organized crime (the Jack Ruby connection). Such rumors, and the evidence to support them, ran so counter to the dominant preference for a clean and simple explanation that a persistent rumble of conspiracy theories continued, fueled as much by suspicion of protected vested interests as by the known facts. The established figures on the Warren Commission had many reasons for not fomenting unrest, and a full criticism of the case of the Kennedy assassination would take into account the possibilities and motives for suppression and distortion deriving from social power and hegemony. Sound criticism requires a sense of history and culture, a willingness to ask difficult questions, and an awareness of underrepresented groups and interests.

In brief, the case-study method selects a problematic expressed in a text (or texts) and then subjects the text to ethnographic description, exegetical clarification, and critical examination in the search for a full understanding of its social origins, meanings, and consequences.

The case-study method has been applied to a wide variety of situations and questions. Presidential assassinations naturally invoke the long-standing debate over violence in the media, a debate to which cultural studies has made important contributions. Curran, Gurevitch, and Woollacott (1982, p. 14) use the issue of research on media and violence to illustrate the differences between behaviorist pluralism and critical cultural studies. They note that "empirical researchers in the liberal tradition have tended to examine media portrayals of violence in terms of whether they promote and encourage violence in everyday life." In contrast, they note, "Most researchers in the Marxist tradition in Britain have approached this question in terms of whether media portrayals of violence have served to legitimize the forces of law and order, build consent for the extension of coercive state regulation and de-legitimize outsiders and dissidents."

As an example of the case-study method, Hall, Chritcher, Jefferson, Clarke, and Roberts (1978) have examined street muggings in *Policing the Crisis: Mugging, the State, and Law and Order.* They locate the mugging phenomenon and its popular interpretations squarely within a historically developing "crisis of hegemony" in which the bases of political and cultural authority become exposed and contested. Finding increased anxiety about mugging by the press and politicians to be largely unfounded in fact and misleading in presentation, *Policing the Crisis* argues that a closer look at the facts of crime and the symbolic descriptions of mugging unmasks the use of force and coercion against citizens where consensus has failed. Seen in the context of the characteristic structure of feeling of "a whole way of life," mugging itself is not an isolable problem to be attacked but, rather, the symptom of much more profound realignments of power, influence, and consent.

In a separate case study, "Popular Culture and the State" (1986), Stuart Hall examines the historical relationship between dominant and popular culture. He takes four seemingly unrelated cases—early football, law, newspapers, and television—in order to trace the changing place of the state as an agent of leadership and intervention in British class struggles in the last two centuries.

Hall sets the stage by describing the radically changed place of "football" ("soccer" to North Americans) in the traditional village, where the game was highly irregular, was without standard rules, and sometimes involved hundreds of participants on unmarked fields or town streets. By contrast, the modern game is centrally administered and organized according to universally observed and refereed rules; it has been redesigned for spectatorship rather than participation. Hall observes,

> These contrasts bring out qualitative differences: between a rural society, regulated by custom, local tradition and the particularism of small, face-to-face communities, and an urban-centralized society governed by universally applied rules and a legal and rational mode of regulation. Nor was there any smooth evolution from one to the other. The traditional game became the object of a massive assault by the governing classes and authorities—part of a general attack on popular recreations in order to moralize the poorer classes and make them more regular and industrious in their habits [p. 24].

Hall's larger argument is made by examining three "snapshots" of how the British state has always played a crucial role in making popular culture conform to the dominant culture. First, in the 18th century the role of the law was to mediate cultural relations, but in so doing it served upper-class interests. Second, in the 19th century the popular newspaper press emerged in the transition from state to market regulation, but it did so as "a press *about* and *bought by* but not *produced by,* or *committed to the cause of,* the popular classes" (p. 36). Commercial capital and state intervention ensured that working-class newspapers disappeared and the popular classes entered the free market of opinion under the leadership and hegemony of the dominant classes, rather than through the previously powerful radical working-class press. In his third snapshot, Hall describes the historical development of television in England to the point where

> television is linked, in a multitude of visible and invisible, direct and indirect, ways, to the state. . . . Broadcasting does not illegally swing its weight behind one political party or another, but it does respect and cherish the whole ideological framework, the basic structure of social relations, the existing dispositions of wealth, power, influence, prestige, on whose foundations it ultimately rests [p. 46].

The purpose is to discover "how cultural institutions and practices institutionalize (settle, fix, secure, stabilize) a particular pattern of relations between the cultures and the classes in society" (p. 47). These patterns shift over time and refashion the nature of cultural leadership and consent in society. For Hall, the restructuring of cultural relations "is central to the processes by which hegemony—a condition of social ascendancy, of cultural, moral and political leadership by a particular social bloc—is, or is not achieved, in particular historical periods" (p. 47). In this way, Gramsci's point is affirmed: that in mass democracies, hegemony is increasingly reliant on the enlarged cultural role of the state. This, in Hall's view, applies also to press and broadcasting, despite their claims to being operations "free" of government influence. As Hall and others illustrate, the case-study method is neither rigid nor guaranteed, but is employed in a variety of ways in cultural studies.

A Summary of Approaches to Media and Culture

The depth and breadth of experiences of super media have occasioned a variety of analytic approaches. In this chapter cultural studies has been presented as a metadiscipline that critiques these approaches and synthesizes the best of them. Taken together, empirical, structural, critical, and ritual analysis each contribute essential understanding and insight into the super media experience. Table 2.2 summarizes these approaches and relationships. It recapitulates this chapter and the organization of *Super Media* as a whole; the chapter and the book are isomorphic in structure. The summary table lists approaches and sources that have been decisive. Some have been identified in this chapter; others appear later in these pages.

Table 2.2 continues the heuristic task of elucidating the distinctions between behaviorism and criticism of Table 2.1. But instead of being

TABLE 2.2 Approaches and Concepts in Super Media Analysis

Approach	Central Theories and Concepts	Representative Figures	Discipline and Methods
Cultural studies			
a. Social interpretation			
	Text	Geertz	Anthropology
	Interpretation	Carey	Communication
	Ideology	R. Williams Bennett	Drama
	Hegemony	Hall, Gramsci	Culture
b. Popular culture interpretation			
	Genre and formula	Cawelti	Literature
	Popular esthetics	Browne, Nachbar	Popular culture
	Taste cultures	Gans	Sociology
	Elite/folk/mass	Nye	Literature
Subdisciplines			
1. Empirical analysis			
a. Individual:	Propaganda	Lasswell	Political sci.
	Persuasion	Hovland-Janis	Experim. psych.
	Consistency	T. Newcomb, Festinger	Functionalism
	Limited effects	Klapper	Behaviorism
b. Social:	Two-step flow	Berelson	Political science
	Personal influence	Lazarsfeld	Social psychology
	Soc.-psych. variables	Cantril, Merton	Sociology
	Gatekeeper	Westley-McLean	Journalism
	Cultivation	Gerbner	Communication
	Agenda setting	McCombs-Shaw	Journalism
	Diffusion	Rogers-Shoemaker	Communication
	Luddites vs. technologists	Mumford, Bell	Planning-design
c. Uses and gratifications	Consumer needs	Katz	Sociology
	Active audience	Blumler	Communication
	Competing media	Rosengren	Communication

(continued)

TABLE 2.2 Approaches and Concepts in Super Media Analysis *(Continued)*

Approach	Central Theories and Concepts	Representative Figures	Discipline and Methods
2. Structuralist analysis			
	Language	Saussure	Linguistics
	Signs and codes	Peirce	Semiotics
	Encoding-decoding	Barthes	Literature
	Binary oppositions	Levi-Strauss	Anthropology
	Ideology	Althusser	Philosophy
	Polysemy	Fiske	Communication
3. Critical analysis			
	Political economy	Marx	Economics
	Culture industry	Frankfurt School	Criticism
	Pol. econ. of culture	Garnham	History
	Cultural domination	Schiller	Economics
	Media institutions	Smythe	Economics
	Transnationals	Hamelink	Communication
	Information/ideology	Slack	Communication
	Ideological crit.	Wander	Speech
	Mediations	Martin-Barbero	Communication
	Alternative media	Kellner	Philosophy
	Le technique	Ellul	History
	Film theory	Eisenstein, Bazin	Esthetics
4. Ritual analysis			
	Expressive rites	Carey	Communication
	Media ritual event	Katz	Sociology
	Liminality	Turner, Silverstone	Anthropology
	Cultural forum	H. Newcomb-Hirsch	Literature
	Consensus narrative	Thorburn	Literature
	Oral culture	Ong	Theology
	Literate culture	Innis	Pol. economy
	Electronic culture	McLuhan	Literature
	Literacy	Postman	Literature
	Mythic functions	Breen-Corcoran	Communication

presented as oppositional, here the approaches are coordinated and made mutually beneficial. The classifications are highly impressionistic: the "Central Theories and Concepts" are far from perfect one-word codes to suggest an emphasis; the "Representative Figures" are a *few* of the researchers associated with the emphasis; and the "Disciplines and Methods" illustrate the variety of sources from which media understanding has originated. Cultural studies appears first, not merely as one approach among others but as a vantage point from which to utilize selectively the positive contributions of each.

The general purpose of the table is to indicate both the rich variety of approaches to media and the interrelationships among these. Many academic disciplines and methods have contributed to our understanding of our media and, therefore, ourselves. We can learn from their findings and select from their methods, as the following chapters illustrate.

However one describes its place and methods, at its most basic, cultural studies appreciates the importance of media, probes beneath the surface, questions dominant meanings and ideology, seeks out suppressed interpretations, and takes culture and history seriously. One of Hall's guiding phrases is "People make history but out of conditions not of their own making." This phrase preserves a sense of the force of inherited practices and political-economic institutions even as it invokes the power of people to seize and shape the future. A past presidential assassination in Sweden, Egypt, India, the United States, or elsewhere cannot be changed. It is a condition not of our own making. But from an interpretive understanding of that event, like a phoenix rising from the ashes, there can arise a new sense of the culture we deal with and the history we can make.

Gradually the attempt on the ex-actor's life recedes into history. First reported as minor, with a joking president walking into the hospital, it proves to be a most narrow escape. Sympathy for his injury improves his standings in the opinion polls.

In much the same way, Americans of 20 years earlier had become accustomed to the fact that their young president was gone. His death was soon overlaid by the similar fate of others. His brother was gunned down as he sought the presidency; civil rights leaders were slain; a decade of assassinations left its bloody legacy.

Nothing much changes. Handgun legislation stalls up against the lobbying of the National Rifle Association. Organized crime remains successful. The movies continue to provide role models for assassins. Cold War antagonisms are more frequently exploited than modified.

Only here and there do a few continue to think about events and about interpretations of events, as their seamless web is reshaped into memory.

Questions

1. Identify central contrasts between behaviorism and criticism as they apply to super media.
2. What is the importance of the terms *text, context, meaning, interpretation, ideology,* and *hegemony?*
3. How might those terms be useful in interpreting political events, labor news, feature films, music videos, television commercials, and other cultural expressions?
4. How is an expanded definition of culture important to the origins and focus of cultural studies?
5. Which aspects of empirical media-centered research does cultural studies accept and which does it reject?
6. What can structuralism, polysemic texts, and stratified audiences reveal about the experience of super media?
7. How can political economy, ideology, and hegemony affect media texts and their interpretations?
8. What dimensions of super media become clearer when they are considered as a ritual experience?
9. What steps are usually implicit in the case-study method of cultural studies?
10. How do super media present presidential assassinations and how does cultural studies attempt to interpret them?

Notes

1. Hall (1980) traces the origins of contemporary British cultural studies as a distinctive problematic to the mid-1950s, with the publication of Richard Hoggart's *The Uses of Literacy* (1957) and Raymond Williams's *Culture and Society: 1780–1950* (1958). Hall adds E. P. Thompson's *The Making of the English Working Class* (1963) and Williams's *The Long Revolution* (1962) to his short list of seminal and formative texts in the development of cultural studies.

2. Is communication an academic discipline? In two classic essays, "Overcoming Resistance to Cultural Studies" (1985) and "Mass Communication Research and Cultural Studies: An American View" (1979a), Carey takes a position on this question similar to that of Hall, Raymond Williams, and most cultural studies advocates. Answering nega-

tively, he proposes that cultural studies centers "the mass media as a *site* (not a subject or a discipline) on which to engage the general question of social theory" (p. 37). Carey and Hall find the social arena of communication today to be the crucial grounds for struggle and power, making it an important site demanding critical attention. They prefer to approach communication, media, and information without the artificial boundaries of academic disciplines.

Mainstream mass communication research has sought both "scientific" and "disciplinary" status, in Carey's view, for purposes of prestige and bureaucratic autonomy on campus as much as for intellectual reasons. Carey finds the resulting independent growth in students, journals, and faculty an inadequate reward as the field becomes "intellectually stagnant and increasingly uninteresting" (Carey, 1985, p. 28). Carey's Illinois colleague Lawrence Grossberg makes the same point in speaking of "a new generation of critical communications researchers who . . . seek ways to integrate communication into a larger theoretical framework" (Introduction to Slack, 1984, p. x). Latin American media researchers, in the words of Juan Diaz Bordenave (1988), seek "to transcend communications issues per se and to deal, through them, with the totality of economic, social, political, and cultural relations in society" (p. 146). This contrasts, for example, with the position of a dominant textbook, *Theories of Mass Communications* (DeFleur & Ball-Rokeach, 1982, p. 254), which presents the study of mass communication as "one of our newest academic disciplines," or Alexis Tan's book *Mass Communication Theories and Research* (1985, p. 4), which asserts that mass communication has achieved the status of a "scientific discipline," based on its research methods, advanced statistical tools, and mathematical models.

Placing somewhat less emphasis than Hall on ideology and hegemony, Carey presents cultural studies through a consideration of the contributions of Clifford Geertz (Carey, 1975a), Harold Adams Innis (Carey, 1975b), Marshall McLuhan (Carey, 1968), and Lewis Mumford (Carey, 1979b), as well as the classics of John Dewey, Max Weber, C. Wright Mills, Kenneth Burke, and even occasionally Vico or Descartes (Carey, 1981b). Carey has clarified the contributions of popular culture and its uses and gratifications (Carey & Kreiling, 1974) and has spelled out the nature of qualitative studies (Carey & Christians, 1981).

3

Empirical Analysis:
The Academy Awards

You enter with friends and find a seat. The house lights go down. An expectant hush settles over the audience. Eyes focus in anticipation toward the front. The audio system brings back the first crisp, clear sounds to the assembled faithful.

For a prolonged period your feelings, your imagination, your mind are captured and held. Like a magic token, your ticket has given you entrance to this sacred experience. Your loftiest dreams and your darkest fears, your most gut-wrenching losses and your profoundest joys, love and death, vulgar manipulation, transcendent beauty, laughter and tears—all these and more are yours as they are acted out before your eyes and ears. You are experiencing once again in all its immediacy the power of super media.

Once each year the magical power of this filmic experience is celebrated through television. For that Oscar event, designer gowns and tuxedos glamorize the familiar screen stars and movie moguls. Celebrities share a microphone to introduce the awards. We hear the familiar words, "The envelope, please." It is nervously opened: "And the winner is . . ."

The Academy Awards telecast is the most widely viewed annual media event originating from the United States. Its 50 million American viewers fall well short of the Super Bowl audience of 120 million. But the Academy Award (or "Oscars") telecast attracts another 200 million viewers overseas in countries where the Super Bowl is virtually unheard of. "Roots" or *Gone With the Wind* may break American television ratings records, but they do not go out live at one moment to the whole world the way the Oscar telecast does. Even the Olympics and World Cup playoffs, which attract world audiences of a billion or more, do not attempt to repeat themselves oftener than every four years. The Oscars are a uniquely interesting transnational media event.

The annual Academy Awards celebration means different things to different people. To ABC television, the Oscar show means an audience of more than 250 million people in 75 countries. To those millions of viewers, the Academy Awards telecast means three hours of celebrities, glamour, and coveted awards—interspersed with tedious walks to the stage, rambling thank-you's, and some obscure prizes. To the movie studio winning a Best Picture Oscar, the award means $20 to $50 million in increased box office revenues for that film. To cultural studies, the Academy Awards means a subject worthy of analysis, a multilayered televised text produced by transnational corporations and interpreted by diverse persons in many countries. To empirical research, the Oscar event means a challenge for measuring audience reactions, quantifying content categories, profiling production procedures, and assessing economic factors and effects.

The Academy Award telecast powerfully combines the resources of the Hollywood film industry and the American television industry to produce a lucrative "media event." Such media events provide, in the words of Elihu Katz (1980), the "high holidays" of contemporary daily life. Whether a "contest," as in a Wimbledon playoff, or a "conquest," as in a Middle East war, or a "coronation," as in a royal wedding, these events capture the attention of vast populations and elicit collective excitement, celebration, and mourning. The Oscars capture all this. They are a contest among films, a coronation of winners, and a conquest over moviegoers by the colossal commercial that is the Academy Awards.

A series of legends confuse our judgments of the Oscars. The Academy of Motion Picture Arts and Sciences is a disinterested, objective body sharing its professional, impartial evaluations, is it not? Television carries this awards event as a public service similar to political conventions and debates, does it not? Members of the public participate and agree on what they like best in this event, do they not? The availability of this service informs the international public by spreading before it the widest possible range of cultural goods, does it not? This is art, not industry, democracy, not autocracy, right? Are these legends fact or fiction? What do we reliably know about Oscar-winning films and the Oscar event?

Traditional Mainstream American Media Research

Theory and research on super media are "contested terrain," in the words of Stuart Hall. Disagreements keep the field lively and make the present a crucial time in the evolution of media understanding. Cultural studies provides an interpretive frame and metadisciplinary flexibility, but many other specific communication research techniques and concepts have contributed to our ability to examine and explain media. The unique value of no single technique or insight outweighs the value of all others. This chapter reviews and applies the more micro and behavioral approaches to media, those that are centered more on media than on culture. What does American empiricism tell us about super media and the Academy Awards, celebrated each spring as the Hollywood film industry pats itself on the back before a huge international television audience?

Media-centered empiricism emphasizes factual certainty in knowledge. It grew from the early applications of the methods of social psychology and survey research to the subject of mass communications between the first and second world wars. In response to rumors of massive media effects, it set about precisely measuring what did and did not play a direct part in specific media experiences and their consequences. As the Academy Awards began in 1929, research efforts were developing ways of answering specific questions. How many people read about the awards in the following day's newspaper? Were they influenced to feel more favorably about the winning films? What kind of people were most likely to notice and appreciate the awards? These were questions to which newspaper, film, and other media owners and managers wanted answers. With their financial support, that form of behavioral research grew. World War II strengthened the prestige of such "hard" science, and its methods became entrenched in universities, research institutes, and media organizations.

Out of this empirical research emerged a "dominant paradigm" of the communication process. Certain "classics" of media analysis provided the fundamental frame for understanding media. One such classic was Harold Lasswell's (1948/1960) widely used segmentation of the communication process into five steps, or stages:

Who
Says What
Through Which Channel
To Whom
With What Effect?

This five-part designation resembles the stages in the Shannon and Weaver model (1949), the Berlo model (1960), the Schramm and Porter model (1982), and others. From the sender the message is encoded, travels through the channel, and is decoded to reach the receiver. A caller speaks into her telephone, which encodes the words as electrical signals. These signals are then transmitted through the channel of telephone lines to a decoder, which translates them back into spoken words heard by the listening party, who in turn responds. This popular "bullet" or "railroad" model of the communication process has dominated media research, with particular emphasis on receivers and effects. The paradigm underlies the majority of conventional American media-centered research and theory: source (Who), message (Says What), medium (Through Which Channel), audience (To Whom), and feedback (With What Effect). The history of this approach, with its peculiar strengths and weaknesses, is well documented and evaluated (McQuail, 1987; Delia, 1987; Lowery & DeFleur, 1983; Wartella & Reeves, 1985; Gitlin, 1978).

The "who" of the Academy Awards telecast is the academy itself, which produces the show under contract to a television network. The "says what" is the three-hour telecast. The "through which channel" is the television network that transmits the signal from the Los Angeles venue through relays to viewers. The "to whom" is the audience member viewing from home, a pub, or elsewhere throughout a large part of the world. The "effect" is any modification of behavior, such as conversations about the awards.

Super media do for human culture today what primary group communication does for lower organisms—animals, insects—and what internal biological messages do for the individual organism in providing growth, movement, healing, and ultimate deterioration. This idea originated in another early "classic" of conventional media analysis, Lasswell's (1948/1960) "The Structure and Function of Communication in Society." Effective communication must serve a unit of whatever size, from organism to United Nations, with three standard functions:

- Surveillance of the environment (the news function)
- Correlation of the parts (the editorial function)
- Transmission of the social heritage (the education function)

As Lasswell pointed out, even ant societies have scouts, organizers, and teachers, and human society parallels these fundamental communication functions on a larger scale. Now, in the age of super media, these functions move to transnational levels. Through its extended transmission, the Academy Awards event performs Lasswell's three social functions. It surveys the film world environment by presenting an array of stars, films, songs and attendant glitter as the approved frame of reference for prestige films from Hollywood. It correlates the parts by giving awards to what the Hollywood filmmaking community considers the most worthy. And it transmits the social heritage by teaching celebrity-watching, filmgoing, humor, art, competition, commercialism, and the other values emphasized throughout the ceremony.

Sources, Transmission, Institutions: Who Says Through Which Channel

What do we know of the source (Who) and transmission (Which Channel) of the Academy Awards telecast?

The Oscar celebration is not a preestablished and self-contained ceremony that just happens to be telecast. Instead, it is a "media event" inseparable in its planning and execution from the media carrying it. The academy was founded in 1927, and its first awards, in 1929, received newspaper and magazine coverage. For the second awards presentation, in 1930, live radio coverage was added and, in 1953, television. If these had been industry awards for computer software or auto design, the ceremony would have received limited media coverage, and that coverage would have been in the form of independent news coverage controlled exclusively by the media reporting it. In contrast, the Academy of Motion Picture Arts and Sciences exercises an unusual amount of control over this media event, considering that the academy is an outside agency contracting with the network to have its awards ceremony covered. The academy names the show's producer—usually a Hollywood industry fixture, such as Jack Haley or Howard Koch or Norman Jewison—as well as controlling the nomination and granting of the Oscar awards themselves. The producer maintains ultimate control over the entire show, even though the network names the television director—Marty Pasetta in recent decades. Everything in the ceremony is planned with regard to how effective it will be on television in serving the interests of the film industry.

It soon becomes clear that to understand the creation and transmission of the Oscar telecast, we must look at questions that empirical research has largely ignored. This lack of attention to "Who Says Through Which Channel" came about because the study of super media in schools of journalism and mass communication was originally considered only in terms of the skills of the trade: observing, interviewing, writing, editing, shooting film, videotaping, selling advertising, building circulation, managing the newsroom or studio, and so on. These professional interests led early to concerns with audience testing and measurement and the development of public opinion. But in so doing, researchers looked only at the latter half of the communication sequence: they examined messages, audiences, and effects. Except for biographies of media barons, little mainstream media research was conducted on the first half of the process: sources and media structures. Even today the volume of published media research is heavily skewed toward audience data, but cultural studies insists that the front half of the process cannot be overlooked. This is where artists and businesspeople, individuals and institutions collide or cooperate as they originate messages for the channels of technological media. In addition, the dominant paradigm has emphasized *intentions*; yet, plainly the explicit high-minded communication intentions of the artistic source are not the only consideration here. They take second place to the real *motives* behind the production, motives that are more institutional and tangible.

The economic payoff of the Oscars is obvious. The annual awards ceremony funds most of the academy's annual expenses, makes profits for the television network, and promotes Hollywood films. Advertising rates for a thirty-second commercial are some $250,000, bringing ABC well over $8 million in revenues. In a given year, six sponsors may each pay $1.5 million for three minutes of commercial time to sell cars, cameras, or cosmetics. The academy, in turn, receives more than $2 million from ABC for television rights and spends only about half that amount producing the awards ceremony. Production costs are low primarily because the normally expensive celebrities appear in person at the Oscars without pay, except for a stipend for one or two hosts.

What the political economy of the awards means is that the institutional sources of the event—the film industry through the academy and the television industry through ABC—have strong commercial incentives and returns. The Oscars do enable film artists to recognize the achievements of other film artists, but that factor has little to do with the prominence given this event. It serves as a moneymaker all around and serves the film industry in particular on a fundamental level as an inexpensive and widely viewed three-hour advertisement for films.

The academy and the television network determine what message goes out to the audience in the classic manner of gatekeepers. The idea of the "gatekeeper" (White, 1950; Breed, 1952) underlines the role that reporters and editors play in the constricting of messages between events and the public. Four obvious gatekeeping stages can be seen among the many steps that reduce the impossible range of happenings in the world into what the individual receives as news. (1) A reporter's story summarizes (and so reduces) an event. (2) This is then edited down for local publication or broadcast. (3) A portion of these stories are further abbreviated and sent over wire services to other media, where (4) a still smaller portion may be briefly mentioned. As a result of the selective gatekeeping at each step, at the receiver end of this trunk only a tiny fraction of the originally gathered news of the day is finally available. These gatekeepers are "co-oriented" (Westley & MacLean, 1957) in one direction to news sources and in the other direction to audiences. Personal judgment and institutional pressures shape the resulting decisions (Gans, 1980; Hirsch, 1977). Organizational, genre-related, and sociocultural factors influence the selection of messages as well (Galtung & Ruge, 1965).

Despite the telecast's international distribution, the Oscar media event has a narrow geographical base. The first gatekeeper is the Los Angeles film industry. Only about 200 of the 3,500 voting members of the academy live outside the Los Angeles area, and in all 24 categories except for Best Foreign-Language Film, Oscar nominations are open only to films that have played in the Los Angeles area before the preceding December. The second gatekeeper is the American national television network, and, whereas the Oscars go out to the world, no foreign film award ceremony is beamed back into the United States. This geographical narrowness and the one-way flow lead many critics to see the Oscar ceremonies as cultural domination rather than genuine international exchange. From time-to-time British films—*Hamlet, Gandhi, Chariots of Fire*—have earned Oscars, but Hollywood products usually dominate. Even a winning film made in China by an Italian director, *The Last Emperor*, was financed by Hollywood. The gatekeeping also favors American performers. More than three out of four (76.1%) Oscar-winning performances have been by American actors and actresses; 16.5 percent have been by British performers; and 7.4 percent have been performers who were neither British nor American

(Levy, 1987, p. 348). The Oscar gatekeeping clearly serves culturally and economically to benefit Los Angeles–based and American-financed filmmaking above all others.

The Oscars are also affected by social routines among production personnel and by institutional alignments. Ethnomethodological studies (Tuchman, 1978; Altheide, 1976) describe how social routines in a newsroom and social definitions of reality shared by newspersons and entertainers determine the possibilities of what becomes super media content. For example, assigning a "beat" reporter to the police station may lead to stories favoring official police versions more than grass-roots community versions of conflicts. Historical studies (Curran & Seaton, 1981; Barnouw, 1975, 1978; Halberstam, 1979) describe a prior linkage between the interests of media owners or managers and the mentality of those they direct and promote. Work on the "production of culture" (Hirsch, 1977) develops analogues in the creation and transmission of art, science, and religion in technological societies. The Nashville-based country-western music industry, for example, illustrates how organizational and institutional models of behavior explain the standardized and controlled industrial production process that brings the Grand Ole Opry and its "folklore-fakelore" to the public (Peterson, 1976). These gatekeeper, ethnomethodological, and production-of-culture models move analysis beyond the atomistic individualism that plagued earlier behavioristic audience research and popular culture critiques.

What is the nature of the creative production process that goes into the Academy Awards show? To Marty Pasetta, director of the event each year since 1971, the Oscar telecast means work and pressure. It is he who must prepare and keep straight all the stars, film clips, dance numbers, nominations, commercials, and time schedules and must resolve unforeseen controversies as the events unfold live before the largest audience of any annual American television show. As a veteran director of this and other live television specials, Pasetta has learned to live with the pressure of knowing that any mistake he makes will be seen immediately by 250 million people. Director Pasetta controls the event from a van wired into the Dorothy Chandler Pavilion or the Shrine Auditorium, where the ceremony takes place. ABC television and the academy have millions of dollars and vast technology and expertise invested in this event. Typically Pasetta has 17 cameras, 45 monitors, 15 video decks, numerous items of special-effects equipment, and an extensive crew to cover it. But, admits Pasetta, "It all comes down to me in that truck that night."

When the show runs behind schedule, as it invariably does, it is Marty Pasetta who decides that the world will *not* see film clips of nominees for Best Documentary or Best Supporting Actress, because dropping the film clips may save a precious 90 seconds. If personnel or equipment malfunctions, as his line carrying commands to the stage once did, Pasetta must find ways for the telecast to continue flawlessly without interruption. That year he commandeered the auditorium public address system to give cues after commercial breaks to the host—and the whole auditorium.

The show is a vast headache of production details for the director. Pasetta begins setting up the overall script, set design, major production numbers, and special awards in January. Other plans await the announcement of nominated films in February. Then the director and producer jointly decide on the running order of the show, which celebrity presenters to invite, and the seating chart for nominees and presenters. Pasetta must avoid having a winner cross in front of a nominee defeated for the same award or using a presenter who has won an Oscar earlier that evening. In rehearsals, he cues cameras to exact seats with three-foot name cards placed on them. Still pictures of every nominee must be electronically stored to represent nominees who fail to attend the awards ceremony.

Friday evening, only three days before the telecast, is Pasetta's first opportunity to work in the auditorium and complete a technical check of equipment and facilities. Rehearsals begin on Saturday with the orchestra, singers, and dancers, at the same time as special effects are being constructed. On Sunday afternoon, the stars walk through their parts. On Monday, while the stars get their hair and nails done, fit dresses and tuxedos, and await limousines, another run-through takes place. All in all, during this final weekend, Pasetta is lucky to get two hours' sleep a night. The artistry required is that of an entertainer, a diplomat, an executive, a workaholic, a person of steel nerves, and a very reliable company man.

The resulting telecast is beamed out internationally via satellite in two versions. The full-length live version is distributed to most of the countries receiving the event. For example, high school students throughout Latin America can watch the full-length version live and talk about it the next day with classmates. Across the world in Taiwan the full-length version is tape-delayed from morning until evening prime time, which means viewers have already read of the winners in the newspapers and must enjoy the ritual without the suspense. These full-length foreign-language versions are transmitted instantaneously from a series of booths in the rear of the pavilion, where announcers speak over the live soundtrack to provide both announcing and simultaneous translation. The receiving country has the option of transmitting live, delaying the show for hours, or, in some cases, delaying it for weeks.

Another version, a shorter one-hour version, is edited down by Pasetta as gatekeeper immediately after the live ceremony and beamed out within eight hours to England and a few other European countries for prime time there. The one-hour version limits itself to the 11 major awards, including, of course, Best Actor, Best Actress, and Best Picture. In his editing decisions, here as elsewhere, Pasetta thoroughly reflects his well-developed sense of what Hollywood and ABC want. He is acutely tuned to the entertainment industry and can anticipate the wishes of industry leaders in every decision.

In the creation and transmission of the Academy Awards telecast one can find gatekeeping, routines, institutions, economics, tradition, technology, and other empirically documented forces at work in shaping the text that is finally made available to the world. This is in measurable ways the opposite of the creative act of the lone artist freely composing in his or her garret. Following Hirsch (1977), we find here three levels of mass-media operation:

- Occupations
- Organizations
- Societal environment

On the first level, Pasetta represents an *occupational* role that serves to relate individuals to media organizations, represented, in Pasetta's words, by "the ABC executives watching over our shoulder." On the second level, the film academy and the television network represent *the organization as a whole*. On the third level, the international socioeconomic position of the television and film industries represents *the relationship between the occupations or organizations and the larger societal environment*. The entertainment industries know the societal environment as a market and act accordingly.

This process represents the mechanisms of the "industrialization of culture," a process that creates texts that Enzensberger (1974) warns can lead to the "industrialization of the mind" by the "consciousness industry." But, while the process resembles industrialization in a mass sense, it is also a kind of culture by consensus, a consensus in which no individual plays an independent role. This brings to mind democracy and the question of "democratization of culture" in all its complexity. But does one want merely a rounded and shaved-off culture, one devoid of idiosyncrasies? The excitement created by "controversial incidents" at the awards show indicates a taste for the unusual and the unpredictable that such overdemocratized and industrialized products have little of. When Billy Wilder reminisces at length about an immigration agent, or Jane Fonda protests against *Deer Hunter's* Oscar, or Marlon Brando sends Sacheen Littlefeather in his place, or a streaker dashes across screen in the background, or any other incident outside the script takes place, there is unusual excitement about it. Culture by consensus may reach the largest audience, but it can easily lack diversity or originality. All this points to the conclusion that the process of creating and transmitting a cultural product like the Oscars through super media is more industrial than democratic.

Message Content of the Text: What Is Said

The telecast content of the Academy Awards show brims over with stars and glamour, with competition and winning, with high-blown rhetoric and glittery production. Hundreds of millions of persons around the world recognize the inset windows of nominees awaiting a decision and the famous line "And the envelope, please." Anyone viewing knows the content at least superficially, but what is it finally? What kinds of material dominate the Oscars? What genre of show is this, and what are its messages about gender, celebrity, competition, ethnicity, and other values?

Message research concerns the content of what is received through the channels of super media; it links source/transmission research with audience research. In contrast to the manner in which most source and audience research is conducted, message analysis is not the exclusive domain of social scientists. Scholars from the arts and humanities elbow their way into the operating theater with instruments of textual analysis and esthetic theory poised next to behaviorist tools for data quantification and processing.

Among social scientists the most common methodology for studying mass communication messages has been quantitative content analysis. O. R. Holsti (1969, p. 13) defines the method as "any technique for making inferences by objectively and systematically identifying accurate characteristics of messages." In its most common applications, content analysis seeks to take systematic samples and quantify the manifest content into categories as objectively as possible. Despite the subjective difficulty of identifying accurate categories and coding content within them, content analysis has been consistently developed and employed in American mass communication research since the late 1930s (Delia, 1987). Content analysis reveals the frequency and distribution of types of broadcast programs; themes of television drama; portrayals of race, class, and occupations; news bias; and trends in violent content. (See, for example, Comstock, Katzman, McCombs, & Roberts, 1978.) Content analysis—from its use by the BBC and the United States Information Agency in tabulating foreign propaganda, to its application by women's groups for identifying sex-role definitions in commercials and children's programs—provides a usually reliable basic score-card for identifying tendencies and tracing trends in the message content of mass communication.

To apply quantitative content analysis to the Academy Awards show: How much airtime is given to each aspect of the Academy Awards telecast? A typical Oscar telecast spends half an hour showing winners receiving awards but even more time showing celebrities walking on and introducing awards. Almost as much time is given to commercials as to film clips from nominated films. Videotapes and transcripts of the past ten Oscar shows yield the typical proportions in various categories shown in Table 3.1.

The categories are familiar to Oscar viewers and relatively self-explanatory, with a few exceptions. The nearly half an hour of special awards is for career achievement, humanitarian contributions, or scientific and technical contributions. Twenty-five minutes are eaten up by winners' acceptances, those gushy thanks to lists of unknown people. Almost as long are transitions, which include connecting comments made by the host, applause, walks to the microphone, reading the academy rules, and other less-than-memorable moments. Celebrities take 18 minutes as presenters who introduce each award and name the winner. Songs and dances include the five songs nominated for an Oscar

TABLE 3.1 Percentage of Airtime in Ten Categories in a Typical Oscar Telecast

Category	Percentage 0 1 2 3 4 5 6 7 8 9 10 11 12 13 14 15 16	
Film clips (28 min.)[a]	————————————————————	15.5
Special awards (27)	———————————————————	15
Winner acceptance (25)	——————————————————	14
Transitions (22.5)	————————————————	12.5
Advertisements (20)	—————————————	11
Presenters (18)	————————————	10
Nominated songs (13.5)	—————————	7.5
Song/dance (12.5)	————————	7
Host monologue (7)	————	4
Opening/closing (6.5)	————	3.5
TOTAL (180 min.)		100.0

[a]Total minutes for a typical three-hour Oscar program are shown in parentheses.

and take up 26 minutes in the form of production numbers that attempt, Las Vegas style, to liven the festivities. The opening includes the arrival of celebrities and the closing includes lengthy credits.

Genre

To what genre of super media content does the Academy Award telecast belong? Standard television exegesis places the Oscar program as an eclectic "television special," reminiscent of many types of television and film: the variety show, the talk show, stand-up comedy, celebrity roasts, movie reviews, golden oldies, sports competition, and even the game show. But Arlen (1979) suggests that the event is more a "ceremonial parade" similar to events staged by the British Crown. If indeed Hollywood stars are America's royalty, a theme developed by various observers, this event is a Yankee equivalent of weddings, coronations, christenings, and other media celebrations connected with the British royal family. Neither the royal family nor Hollywood has direct political power today, but both exercise a kind of symbolic leadership and escapist compensation replete with well-publicized glamour, luxury, privilege, and performed duty. This might be called their ideological function. The Oscars foreground the filmdom royalty, not in their assumed film identities, but in their actual personas, giving a privileged view of larger-than-life characters as seemingly real people. In this way the event is more news documentary of the royal parade than dramatic fiction.

Among television specials, the Oscar's closest relatives are the awards shows for the Grammys, Tonys, Emmys, Miss America, Miss Universe, and others. These claim smaller audiences than their senior representative, the Oscars, but together they are the ultimate expressions of a genre that, at the grass roots level, features rubber-chicken awards banquets for anything from Little League to local fashion design. The formulas for introducing distinguished guests, presenters, and winners and for interspersing musical and comedic features retain echoes of those awards banquets for commoners but now elevated to the heady atmosphere of royalty. Viewers have experienced awards competitions and can identify with nominees.

Gender and the Oscars

There is no confusion of sexes on the Oscar screen: every male connected with the ceremony must wear a tuxedo, from superstar to delivery truck driver; females wear extravagantly varied and enticing gowns. This is consistent with Hollywood's notorious history of sex-role sterotyping. Emanuel Levy (1987) has examined male and female Oscar-winning roles from 1927 to 1985 in detail. What gender patterns emerge in the Best Actress, Best Actor, Best Supporting Actress, and Best Supporting Actor winning roles?

The film genres with the most Oscar-winning roles have been the serious dramatic picture (59%) and the comedy (15%). Men and women have been equally represented in them numerically, but have differed sharply in age, marital status, and occupation, as will be shown. The second most frequent genre for male winning roles is the action-adventure film, which has provided 19% of all male Oscar-winning roles but only 6 percent of female roles. The female "equivalent" has been the romantic melodrama, with 14 percent of the female roles (19% of Best Actress winners) and not one male Oscar winner. These differences indicate that not only does Hollywood portray men and women differently, but there are certain types of films regarded as appropriate for men and others for women.

Matching age with gender reveals further disparities in Oscar-winning roles. Only 16 percent of male Oscar roles have been of young characters, while 62 percent of female roles have been young. Only 22 percent of female characters have been middle-aged, while 57 percent of males have been. Of male roles, 27 percent have been of elderly characters, compared with only 13 percent of female roles.

Movies tell whether women are married or not, but not always whether men are. No reference to marital status occurred for 18 percent of the male Oscar roles, but this was true of only 3 percent of the female roles. The marital status of *every* Best Actress winner was provided.

Occupations also vary with gender in Oscar-winning roles. Almost all male winners (97%) had identifiable occupations, but only 64 percent of the female winners did. Moreover, males have been portrayed in three times as many occupations as females. The two most frequent occupations among males were soldier (14%), as in the winning roles of George C. Scott, Jon Voigt, Christopher Walken, and Louis Gossett, Jr., and law enforcer (9%), played by Gary Cooper, Rod Steiger, and Gene Hackman, among others. Males have also played kings, politicians, judges, lawyers, and priests in winning roles. In comparison, prominent female roles have been in service occupations, such as teacher, nurse, or secretary, and in entertainment occupations, such as actress, singer, or dancer. The two most common occupations for female winning roles have been actress (15%) and prostitute (12%). As Levy (1987, p. 191) notes ruefully, "At least one out of every three gainfully employed woman has been an actress or a prostitute and, at times, both actress and prostitute"—as in the case of the Jane Fonda character in *Klute.* Other women's roles have been in family settings as wives, mothers, and daughters, often with a generous sprinkling of suffering and victimization. Fully 42 percent of the Best Actress roles have portrayed victims of their spouses or lovers, compared with 2 percent of the Best Actor roles. Moreover, as Levy (1987, p. 198) notes: "Any attempt by screen women—until the 1970s—to deviate from their prescribed, stereotypical roles has been consistently and continuously punished . . . from the most extreme sanction, death, to lesser sanctions, such as humiliation, ostracization, and relegation to domestic life." Career women are generally dehumanized, as in the case of Big Nurse Ratched, played by Louise Fletcher in *One Flew Over the Cuckoo's Nest,* and the power-hungry television executive played by Faye Dunaway in

Network. A notable exception occurred in 1977, when four of the five Best Picture nominees were films about women: *Annie Hall* with Diane Keaton, *The Goodbye Girl* with Marsha Mason, *Julia* with Vanessa Redgrave, and *The Turning Point* with Shirley MacLaine and Anne Bancroft.

In Oscar-winning roles, men are recognizable *types*, but women are confined and rigid *stereotypes*. Levy (1987, p. 202) points to the basic problem this indicates:

> The function of the male types and female stereotypes, from the point of view of dominant ideology, is to keep women in their place, to reward them for accepting their traditional roles and for *not* challenging the status quo. These screen roles have provided an ideological rationalization much needed to reconcile women to marriage and family life. Comprehensive and all-embracing, these images go beyond the socioeconomic area, providing a mental state of mind, a whole way of life for women.

Content Values

In addition to questions of genre and gender, the televised content of the Oscar ceremony provides a positive valuation of celebrity, competition, tradition, ethnocentrism, regionalism, and nationalism. The first level of the polysemic text consists of the awards, personalities, songs, and so on. The second level contains the values proposed and reinforced. The values of celebrity and competition predominate: the show attracts an audience by presenting a vast number of popular stars (celebrity) and by creating suspense over who will win (competition). Tradition is present in the sense of historic grandeur evoked by film clips of past Hollywood classics and by the honored presence of elderly stars and directors. Ethnically, fewer than 5 percent of the featured celebrities are non-White, a figure dramatically below non-White proportions in United States and world populations. Regionally, as we have seen, this American celebration represents the narrow Southern California domination of electronic entertainment, a domination that competes with East Coast domination of literary, political, and economic power. In terms of nationality, fewer than one fourth of the presenters or winners are non-Americans in a super media event through which cultural norms are proposed to peoples scattered throughout the world.

Audiences and Interpretations:
To Whom With What Effect

Who watches the Oscars, and how does this telecast affect its viewers? This is without doubt the most traditional and widely researched kind of question in the history of mass communications. Audience surveys and ratings measure the effects of media messages on audiences, generally with the methods of social psychology. The emphasis in on measurable change in audience attitudes and behavior in relation to information diffusion and influence. Public opinion polling, television ratings, and measurement of product and candidate advertising have made audience research especially lucrative and visible. Although this effects research examines the audience, it is in fact most frequently conducted not for the sake of the audience but for the sake of the producers of cultural products so that they can maximize their audience and the effect of their messages. Thus, using the Lasswell model, it serves the interests of the first part, the sources of communication, even though it generates information about the last part, the audiences. The reverse seldom occurs in traditional empirical research. That is, traditionally the audience does not have access to detailed research data about the sources who create the communication messages. Once again, there is the appearance of aspects of *democracy*—surveys find out "what the people want"—but the information is gathered and assessed in service to the *industrial* system of cultural production and profit. Uses and gratifications research has broken with this tradition partly, and political economy research reverses the sides completely.

To examine the typical Academy Awards audience and its interpretations, a telephone survey was conducted, drawing on a random sample of metropolitan residents of a city in the southwestern United States (Real & Hassett, 1981).[1] The 141 completed questionnaires matched the proportions of the adult population of the United States by age, income, education, and other demographic variables. The survey was conducted during the four days following the awards telecast.

Approximately half of the survey respondents had watched the telecast. Specifically, of the 141 respondents, 71 had *not* watched the telecast, 42 had watched *some,* and 28 had watched *all* of it. Viewing the Oscars appears to be a pattern over time for most. Those who had not watched had previously watched a mean of only 1.67 Academy Awards telecasts in the past five years; those who had watched some had watched a mean of 3.26 shows of the last five; and those who had watched all had watched a mean of 4.07 of the last five. The roughly 50 percent viewing among the survey population appears a bit lower than the Oscars' 65–70 percent share of American television households reported in Nielsen ratings. In any case, its 75 million American viewers places it close behind the Super Bowl, but this number is only one third to one fifth of its total estimated international audience.

Do the Oscars and other super media content "cause" specific effects in the audience? There have been conflicting positions on that question for decades, as the first chapter hinted. One extreme sees media as all-powerful, the other as powerless.

The first extreme would have the Oscars cause direct effects. It is often characterized as the "hypodermic needle" theory, in which media are believed to have an automatic one-to-one stimulus-response effect on the audience. This position was popular in the 1930s, as exemplified by reactions to Hitler and Roosevelt and public outcry over Orson Welles's famous panic broadcast, *The War of the Worlds,* in 1938. Remnants of the position can still be found in certain fundamentalist fears about the effects of portrayals of sex and related elements in the media. But research during and after World War II contradicted such oversimplifications. Hadley Cantril's (1940) research on the Welles broadcast highlighted the *uniqueness* of the social and historical conditions and the style of the broadcast, which made possible its panic results. The seminal analysis of voting preferences in Erie County, Ohio, in the 1940 presidential campaign, published as *The People's Choice* (Lazarsfeld, Berelson, & Gaudet, 1944), gave birth to the immensely productive research tradition centered on *social relations, personal influence,* and the *two-step flow* of communication from media to influentials (step one), and from influentials to the less active sectors of the populace (step two). This emphasis on social process variables intervening between the transmissions of mass media and the behavior of the audience was complemented by persuasion research conducted during and after World War II by Hovland and others (Hovland, Lumsdaine, & Sheffield, 1949; Hovland, Janis, & Kelley, 1953). This series of psychological experiments confirmed the presence of individual differences and personal judgment variables, factors that modified or prevented media effectiveness.

The second extreme would have the Oscars cause no effects. With the impetus of the aforementioned skeptical research around midcentury, generalizations began to swing in the opposite direction and imply that mass media were virtually insignificant as social forces. By the 1960s misreadings of earlier research, such as the two-step flow, and of Klapper's (1960) limited-effects summary led to the opposite extreme, where media were assumed to have no effects. This crept into textbooks and led to a condescending attitude among some in media professions and research, who dismissed all effects concerns as if they were the old oversimplifications of the hypodermic needle argument. In the last two decades, the pendulum has swung back toward belief in media effects but in carefully defined ways. The unequivocal empirical evidence of media's ability to cause measurable effects becomes clear in such places as the historic and ground-breaking studies gathered by Lowery and DeFleur as *Milestones in Mass Communication Research* (1983).

An alternative to the effects debate would speak of the Oscars' "audience functions" rather than effects. What functions did the Academy Award telecast perform for viewers? "Functionalism" is the label applied to traditional American psychosocial explanations of audience effects and responses. In a benchmark essay (Lazarsfeld & Merton, 1948/1957), two of the most respected contributors to this tradition summarized media effects on audiences with three phrases: status conferral, enforcement of social norms, and narcotizing dysfunction. These functions can be found in the Oscars audience.

In the *status-conferral function* "the mass media confer status on public issues, persons, organizations and social movements," giving them recognition and legitimization. This anticipates the *agenda-setting function* of the mass media (McCombs & Shaw, 1972), in which, as political issues rise and fall in the public agenda, a similar change occurs in the media agenda slightly *before* the change in the audience agenda. In other words, the press "may not be successful much of the time in telling people what to think, but it is stunningly successful in telling its readers what to think *about*" (B. Cohen, quoted in Schramm & Porter, 1982, p. 239).

This status-conferral function can be seen at work with Oscar viewers. Asked to rate on a 5-point scale the importance to them of each of eight motives for viewing, survey respondents rated most highly "To find out the winners" (4.5) and "To see the celebrities" (3.5). After those came "To see the dances and hear the songs" (3.2) and "To see the film clips" (2.9). The lowest rated motives all received ratings of 2.2 or 2.3: "For the celebrity chitchat," "Because nothing else was on," "To be able to talk about it," and "To share time with others." Wanting to find out the winners is a request for access to the act that confers the status of winner. Wanting to see the celebrities recognizes that status has been conferred on these people worth watching. What they say (celebrity chitchat) is less important than who they are (celebrities to see) and significantly less important than being current about those on whom status is being conferred that night (finding out the winners).

At the same time as super media coverage confers status on selected persons, policies, and groups in *the enforcement of social norms,* "mass media clearly serve to reaffirm social norms by exposing deviations from these norms to public view." Televised congressional hearings— the 1954 Army-McCarthy debate, the 1974 Watergate hearings, the 1987 Iran-*contra* investigation—are examples of public super media rituals to expose and exorcise deviant abuses of political power. More subtle norm enforcement occurs throughout media as standards of honesty, heroism, sexual conduct, racial attitudes, violence, and other behaviors are approved as models or impugned as deviations. A more developed *"cultural norms theory"* (see DeFleur, 1966) holds that individual behavior as a whole is guided by the individual's perception of cultural norms and that the mass media, through selective presentation and emphasis, establish audience impressions of such cultural norms. It thus argues the indirect rather than direct effectiveness of media, through modification of the audience's assumed definition of a situation.

Hollywood films and the Oscars telecast are associated with a variety of subtly enforced social norms. The majority (57%) of respondents agreed with the statement "I enjoy the beauty and fashion displayed at the Academy Awards telecast." Certainly films themselves help establish norms of beauty and fashion. Clark Gable was a paragon of American male attractiveness, and when, in *It Happened One Night,* with Claudette Colbert, he removed his shirt and was seen to be wearing no undershirt, the sale of undershirts plummeted. The young John Travolta sped along two fashion trends, one for disco attire in *Saturday Night Fever* and the other for western outfits in *Urban Cowboy.*

In the *narcotizing dysfunction* of the media "increasing dosages of mass communications may be inadvertently transforming the energies of men from active participation into passive knowledge," leaving "large masses of the population politically apathetic and inert." Not only escapist media—entertainment television, sexy tabloids, seductive or screaming ads, lobotomized music—but *all* media can have this cumulative effect. And all readers, even those intent on staying informed through the elite press, in the judgment of Lazarsfeld and Merton, are exposed to the danger of having no time left to act effectively in society.

Certain audience responses to the Academy Awards telecast suggest the passivity of the narcotizing dysfunction. Two thirds (66%) of the respondents agreed with the statement "I enjoy watching the Academy Awards show." But only one third (34%) agreed with "I look forward to the Academy Awards each year." If this is generally true, then one third of the audience, or more than 100 million people internationally, do not look forward to the Oscars, but enjoy them, revealing in their unplanned viewing a vague sense of accepting whatever enjoyable comes down the line, a passive and almost Pavlovian approach to television viewing. Almost two thirds (64.5 percent) *disagreed* with the statement "I talk about the nominations with friends before the awards are given," and 44 percent disagreed with "I usually have my personal favorites picked out before the awards show." Active opinionizing is not required but its absence can be taken as an indication of low involvement and participation in the viewing event, despite the nearly three hours the event takes up. Heavy and passive television viewing has long been associated with social disengagement, even to its being called "the plug-in drug" (Winn, 1975).

The status-conferral function, the enforcement of social norms, and the narcotizing dysfunction remind us that, if super media are not omnipotent, neither are they sterile or impotent.

How do audience members use the Academy Awards, and what gratifications do they seek? Emerging in recent decades as a major force in audience analysis, *uses and gratifications* research focuses on the needs perceived and satisfied by individual consumers in using the media, without regard to the effects sought by the media producers. Audiences are considered active and goal directed, able to articulate their motives and select from competing sources what will satisfy their needs. In this indirect way, uses and gratifications research reverses the direction of assumed causality in media: audiences "cause" media effects by their selection of media, while producers provide only the raw material. In this perspective, one examines the popularity of U-2 or Michael Jackson not in reference to marketing or promotion or economics, but in terms of what adolescents in their own words seek and find in those teen idols to gratify their personal and social needs.

Oscars viewers used the ceremony for various gratifications. Asked, "Are you more likely to see a certain movie because it has won an Academy Award?," 45 percent answered yes. If a film was merely nominated, 34 percent were more likely to see it. This means that viewers were using the telecast awards to gratify their need for guidance in selecting which films to see. But this example is also a classic "effect." One of the show's basic intents is to promote films and filmgoing, and the studios' campaigns to win nominations and Oscars are undertaken in pursuit of the effect of causing more people to watch their films. Moving to a different example, among the motives for viewing, three were of moderate importance rated at 2.2 or 2.3 on the 5-point scale, and were clearly audience-centered uses and gratifications: "To share time with others," "To be able to talk about it," and "Because nothing else was on." These were not intended effects of the producer but, rather, active uses by the audience, gratifying needs for sociability, conversation and entertainment.

Frequent filmgoers and heavy television viewers seem to be two very different groups of users of the Oscars. Moviegoers are younger and television viewers are older. The mean age of frequent moviegoers was 30 years, while that of nonmoviegoers was 46. The mean age of heavy television viewers was 44, while that of light viewers was 31. Likelihood of viewing the Oscars telecast varied with television viewing but not moviegoing. Heavy and moderate television viewers had watched more of the past five shows (mean = 3.2) than had light or very light television viewers. Frequent moviegoers, however, were no more likely than moderate or nonmoviegoers to watch the Oscars. This would indicate that the Oscars event is used more directly by television viewers than by filmgoers, a fact that may please ABC Television more than the Academy of Motion Picture Arts and Sciences. Both in face value and in viewer uses, the Oscars ceremony offers the gratifications of television viewing more than of filmgoing.

Do Oscars viewers really care about the show? Standard audience ratings emphasize how large the audience is but not how deeply audience members care. To get at this more qualitative issue, viewers were asked what their reaction would be if the awards were not televised and if the awards were abolished altogether. If they were not televised, 82 percent would be indifferent and only 13 percent would be upset, while 4 percent would be happy. This means the audience watches, but only a tiny proportion care much about it personally. Asked their reaction if the awards were completely abolished, a smaller number (63%) indicated indifference and 33 percent said they would be upset, while again the same 4 percent said they would be happy. The net impression of these replies is that only a small minority (1 in 7) care deeply about seeing the awards, a larger minority (1 in 3) value the awards, a solid majority could live without the awards (almost 2 out of 3) or the telecast (more than 4 out of 5), and a few beleaguered souls (1 in 25) personally resent the whole affair.

"Promotional culture" is one of the classic labels for the world of super media (Lazarsfeld, 1941). This promotionally overheated culture, permeated by advertising, marketing, public relations, and every level of promotional activity and incentive, is inseparable from the media and has come to be a central characteristic of American capitalist culture. Are audiences aware of this in any degree?

As a "cynicism index," the Oscars survey respondents were asked whether they agreed with the statement "The Academy Awards are nothing more than a public relations event for the film industry, in an effort to focus attention on films and increase moviegoing by the public." More than half the sample (55%) agreed with the statement. The strong phrasing "nothing more than" did not scare away respondents; only 27 percent disagreed with it. Another 18 percent had no opinion on the statement. Audiences perceive the "hype." As noted above, however, viewers are more likely to see a movie that has received an Oscar or even a nomination. The Oscars do work as promotional devices. Fully 77 percent agreed that "a movie's earnings are greatly increased by winning an Academy Award." Only 3.5 percent felt winning had no effect on a film's success or an actor's career. A slight majority (50.4%) agreed that "films with larger budgets are more likely to be nominated for an Academy Award." Given the choice not now available except in England and a few other countries, approximately half the respondents (49.6%) would actually prefer "a one-hour program of awards for best film and best acting." Audience responses indicate not only the presence of Lazarsfeld's promotional culture but also a critical self-awareness of that culture and its promotional obsessions.

Relative to media theory, perhaps the greatest limitation on audience theory, whether effects- or gratifications-oriented, is that it has been blessed with such a quantity of empirical data and has developed so many related or contending concepts that it has tended to remain self-contained. Rather than being a major contributing part of a full-blown media theory or theory of mass communication *in toto,* audience research has pursued its own purposes. Those who have built the sturdy base on which media analysis stands, the audience effects tradition, have not consistently integrated that work into an overall theoretical frame inclusive of sources, transmission, content, interpretations, and cultural impact. By looking beyond media-centered analysis to a culture-centered approach, it is possible to overcome this limitation, but not without also questioning certain assumptions and limitations that are central to the empirical behaviorist tradition.

Empiricism and Cultural Studies

As noted in the preceding chapter, the conflict between behaviorism and criticism concerns the decisions about which evidence will be sought, the method of gathering, and the context of interpretation (Melody & Mansell, 1983). Will the interest of powerful media sources be served or those of subordinate groups? All research has in this sense an "ideological perspective," especially in the researchers' treatment of results (Smythe & Van Dinh, 1983, p. 118). For many, "the political question of social power, linked with the epistemological question of causality, is what ultimately distinguishes the critical approaches" (Slack & Allor, 1983, p. 215). Positivist behavioral research distorts truth by removing facts and phenomena from their social and historical contexts (Mosco, 1983). Ewen (1983, p. 223), argues, "Rather than media/audience relations being abstracted as discrete from the world they inhabit, they must be vigorously situated within that world and its history."

In this critical context, the accuracy of audience ratings for the Academy Awards telecast or the number of viewers who go to Oscar-winning films is a first-level fact, which provides only a possible beginning to research and interpretation. Culturally important questions would be, What do the Oscars mean in a fully human sense to viewers? At this time and place in history, whose interests are being served in what way by the massive spectacle of the Oscars? What needs and interests are left out or distorted by this popular event?

Cultural studies rejects neither the empiricism nor the findings of traditional media research, but it does radically change the emphasis. One finds this in calls for a shift in disciplinary alliances of communications "from the behavioral sciences to the cultural sciences and humanities" (White, 1983, p. 283). The cause-effect transportation model of communication is replaced by a ritual model through which a shared culture is created, modified, and transformed: "Meanings do not originate with some abstract sender, but are derived from a historical-cultural tradition and a concrete political-economic context"

(White, p. 293). Cultural studies employs logic, debate, history, context, epistemology, and theory building, sometimes instead of, and sometimes in addition to, the contribution of positivism and behaviorism in the form of tightly constructed facts and elementary level conclusions. Thus, they are in conflict insofar as each considers the other not complementary but oppositional. And the conflict becomes obvious in such forums as the international review and debate titled *Ferment in the Field* (Gerbner & Siefert, 1983). To some extent, therefore, a communication scholar must choose between the two. One cannot devote full time to both.

At present no single overriding theory of media dominates the field of communication research. If theory embraces intellectual depth as well as testable hypotheses, any fully developed media theory will be critical in essence even as it takes into account empirical, behavioral findings. As Chomsky (1983) has argued, it takes deductive, conceptual thinking to create explanatory theories; inductive empirical data themselves cannot do this. Can there be a "theory of media" which is at once holistic and integrative of the entirety of media, and which, at the same time, accounts for social institutions and complex channels, guides the interpretation of message and symbol systems, addresses policy questions, provides for factors of history and context, and empowers people? Perhaps not. But if there can be, it will draw on the structural, critical, and ritual thrust of cultural studies as well as on the empirical media-centered findings of behaviorism.

The legacy of critical theory and cultural studies has been to force media theorists to face the full implications of the political economy of institutionalized transmission systems, the ideology of message systems, and the consciousness resulting from changed, modified, or reinforced audience attitudes and behavior. Productive policy decisions, significant research projects, and humane media practices require media theory and research that confront rather than skirt the difficult questions. If seven decades of growing empirical understanding of super media tend to any single moral, it is this: that few questions are more central to our collective future than the accurate assessment and positive utilization of the realities and potentials of super media.

> The show ends. The lights come back on. Gradually you reenter normal life. But for a time you were somewhere else. Where did that experience come from? How did it get here? What was in it? How did it affect you? How can you use it?

Thanks to media research, we can answer those questions, although we do not usually need to. We let the immediate experience work on us. But it is nice to know we can cognitively take it apart and understand it, as well as affectively appreciate it. And it is nice to know what questions we have not fully answered.

And now, for filmgoer or television viewer, it is on to the next super media experience.

Questions

1. What aspects of the Academy Awards make them particularly worth investigating as a case study of super media?

2. What is "empirical media-centered research" on super media?

3. How does the political economy of the sources transmitting the Oscars affect their gatekeeping of the message?

4. What can content analysis tell us of genre, gender, and values in Oscar-winning films and the Academy Awards telecast?

5. How are the audience effects of the Oscars different from audience uses and gratifications?

6. How do the Academy Awards provide each of the following: status conferral, enforcement of social norms, surveillance of the environment, agenda setting, two-step flow, personal influence, and uses and gratifications?

7. What might critical research examine in the Academy Awards that behavioral research would ignore?

Note

1. The audience survey reported here is especially indebted to the research work of Chris Hassett and a graduate student research team at San Diego State University using the Social Science Research Laboratory. More details of the survey are available in a different publication of findings from the Oscars research project (Real, 1985b).

4

Structuralist Analysis 1:
Bill Cosby and Recoding Ethnicity

In expressing love we belong among the undeveloped countries.
—Saul Bellow[1]

William H. Cosby, Jr., emerged in the last third of the 20th century as one of the great popular artists of the age. His genius at tapping the popular sensibility placed him in the tradition of Charlie Chaplin, Walt Disney, Lucille Ball, Steven Spielberg, Monty Python, and precious few others. As both performer and producer, Cosby achieved the stature of an institution, eventually being featured on the cover of *Time* (September 28, 1987) as "Cosby, Inc." Considering that as a Black American male, he was both heir to a strong entertainment tradition and victim of a stereotype, Cosby's achievement was especially interesting. From minstrel shows to *Birth of a Nation,* from Stepin Fetchit to "Amos 'n Andy," the Black male in particular has been the subject of sterotyping. Even today representations of the Black male in the mass media tend to be confined to comedy (Bill Cosby, Richard Pryor, Redd Foxx), sports (Michael Jordan, Dwight Gooden), and music (Lionel Ritchie, Michael Jackson, Prince), and to lack the full range of fictional and nonfictional roles available to White men and the different but restricted roles available to women.

Cosby's representation of ethnicity and gender, especially in his successful father role on prime-time television, occurs in a challenging context. Black scholarship, especially in film theory and practice, draws from semiotic and mythic analysis to describe and prescribe the Black presence in the image industries of super media. Snead (1985), Davis (1985), and White (1985) articulate a call for new forms and techniques in the mythic media construction of Afro-American experience. The

---

AUTHOR'S NOTE: *Carroll Parrot Blue coauthored material on* Black encoding and recoding *for this chapter.*

portrayal of Black ethnicity in "The Bill Cosby Show" contrasts with traditional stereotypes and, in the process, brings up for conscious consideration structures for coding and recoding the myth of Blackness and all it stands for in super media today.

This chapter, on ethnicity, and the next on gender, employ structuralist analysis to examine the most popular television show of the 1980s and the most financially successful male- and female-directed films.

Icons, Formulas, and Genres in the Mythology of Super Media

Structuralist analysis, a technique employed in cultural studies, identifies the structure of linguistic and other sign systems used for expressing and communicating. *Codes* organize signs into systems—for example, when grammar organizes words into sentences. Certain structural features, such as binary oppositions of Black and White or male and female, appear in the signs and codes of verbal expression, social relations, and mental categories. These structures exist as codes that relate the signifying practices of super media to the personal identity of members of the public. Myths tell a culture's stories through its signs and codes.

"The Bill Cosby Show," in its years atop American television ratings, managed to cleverly entertain as it carefully wound its way around and occasionally challenged the mythic stereotypical structuring of Blackness that preceded it. Stereotypes, racial and otherwise, serve as shorthand codes of representation and social control. Myths construct narratives around types and stereotypes, and in the words of Kellner (1982), "the myths of a society are the bearers of its ideologies" (p. 134). In this sense the ideology of racism has been coded into American mythology from the earliest days of the Republic. In the popular culture of Joel Chandler Harris, Stephen Foster, and many others, the dominant mythology about Black Americans pictured slaves and ex-slaves on the plantation as happy-go-lucky singing and dancing servants.

The structure of myths of Blackness, before and after Cosby, emerges from the psychology of American emotions and cultural life, in the same manner as all myths arise from and express collective emotions and culture.[2] For Ernst Cassirer (1946), the key to explaining myth is the function of myth in human social and cultural life. Myth is not merely an erroneous prescientific explanation of nature and life originating from faulty reasoning. For Cassirer, myth expresses something between our direct sense impressions and our logical rational thought, our *"feelings,"* centered especially in the human feeling for the unity of life. In addition, myth reflects and expresses *social,* not individual, life experiences and constitutes a collective representation. Through signs, codes, and myths, human society seeks to symbolize and control the environment. For Cassirer, the power of myth, and its place as ritual in culture and daily life, flows from its role as a system of personal and social representation and communication.

Television, more than any other super medium today, provides mythologies that play fundamental roles in expressing and representing human feelings and social life, including ethnicity, gender, and political ideology. The powerful dimensions of myth that make it omnipresent in contemporary television are summarized by Douglas Kellner:

> Television images and stories produce new mythologies for problems of everyday life. Myths are simply stories that explain, instruct, and justify practices and institutions; they are lived, and shape thought and action. Myths deal with the most significant phenomena in human life and enable people to come to terms with death, violence, love, sex, labor, and social conflict. Myths link together symbols, formula, plot, and characters in a pattern that is conventional, appealing, and gratifying [Kellner, 1979, p. 22; see also Kellner, 1980, 1981, 1984, 1988].

Unfortunately, for most of its history, and well before television, the dominant mythology in Western popular culture has included stereotypical symbols, formulas, and characters for virtually all non-Whites. Roland Barthes's famous description in *Mythologies* of the picture of a Black African soldier saluting the French flag on the cover of *Paris Match* illustrates the subtleties of these representations. The picture conveys in a single image a mythology and an ideology of French imperialism, the integration of Blacks, and the honor of the military, all of which were debated points at the time that *Paris Match,* without comment and in all likelihood without self-conscious intent, selected this mythically rich and biasing image. Even in news stories the demands of storytelling constantly pull media beyond the transmission of information and toward mythically shared expectations and forms, a pull that easily leads to stereotypical coding. (See, for example, Tuchman, 1978; Bennett & Edelman, 1985.)

Literature and the arts have given rise to a form of interpretation that contrasts sharply with the traditional quantitative content analysis employed by empirical social scientists. Where content analysis, in the interest of quantification, takes many messages, shaves off the idiosyncrasies, and tallies the uniformities, the interpretation of popular esthetic codes, in the interest of qualitative analysis, zeroes in on the single expression, relishes its uniqueness and style and explores meanings and parallels emanating outward. The former tells us how many karats a jewel has; the latter examines its luster and beauty. Quantitative content analysis tells us the ratio of Blacks to Whites in the events of the Huxtable household in "The Bill Cosby Show." Qualitative content analysis tells us what these Blacks and Whites are like.

Powerful elements at work through myth include icons, formulas, and genres. Signs and codes are primary structures always present in messages while myth, icon, formula, and genre are secondary structures available to provide the standardized conventions of message content in super media texts. These secondary and aesthetic codes provide the well-recognized structures through which the popular arts are expressed and understood.

Bill Cosby personally, and his mythical television family collectively, have become *icons* of super media. Icon analysis is a form of message interpretation. Marshall Fishwick (1970, 1978), drawing from Herbert Read and Erwin Panovsky, has described the place of contemporary icons. The word *icon,* based on the Greek word for image, refers to "an object of uncritical devotion" and denotes medieval religious images painted on wooden panels. More generally, icons are external expressions of internal convictions tied to myths, legends, values, idols, and aspirations. Panovsky defined iconography as "the branch of art history that concerns itself with the subject matter or meaning of works of art, as opposed to their form." He distinguished surface data, which require identification, description, and authentication, from interior qualities, which call for deeper evaluation and interpretation.

"The mainstream of iconology in our time—because of its dissemination through mass media—is the popular stratum of our culture," according to Fishwick (1970, p. 6). Media icons are as diverse as the superchild Shirley Temple, the Beatles, comic strip characters, the cowboy, and sports stars (Fishwick, 1970, 1978). Icons are the static visual representations of our myths. Following Elíade, Gregor Goethals (1982) finds in both classical and popular icons the power to provide a sense of meaningful order and to integrate the personality of the viewer into that order.

How did Bill Cosby become an icon of American popular culture? First emerging as a vivid and hilarious stand-up comic, Cosby developed routines about his boyhood friends, his brother and himself, his family and neighborhood, sex and marriage, all delivered with vocal dramatics and masterful timing—nuanced and telling stories of everyday experience. These routines became popular records as well. With Robert Culp, Cosby costarred in a dramatic television series, "I Spy." By the early 1970s Cosby was providing voices and direction for the popular Fat Albert television cartoons, which also spun off two books, *The Wit and Wisdom of Fat Albert* (1973) and *Fat Albert's Survival Kit* (1975). As the commercial spokesman for Coca-Cola and Kodak, Cosby developed into one of the most credible pitchmen in the history of television, eventually registering the highest "Q Score" for audience appeal in history. As "The Cosby Show" sat as the number-one rated television program from its beginnings in the fall of 1984 through the 1980s, Cosby also authored best-selling books. His first, *Fatherhood* (1986), sold 2.6 million in hardback, breaking the record held by *Iacocca*. At this point his annual earnings were the highest in the United States, averaging some $57 million. His iconic presence had become unavoidable in the super media.

The media icon may differ significantly from the real person. With a public persona as straightforward and comfortable as they come, Bill Cosby's actual persona was complex and almost contradictory. Relaxed and easy on stage, he could be intense and determined off it. In his chauffeured BMW, he preferred to ride in front next to the driver. Symbol and spokesperson for marriage and family, he was for years a regular at Hugh Hefner's Playboy mansion. Wearing a silver bracelet that proclaimed him "Camille's Husband," he nevertheless confessed to *Ladies' Home Journal* (January 1988) that he had "never been a saint. I'm sure if anyone wanted to get me on my past, they very well could." Always best at reaching the popular, mass mainstream tastes, Cosby himself had personal tastes that were more elite. He developed an extensive art collection and, after going through college playing football, proceeded on to graduate school, despite a busy professional life, and was immensely proud of his doctorate. Carefully avoiding controversy in his prime-time program, Cosby was a generous supporter of Jesse Jackson, the antiapartheid movement, and other political causes. One-dimensional, Cosby was not.

The symbolic icon, Cosby, has chosen to use the "genre" of domestic situation comedy as his vehicle. A *genre* is a secondary code present in a creative work as a combinations of setting, characters, dress, plot lines, and other elements regularly found in a widely recognized grouping of works (Cawelti, 1976). By now a number of standard genres dominate super media films, television, books, and magazines: science fiction, westerns, gangster stories, detective mysteries, horror, combat, comedy, musicals, serial dramas (soap operas), romance, sports, and news. These and other genres have many subgenres as well. Westerns may be classical, contemporary, Samurai, or even, when made in Italy, spaghetti westerns. Comedy may be situation, stand-up, black, satirical, topical, or slapstick. Movies made for television have developed a tear-jerker disease-of-the-week sub-subgenre featuring athletes, celebrities, and average people melodramatically dealing with trauma. Feature films from India may attempt to combine nearly every genre in a single film. Cosby, veteran of stand-up comedy, spy thrillers, and children's shows, found in the genre of situation comedy the perfect vehicle for his greatest success and for recoding Black male ethnicity.

The genre of situation comedy employs standardized *"formulas"* for structuring its presentation. Myths and genres are universal forms, while formulas are limited; they represent "the way in which a particular culture has embodied both mythical archetypes and its own preoccupations in narrative form" (Cawelti, 1976, p. 6). One safely knows that the Cosby domestic comedy will have humorous situations and clever lines, that it will present plot complications but always end well. The adventures of Cliff, Rudy, Theo, and the other Huxtables follow formulas. Popular formulas rely more heavily on convention than invention. *Conventions* are those parts of a cultural product that exist in similar products in the form of elements known to both author and audience beforehand. Since "All in the Family," situation comedies have been taped before a live audience; "The Cosby Show" employed this convention. Conventions maintain a culture's stability. *Inventions* are those parts of a cultural product uniquely contributed by a particular artist; over time they may modify conventions. "The Cosby Show" offered a perfect opportunity to invent new definitions of the Black male and the Black family. Inventions enable a culture to respond to changing circumstances. "The Cosby Show" was prepared to take full advantage of television conventions distinguished by the intimacy of the small screen, the continuity of characters and series, and the use of contemporary concerns even in historical presentations (Newcomb, 1974, 1987).

The coding of ethnicity in super media icons, formulas, and genres is complex and important, especially in humor. Asians today may be coded in the popular culture as exotic Orientals, overachieving competitors, ethnic gangsters, or stumbling intellectuals. Polish stereotypes run from the heights of the Solidarity movement to the depths of Polack jokes. The coding of Hispanics has "progressed" from lazy siestas under sombreros to Speedy Gonzales, from pistol-waving Zapatas to the Frito Bandito, from superstitious underachievers to undocumented "aliens," and finally to the excellence of *Stand and Deliver, The Milagro Beanfield War,* and "Zoot Suit." A joke about three Jews and a blindfold illustrates the dangers of stereotypical humor (Lewis, 1987). Three Jews are about to be shot and are offered a blindfold by the captain of the firing squad. The first Jew takes the blindfold, the second takes it, but the third refuses it. The one next to him says, "Take the blindfold. Don't make trouble." This example of gallows humor has been cited as "liberating" in an internal Freudian way for Jews, but it may also serve to reinforce stereotypes of Jews as submitting too willingly to victimization. Commenting on this, Paul Lewis insists that "a *good sense of humor* refers not only to someone who laughs readily and often, not only to someone who creates humor easily, but also to someone whose creation and appreciation of humor is mediated by humanity" (p. 71).

The Call for Recoding Blackness

An all-too-typical negative depiction of a Black male occurred in a seemingly exemplary 1986 CBS documentary by Bill Moyers, "The Vanishing Family—Crisis in Black America." That documentary included a 13-minute segment featuring "Alice." Opposite her was "Timothy," the 26-year-old father of her three children. In the course of following and interviewing Timothy, Moyers uncovers that he is also the father of three other children by different women, has not held a regular job in two and a half years, has been arrested several times, and does not contribute to the financial support of any of his six offspring. In an interview Moyers digs out of Timothy his pride in making children: "They're like artwork . . . I'm a babymaker. I guess I have strong sperm." Moyers elicits comments from Timothy that show no regrets that the six children are all supported by Welfare. The representation of Timothy is absolutely everything that a welfare abolitionist and racist could ask.

This portrayal of Timothy is not merely information; it shares in the restricted codes of a historical mythology. What mythic dimension does Timothy take on? The question is not whether the picture is true of not; apparently Timothy is all too real. The question is, rather, what this single case generalizes to, mythically and iconically, in the imagination of the viewer. How does Timothy code and image Black maleness, and what reinforcing or conflicting codes and images surround this representation? Unfortunately, for the health of the popular imagination, steeped as it is in past stereotypical conventions of the image industries, the positive alternatives are restricted and the negative reinforcements numerous and readily available.

Painfully aware of such mythological frames, Black critiques look to create not only new images but a new sensibility about Blacks in film and television. Armond White (1985, p. 40) observes, "How black characters might be presented in a politically correct, emotionally resonant situation depends on the filmmaker's mythic or visionary sense of his subject." Negative myths, stereotypes, and ways of seeing that have shackled Hollywood are to be stripped away and recoded by those who share the subject's own ethnic experience and vision.

In a perceptive analysis, "Recoding Blackness: The Visual Rhethoric of Black Independent Film," James Snead (1985) of Yale remarks,

> Recoding blackness means revising visual codes surrounding black skin on screen and the public realm. In the traditional dialectic of film and audience, the spectator takes pleasure in recognizing what "everyone knows" to be obviously true. Stereotyped images, most notoriously of women and blacks, hide real paradoxes, contradictions, and inequities in society underneath the unthinking pleasure of filmic recognition. Particularly in Hollywood's early character repertoire, black skin signified "subhuman, simpleminded, superstitious, and submissive." Continuous association has fixed and transmitted this falsification, and the repetition of codes seems to validate the first coding as correct and the later versions as obviously true [p. 1].

Drawing on Umberto Eco and Jacque Lacan, Snead points to underlying psychological problems in the need to feel authoritative, the same emotional level of existence where Cassirer places myth. Snead says, "The spectator-subject codes the black as servile or absent in order to code himself as masterful and present. The black serves, in other words, as an 'Imaginary' remedy for the spectator-subject's lack of authority" (p. 1).

Snead takes Roland Barthes's famous concept of "writing degree zero" as a starting point for a strategy to counteract and replace the repetition of the pseudo-validated falsification. He reasons,

> Recoding can arise from the very nature of film language, rupturing previous significations in unexpected ways. Where black skin is already framed, or coded into place, montage might be the only realm of freedom. Semioclasm, the "smashing of codes," does not return the lack to the [b]lack, as coding does, but returns the sign to zero, where it begins afresh, mounted in a new context [p. 2].

A Black esthetic of film calls for new content and form, new film style as well as new film subjects and judgments. Predictability diminishes as Snead applies the work of Christian Metz: "The black filmmaker exercises the freedom to recode blackness. The 'other place' on the filmstrip comes after the coded past and present, no longer addressing the dominant 'I,' but redressing codes in the unknown shot to come" (p. 2).

Codes of Ethnicity in "The Bill Cosby Show"

The centerpiece of Cosby's contribution to super media has been the weekly television program "The Bill Cosby Show." As a prominent social force, can the show "resolve cultural conflict and contradictions" in the way that Levi-Strauss describes myth's structural power? Or does the show "suppress contradictions and idealize existing conditions" in the way that Roland Barthes identifies myth's masking powers? A cultural studies reading of the show's texts over the years sheds light on this question and on the show's self-conscious techniques for recoding Blackness.

"The Cosby Show" as a standard televised situation comedy is centered in the living room and kitchen of the residence of Dr. and Mrs. Cliff Huxtable. He, Cliff, is a obstetrician-gynecologist, and she, Clair, is a lawyer. Their family in the beginning consisted of a college student daughter, Sandra; two teenagers, Denise and Theo; a preteen, Vanessa; and a preschool girl, Rudy. As actors aged, so did their characters and the family life as a whole. Each show opens with a lively jazz score over an introduction to the ensemble cast. Each cast member is shown dancing to the score. Cosby himself is shown first and last in this sequence and sometimes dancing with each of the other cast members. In this introductory montage, as in the shows themselves, each family member is given his or her relatively balanced screen time, but it is clear that Cosby is the focal point. The family emphasis and the centrality of Cosby are among the principal symbolic contributions of the show.

The Father Figure

As a result of antifamily practices during slavery and subsequent discriminatory employment practices, Black families have had a larger-than-average number of single-parent households with female heads. Timothy, in the CBS documentary described above, represents the epitome of the Black male stereotype as absentee father out of the household. The Cosby character of Cliff Huxtable, M.D., the loving, caring, and incredibly *present* father of five, is the antithesis to this stereotype. He shares decisions with his wife but is in charge. He shows unwavering understanding, perceptive advice, and good-humored charm in all his dealings with his children. His character is unquestionably established as a well-employed breadwinner, and yet he is present at home and involved with his children to an unusual degree for a working male of any race. When he takes responsibility—along with his protégé in training for responsible maleness, Theo—for finding and removing the snake in the cellar, or carving the Thanksgiving turkey, or any of a thousand other duties, Cosby is the incarnation of the perfect father figure.

The Strong Nuclear Family Unit

Consisting of two loving parents, five clever and achieving children, and grandparents who visit its solid house, the Huxtable family seems to have moved right out of texts on the sociology of the nuclear family and into our living rooms. The parents have a stable union; they frequently reminisce about when they first met and dated in college, even about failing to tell their parents about everything they did. The children are intelligent and well adjusted; when they have problems with grades or siblings or boyfriends or girlfriends or behavior, they always respond quickly to parental attention and reintegrate into the closely knit family unit. The children have predictable conflicts, as in wearing each other's clothes or demanding the privileges granted another, but they always wind up reinforcing and assisting each other as well as their parents. Against the stereotype of Black families as unstable, full of unwanted pregnancies, and rife with street talk, conflict, and drugs, this family is as stable as the Rock of Gibraltar and as nuclear as anything Einstein ever conceived.

The Professionals

Allegedly, Cosby's real-life wife, Camille, was the one who insisted that Cosby be cast not as a chauffeur, as planned, but as a doctor. Added to this high-status male role is the female role of a wife who is a lawyer. This couple is about as stereotypically upwardly mobile and yuppie as can be imagined. While Ozzie Nelson never had an occupation in that family show, and Archie Bunker was almost never shown working at his, both Cliff and Clair are actually shown from time-to-time in scenes at their work. Cliff instructs and counsels young parents-to-be, and Clair negotiates with her law partners. When Theo gets them arguing over his punishment, Cliff calls from his doctor's office to Clair's law office, and their professional personas are overlaid on their family roles. "The Cosby Show" presents the antithesis to the stereotype of Blacks on welfare and without professional training or gainful employment. Those who object that the Huxtables are "atypical" never seem to raise the same objection against Redd Foxx's portrayal of a junk dealer on prime time ("Sanford and Son"), although being a junk dealer is no more typical of Blacks than being a doctor or a lawyer. In fact, very few portrayals on television are "typical."

Affluence and Fiscal Responsibility

"The Cosby Show" offers no apologies for the obvious affluence that it portrays. The Huxtables own a nice home, two or more cars, excellent wardrobes for parents and children, and the full range of home appliances; they appear to lack for no material goods. They go to nice dinners and nightclubs, take vacations, and send their children to college with no apparent financial strain. Lest their children become financially reckless, however, they instruct them carefully on the realities of living expenses. When Denise wishes to spend all her savings to buy an expensive, attractive, and untested used car, Cliff dissuades her by speaking of costs of gas, insurance, and maintenance. When Theo wants to skip college, get a job, and buy a motorcycle, Cliff gets out Monopoly money to explain to him the hard facts of rent, food, clothing, transportation, entertainment, and other costs when matched against income. All this, of course, counters the Black stereotype of indigent spendthrifts who throw away their last dollars on Cadillacs, clothes, and drink. This Black family's enviable affluence has come from planning, hard work, and fiscal common sense.

The Value of Education

Against stereotypes of school dropouts and poorly educated unemployables, the Huxtable household seems to ooze with affirmations of education and the value of school. Cliff and Clair refer periodically to their years in college and professional school; the children often deal with school issues of homework assignments and grades; everyone plans for college; and the Cosby spinoff "A Different World" is set in a racially mixed but predominantly Black college. The Huxtables' eldest daughter, Sandra, was a success at Princeton, but Denise, after intense lobbying by her father, chose to attend his traditional Black college, Hillman. Consistent with the program's validation, Cosby has personally contributed more than a million dollars to Black college funds. "The Cosby Show" has featured episodes set at college, as when Denise and her grandfather wind up collaborating in stealing the bear's head that is the symbol of their rival college. The show has even showcased a professor as "the master teacher" and commencement ceremonies complete with educational rhetoric and ceremonial music. Cosby's own credit at the end reads: "William Cosby, Jr., Ed.D."

The Multigenerational Family

Although the Huxtables are a nuclear family, they are not without the older generation, since Cliff's father and mother are frequent and good-humored visitors. In addition, Sandra married her likable but slow-witted boyfriend, Alvin, and a new generation can begin. The grandparents are also upscale and articulate, making the program a portrait of three generations of a stable, successful Black family. Any stereotype of Blacks as isolated into discontinuous generations finds its opposite here.

Multiracialism

Although the emphasis is Black, the show is carefully inclusive of a variety of ethnic representations. Rudy has a chubby White playmate, Peter, as well as her Black friend, "Bud." When the experienced Black actor Roscoe Lee Browne plays a Hillman professor of literature, the equally experienced White actor Christopher Plummer enters as a professor of drama at Columbia. Cliff borrows a saw from a White neighbor, and Rudy, feared lost at the plaza, is found at a Chinese restaurant playing with her friend, the daughter of the owner. Clair collaborates with her White law partners and Cliff counsels a pregnant Latino woman. All this helps to counter any charge that Blacks or others live with and care about only "their own."

Racial Pride

Despite its appeal to a broad cross-section of the American television audience, "The Cosby Show" makes deft and frequent reference to elements of Black history and culture. Student essays for school, Black History Week, pictures on the walls in the background, references in conversations, and other opportunities are seized on to refer to historical personages and events in Black American history and culture. Black jazz receives especially prominent endorsement through the taste and conversations of Cliff and his father, and through an occasional guest appearance by a Black musician. Singer Lena Horne is the focus of one episode, when Cliff arranges a family celebration to attend her show and she graciously shares dinner with the family afterward. Another episode is built around Martin Luther King, Jr., when to write an essay for school, Theo interviews his parents and grandparents, who describe the March on Washington. The episode concludes with the soundtrack of King's voice delivering his incomparable "I Have a Dream" speech as the family watches a television documentary. Participation in sports is affirmed as Cliff inspires Theo with tales of his old gridiron conquests, but obsession with them is avoided, in keeping with the falseness of their career promise for most Black youths. Family members never speak in jive or nonstandard Black dialect; although, for example, Theo does perform with his buddy "Cockroach" a rap version of Mark Antony's speech from Shakespeare's *Julius Caesar.* Given the show's popularity in South Africa, NBC was uncomfortable with an anti-apartheid poster on Theo's wall, but Cosby insisted it stay in. All in all, the show manages to affirm Black pride but not in a heavy-handed way. Racial discrimination and conflict are never directly raised, despite the emphasis on Black pride.

Humor Mediated by Humanity

Of course, what makes the show successful is its humor. The Huxtable family, despite their ideal circumstances and values, are still very funny. Bill Cosby personally is something of a comic genius. His nonverbal skills are marvelous. The bell rings, he lifts his eyes, and he does a very subtle dance move across the room to "charmingly" open the door. Nothing has been said, but the live audience responds with genuine laughter. As Cosby does it, it is funny! He can make taking care of a sick child the most delightful experience in the world. In one episode, the germs in the patient Rudy become live characters acted out by Cosby. He makes a tight, prissy little face and mincingly articulates, "Party, party. We're going to party." Then when Cosby gives the spoon with medicine to the child, it is a major nonverbal experience. The airplane roars in carrying the medicine. Rudy sits up in bed transfixed, beginning to smile and giggle contagiously. Cosby continues clowning cleverly and easily with the airplane-spoon. He's got Rudy going, and he's got the live audience going and, one can only assume, he's got the home audience going. It's laughing time. In that moment "The Cosby Show" has created classic Aristotelian humor by surprise. It is the common seen in an uncommon way. There is a shock of recognition as audience members say to themselves, "I've been there!" A basic human experience is created fresh on television, cleverly and as if new.

Cosby's artistic restraint and control strengthen the entire effect. Cosby does not embarrass himself or anyone else with his clowning. It is quite the opposite of the problem depicted so bitingly in Robert Townsend's low budget success *The Hollywood Shuffle* (1986): the negative, insulting "Black" roles to be performed in Hollywood by using bad grammar and hyperactive mannerisms. Cosby will not demean himself for a laugh, as a Stepin Fetchit character was forced to. He does not mock others, as an insulting stand-up comic working the Borscht Belt might. One laughs "with" Cosby, not at him; he knows and intends what is funny.

Broad Popular Appeal

Bill Cosby's comic and naturalistic acting abilities have been central to the appeal of "The Cosby Show." Through these entertainment skills, backed by restless ambition and calculating foresight, Bill Cosby has become extremely successful, to a degree rare for a person of any ethnic background. There is, in his ability to entertain, an echo of the ultimate and absolute genius of nonverbal humor, Charlie Chaplin. There is in all Cosby's work an element one saw in Walt Disney (Real, 1977): an immediate sense of what the largest portions of the public will respond to, an ability to operate in the middle register between the heights of elite culture and the depths of brutal culture. For Cosby this means a sense of "popular taste" perceptively and humorously presented in books, records, television, and live appearances. He is obviously a maestro of modern super media.

Achievements and Limitations in the Cosby Recoding of "Black"

Does "The Cosby Show" serve to (1) "suppress" or (2) "resolve" the social contradictions that surround it? It recodes Black ethnicity around the father figure and the strong nuclear family, an affirmation of the value of education, a sense of affluence with fiscal responsibility, and a population that is multigenerational and multiracial. Does this merely mask and obscure problems through ideological manipulation—one function of Barthes's mythologies—or does this television program actually initiate or reinforce needed catharsis and resolution, as Levi-Strauss saw myths doing? Obviously the question is a false opposition. To some degree the Cosby show does both. First, let us look at the negative "masking" function.

Critics of "The Cosby Show" tend to be cynical about the material comfort and security of two wealthy professionals and their children. Are these "typical" Blacks, or is this not some kind of fairy tale that, in the best Bettelheim tradition, lulls children and adults into believing the myth "Be good and you'll live happily ever after"? Is this not a conformist compromise whose principal ideological function is to convince subordinate groups that they should conform to this society's rules? The answer is a partial yes; this program does not in any overt way attempt to rearrange the power structure in the United States. Many harsher realities of Black existence are ignored or obscured. High unemployment, especially among the young, finds no echoes in "The Cosby Show." Racial discrimination in housing, education, and other areas is not confronted. Police harassment of minority populations receives no attention. What is omitted from the show is significant. The show carefully avoids antagonizing any members of the audience. In this sense, as the saying goes, it "comforts the afflicted" far more than it "afflicts the comfortable." Relative to the dominant ideology, "The Cosby Show" is clearly "reformist conservative" in the manner of a subordinate recoding that attempts to change only one dimension, and not an oppositional recoding that challenges the larger system.

But "The Cosby Show" does have a positive role in the class struggle in precisely the way Stuart Hall, a Jamaican by birth, speaks of that struggle. In his well-known essay, "The Rediscovery of 'Ideology': Return of the Repressed in Media Studies," Hall (1982) describes the political and ideological battle over the principal descriptor to go with the term *Black*. Hall speaks of the class struggle in language that "took the form of a different accenting of the *same* term: e.g., the process by means of which the derogatory colour 'black' became the enhanced value 'Black' (as in 'Black is Beautiful'). . . . The struggle was not over the term itself but over its connotative meaning" (p. 78–79). In discussing Bernstein, Bourdieu, and Volosinov, Hall (p. 79) explains further:

> Of course, the same term, e.g., "black," belonged in both the vocabularies of the oppressed and the oppressors. What was being struggled over was not the "class belongingness" of the term, but the inflection it could be given, its connotative field of reference. In the discourse of the Black movement, the denigratory connotation "black = the despised race" could be inverted into its opposite: "black = beautiful." There was thus a "class struggle in language."

Hall also referred to this as "an ideological struggle to disarticulate a signifier from one, preferred or dominant meaning-system, and re-articulate it within another, different chain of connotations" (p. 80). Hall argued for action: "'Black' could not be converted into 'black = beautiful' simply by wishing it were so. It had to become part of an organized practice of struggles requiring the building up of collective forms of black resistance as well as the development of new forms of black consciousness" (p. 82).

Here, at precisely this point in Hall's description of the coding of Black ethnicity, is where "The Cosby Show" has been most active. It has had potentially decisive effects in convincing middle Americans that a Black man and his family can be their most favored weekly guest. Reversing the tradition of "Amos 'n Andy" in which Blacks were funny because they were different, and even inferior linguistically (see Cripps, 1983) Cosby establishes very firmly a strong, positive role model for father, family, education, career, and pride.

"The Bill Cosby Show" shifts the connotation of *Black* decisively, following on the widespread influence that the historic miniseries "Roots" had on American consciousness. After sitting through a week with Alex Haley's enslaved family tree, as part of the largest American week-long television audience in history, mass-mediated America had reason to be sympathetic to a Black attempting to survive and succeed

in America. Leslie Fishbein's (1983) definitive history of that remarkable American television docudrama, based on Haley's somewhat
mythical genealogy, explains the popular style and emphasis in what
was subtitled and advertised as "the saga of an American family." Note
the two descriptors: *American* and *family.* Fishbein recounts how dramatically influential the series was in focusing national attention on a
long-distorted segment of American history and mythology. And she
suggests that Haley and ABC provided a valuable learning experience
for both Blacks and Whites. She judges they deserved their many
awards even though they significantly distorted historical facts. The
distortions were secondary: "The facts were far less significant than the
myths *Roots* wished to generate" (p. 295). And here, like Cosby later,
Roots centered on family and on America, although its myths were
historical and heroic, while Cosby's are contemporary and domestic.
Both were movements to correct history and recode popular understanding of *Black.*

Before the 1960s, Black Americans were commonly called "Negro."
The first mass-media use of *Black* as a term of pride came in the
declaration of the late 1960s civil rights movement: "I'm Black and I'm
proud!" Since that time no individual has done as much as Bill Cosby
to engineer symbolically a shift in the connotation of *Black* from the
negative one imposed by the historic oppressors to the positive one
sought by self-respecting and proud African-Americans.

There is evidence that both Cosby and the show's "production con-
sultant," his friend Alvin F. Poussaint, M.D., of Harvard, understand
and intend this recoding. A more racially militant Bill Cosby has
appeared on television but rarely. In a memorable sequence in a 1969
segment of CBS's "Of Black America" series, Cosby narrates and
comments on the crucial relationship between media images and children's self-perceptions. Speaking from a quiet classroom filled with
elementary students, Cosby draws on psychological data to indicate in
children's drawings of themselves what weak and inadequate self-
concepts some Black children evidence compared with White children.
He then flips off the lights and flicks on a film projector to show a series
of stereotypical Black portrayals from Hollywood movies of the 1920s
and 1930s. The Black males are slow and dumb. They are superstitious,
and they scare easily, with bulging eyes and quaking knees. Cosby
points out that the nasty Negroes in a segment from *Birth of a Nation*
are actually Whites wearing blackface. The segments show actors
playing dim-witted Black children, women, and men in various roles as

Davis Memorial Library

10/8/2019 01:00 AM

Mass media & the First Amendment : an
introduction to the issues, problems, and
practices / Maurice R. Cullen, Jr.
Cullen, Maurice R.
342.73 C967m

*Get Between the Covers! Developing a
Culture of Reading*

Cosby notes that virtually no other roles were available to Blacks in movies at the time. In one segment even the little White girl, Shirley Temple, is smarter, braver, and more mature than the adult Black servants, who can barely speak and who move gingerly except when they break into a happy dance to entertain the White children at a birthday party. Stepin Fetchit, Willie Best, Bill "Mr. Bojangles" Robinson, and others were hired in films only to play stereotypes. From these vivid segments, Cosby moves into a discussion of a few pioneer Black inventors and leaders and remarks how their achievements "got lost in the history books." This is supported by a passage he then reads from the leading American history text, by Harvard professors Samuel Eliot Morison and Henry Steele Commager. They characterize slavery by writing, "As for Sambo [at this Cosby lifts his eyes from the text and says quietly and sarcastically, 'Sambo, Professor Morison? Sambo, Professor Commager?'], there is reason to believe his lot was not an unhappy one," or words to that effect. Cosby's part of the program concludes with more examples of Black achievement and his final comment, "You've got to give us credit for more than rhythm." The "Of Black America" episode is partly a remnant of a more militant time but also a reminder that "the Coz" is far from unaware of the importance of media stereotypes, images, and labels.

Cosby's emphasis on positive values, of course, goes beyond issues of race as well. The popular priest-sociologist-novelist Andrew Greeley calls Cosby the most popular preacher in America, ahead of any priest, minister, rabbi, or televangelist. Speaking of the quality situation comedies, such as "Family Ties" and "The Cosby Show," Greeley notes,

> His program and the others are based on the insight that implicit ethics and religion in a matrix of humor are highly commercial in a country where meaning and belonging are as important as they have ever been, and where those institutions traditionally charged with meaning and belonging— churches and schools—are failing to deliver sufficient amounts of either [Paulsen, 1987, p. 27].

In Gerbner's sense of television as "the new religion" (1967; see also Goethals, 1981; Schwartz, 1984), a new religion that anchors our values and identities, Bill Cosby and others with television influence have a unique power to serve society in profound and meaningful ways. Cosby's *awareness* of this power, as shown in various ways, including his arguments with Eddie Murphy as Murphy recounts these in his film

Raw (1987), sets him off almost as much as does the success with which he exercises that power.

Cultural studies can affirm "The Cosby Show" for its historic contribution to recoding *Black* and for its other positive services, but, confined to prime-time formulas in a situation comedy genre the show was subject to constraints and goals that prevented it from taking the struggle to a deeper level of coding. The primary criticism here has to do with the high expectations for recoding established by Snead, White, and Davis as described above. They demand not only a recoding of *Black* but also a remaking of the code itself—a more radical task than prime-time entertainment genres and formulas permit. The code of environment and image through which good or bad *Black* is expressed is also posed as part of the problem. Armond White (1985) charges, "The classical filmmaking style, which developed synchronically with the generic myths of Hollywood, never included a realistic or truthful appreciation of black American experience" (p. 40). This absence has created a basic problem for the "black filmmakers' difficult, awestruck efforts to join the general discourse of American films." He warns, "Although blacks and whites have shared the myths of Hollywood— dreaming at the same icons and projecting fantasies into a common pool—it has been an anomalous activity and a deeply superficial relationship" (p. 41).

The challenge of an Afro-American sensibility has also drawn the attention of Black folklorist and filmmaker Gerald Davis (1985). He calls for "the development of a visual product consistent with African-American interior and exterior world views and expressive systems, and visually and conceptually 'different' from the products modelled after the standard and inadequate Hollywood vocabulary" (p. 101). Insiders can do what outsiders, however well intentioned, cannot do. Davis reasons that "if the producer, camera person, and editor consciously understand . . . characteristic emotional, psychic, and intellectual response to African-American existence, . . . the media imager begins to approach a cinematic or video product closely tied to the particular historical matrix we identify as African-American culture" (p. 102). A new Black film esthetic under the control of the Black filmmaker makes it possible, in the words of Davis, "to produce an African-American cinematic way of looking at both African-American phenomena and the workings of the wide world without the self-consciousness and embarrassment that frequently attends watching a film on African-American materials produced from another perspective" (p. 103).

This task and others lie well beyond the possibilities of what a network prime-time entertainment program can hope to tackle, no matter how well intentioned and forward thinking the creators and producers. This is, in fact, probably not a task approachable through popular or mass culture but only through the more rarefied atmosphere of elite culture, in much the way that feminist films have evolved in specialized circles in recent decades. But this distinction takes us from "The Cosby Show" to complex questions of class and power.

Class, Group Identity, and Decoding Culture

"The Cosby Show" recodes Blackness, but it fails to address directly class and group conflict within American society. In super media culture and daily life, social class is one form of subordination alongside patriarchy, racial and ethnic separation, regionalism, nationalism, religious discrimination, and more. Members of the upper-, middle-, and lower-income groups clearly exhibit distinct tastes in much of their selection and appreciation of super media. Social class affects super media because media are decoded by class membership, media products are identified with class taste levels, and hegemony occurs through ruling class influence over media products.

In Great Britain, where awareness of class differences is significantly higher than in the United States, research has established that members of different classes decode media messages in different ways, often consistent with their class membership. Graham Murdock (1982, p. 760) notes that these studies "have reconnected studies of consumption to the sociology of stratification." For example, a working-class laborer has access to social experience and interpretive schemata consistent with his or her place in the stratified social order. If the worker is particularly frustrated, he or she may interpret a story of conflict between Theo Huxtable in "The Cosby Show" and the police in favor of Theo rather than the representatives of law and order, even though the show clearly portrays Theo as in the wrong. A more contented member of the upper class will, in contrast, identify with and favor the forces of established law and order, the police. The Glasgow University Media Group (1976, 1980) has established that conflicts between owners and trade unions are interpreted in broadcast and press coverage in such a way that the interests of the ownership class are more favorably portrayed than those of the working class.

Does Cosby's show favor the interests of the dominant over the subordinate? The degree and manner in which the interests of the dominant class influence popular culture raise difficult questions. Tony Bennett (1986) suggests that Gramsci's notion of hegemony offers a solid middle ground for answering this. On one side, rigid structuralism charges that the popular culture is an "ideological machine" that dictates the thoughts of the people, while on the other side, populist culturalism romantically views the popular culture as the authentic voice of subordinate classes. Bennett emphasizes Gramsci's contribution to resolving this conflict: "In Gramsci's conspectus, popular culture is viewed neither as the site of the people's cultural deformation nor as that of their cultural self-affirmation . . . ; rather, it is viewed as a force field of relations shaped, precisely, by these contradictory pressures and tendencies" (p. 11). Gramsci contended that the antagonistic relation between ruling and subordinate classes was less one of direct "domination" than one of negotiated "hegemony." The interests of the ruling class must contend with a set of opposing class cultures and values rising from the subordinate classes. Ruling-class hegemony is effective to the extent that it is articulated to and incorporates such divergences. Thus members of subordinate classes do not encounter ruling-class culture interests directly but, rather, in this negotiated version of ruling-class culture and ideology. Robert Gray (1976, p. 6, cited in Bennett, Mercer, & Woollacott, 1986) notes that "certain aspects of the behavior and consciousness of the subordinate classes may reproduce a version of the values of the ruling class. But in the process value systems are modified." At the same time, potentially dissident values in the subordinate-class culture are transformed as they are articulated to ruling-class ideology, which prevents the working through of their full dissident implications. The result is a compromise familiar to students of the popular media. Figure 4.1 illustrates this dynamic.

Hegemony can now be seen as the greater power of the dominant against the dissident values in Figure 4.1. Compared to that of England, membership in the American ruling class has been less defined and discussed, but the cultural studies distinction between dominant and subordinate groups raises questions about "The Cosby Show." Is it not convenient that America's most popular television programs do *not* raise issues of disparity and inequality? Redd Foxx in "Sanford and Son" played a junk dealer who seemed no more deprived or unhappy than the affluent, professional Huxtables. Entertainment television meticulously avoids problematic portrayals of class and social conflict

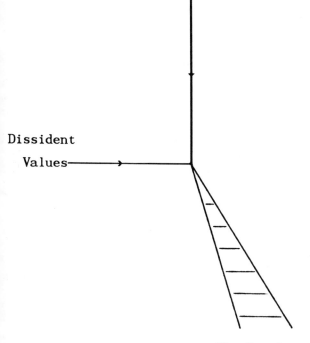

Dominant Ruling

Class Values

Dissident

Values——→

The Resulting
Negotiated Version
of Ruling Class Interests
Operating in Super Media

FIGURE 4.1 Dominant and Dissident Value Conflict in Super Media

except in those rare adventurous shows from Norman Lear and Tandem Productions. Even "Miami Vice" and "Hill Street Blues," for all their ethnic and criminal conflict, do not draw attention to possibilities for social structural change. Why?

The answer lies with control of the television text. Do audiences really determine programming? Recent American sociology questions the absoluteness of programmers' claims about this. Ball-Rokeach and Cantor (1986, p. 18) note that, despite communicators' claims to be answering to an audience, "most research shows that the audience's input remains indirect and obscure." Special interest groups, such as gays (Montgomery, 1981) or Action for Children's Television, can over time make inroads against unwanted media portrayals. But, among groups trying to affect media content, "some have greater access to the media due to their higher class or status, as, for example, economic and political elites," in the words of Ball-Rokeach and Cantor (p. 18).

Do creative artists determine television programming? The sociology of organizations that produce culture reveals the importance of group membership within the media organizations. This membership produces a narrowed frame of "professionalism" that is inhibiting (Tuchman, 1978) and ideologically restricting (Golding, 1977). More generally, Ball-Rokeach and Cantor (1986, p. 15) note that recent sociology confirms, "Power over what is shown rests finally with those who own or finance the media, rather than with the individual creators." They also note, "Usually there is general agreement within an editorial staff or on a set because both the creative people and the decision makers subscribe to the same basic values and norms." This belief consensus becomes tighter toward the top. The same authors observe that only media workers who subscribe to "the values and beliefs of those who control the organization are likely to be offered elite positions within those organizations" (p. 16). These restrictive filters are the mechanisms of "ruling class negotiated domination" in "The Cosby Show" and other American television.

In "The Political Economy of the Television (Super) Text," Nick Browne (1984) explains "the direct role of economy in shaping the form of American television texts" (p. 175). The "supertext" of television includes all programs, commercials, announcements, and so on. He finds that serial forms, such as "The Cosby Show," "serve to continue the subject along the itinerary of habituated consumption" (p. 178). Ultimately, "in the television age, consumption and social control have become linked" (p. 181). Diversity and change are unlikely against the "megatext" of the television schedule and history.

The control, however, is negotiated, not absolute. Horace Newcomb (1988) points this out by applying the notion of "semiotic excess" proposed by Hartley (1984) and Fiske (1986). The idea of semiotic excess is that "once the ideological, hegemonic work has been performed, there is still excess meaning that escapes the control of the dominant and is thus available for the culturally subordinate to use for their own cultural-political interests" (Fiske, 1986, p. 401). When meanings proposed by television conflict with viewers' beliefs, the possibility for aberrant decoding and dissent arises. Similar to the notion of polysemic readings of a text, Bakhtin's notion (1981) of "heteroglossia," or multiple speaking in a text, emphasizes ideological struggle and the possibility of freedom even where the forces of domination are apparent.

Television is constrained by the demands of its own "consensus narratives" as much as by dominant ideology. David Thorburn (1988) finds a consensus narrative has "the ambition or desire to speak for and to the whole of its culture, or as much of 'the whole' as the governing forces in society will permit" (p. 56). Its task is "to articulate the culture's central mythologies in a widely accessible 'language,' an inheritance of shared stories, plots, character types, cultural symbols, narrative conventions" (p. 57). This it does by storytelling in a popular language legible to the common understanding of a majority of the culture. The communal and collaborative nature of such storytelling confines it to the "dominant pieties of the culture." As the chief carrier of the lore and inherited understanding of its culture, consensus narrative is essentially conservative, but it is not closed. A continual testing, rehearsal, and revision of cultural experience and values takes place within consensus narratives.

Within the negotiated dominant ideology and consensus narratives, there is yet a semiotic excess through which "The Cosby Show" attempts to bring about limited but real change. The change is real in recoding Blackness, particularly in inserting a positive icon to replace negative stereotypes of Black males in family life. But the change is limited, given the centrist demands of prime time, to inventions of recoding Blackness while accepting the framing conventions of situation comedy formulas and genres. Recoding Blackness in this manner serves liberal progress but does not directly threaten any of the protected interests of super media ownership and the dominant class. It is, in the classic phrase of Daniel Hallin (1986), "reformist conservatism."

Placed in the context of theories of codes, myths, icons, genres, class, and ideology, the positive and negative portrayals of Black males, from Stepin Fetchit to Bill Cosby, serve to illustrate the mechanisms on a broad cultural level through which super media as a whole create, sustain, and reflect meanings and the interpretation and structuring of existence. Pro and con, the conflicting portrayals become differently refracting prisms through which current cultural struggles are expressed.

In its general implications, "The Cosby Show" does serve to "resolve" America's racial failures by powerfully recoding *Black* and effectively countering generations of negative stereotypes. At the same time, the show "suppresses" other problems and solutions by omission through the program's own choices and, especially, through the limitations imposed in subject and style by the political economy of mainstream popular super media.

Bill Cosby's role in super media, together with gender in film directing as described in the next chapter, both illustrate structures of subordination and struggle within the symbolic world of super media. As women and ethnic minorities seek better employment and portrayals, they will continually challenge inherited practices and values in super media and make those challenges larger than any one individual or any one group. Media are an essential component of "self-determination" today, and restricted media access and control for any group is a social deficiency doing a disservice to all. If it is true that the absence of freedom for anyone diminishes the freedom of all, then efforts toward gender and ethnic parity in super media deserve universal support and gratitude.

Questions

1. In super media's role as mythmaker, what signs and codes of Black males have been prominent?
2. What role do icons, genres, and formulas play in "The Cosby Show" and similar super media?
3. What are the rejected previous codings of *Black,* and what are the new codings proposed in the portrayal in "The Cosby Show" of the father

figure, the nuclear family, professionals, affluence and fiscal responsibility, education, cross-generational and multiracial themes, racial pride, humor mediated by humanity, and broad popular appeal?

4. How has "The Cosby Show" recoded *Black* and in the process both resolved and suppressed social tensions?

5. How do negotiated interpretations emerge from the conflict of dominant and dissident values in super media?

6. Who has the strongest say in what appears on television—audience, artists, or owners?

7. In the tension between the restrictions of consensus narratives and the opportunities of semiotic excess, how does "The Cosby Show" find a compromise between convention and invention?

Notes

1. Gardner, J., & Reese, F. (1975). *Quotations of wit and wisdom.* New York: W. W. Norton.

2. The power of myth in accounting for significant dimensions of contemporary media has received increasing attention from communication scholars, most notably Roger Silverstone (1981), James Carey (1988), Douglas Kellner (1979, 1982), Hal Himmelstein (1984), Gaye Tuchman (1978), and Len Masterman (1984). The writings of Ernst Cassirer (especially 1946, 1944) on myth as a symbolic form in all human life provided the first detailed explanation of the role of the psychology of emotions in myth.

5

Structuralist Analysis 2:
Gender in Film Directing

It is election night. Reporter Lesley Stahl is one of four principals in CBS election night coverage.

She walks on the set. The names on the chairs read: "Cronkite," "Mudd," "Wallace," and "Female."

She is reminded of Simone de Beauvoir's warning that women are identified simply as "the other," and James Baldwin's charge that, for minorities, "Nobody Knows My Name."

Lesley Stahl survives the insult and continues her successful career, eventually anchoring CBS's *Face the Nation* and serving as national affairs correspondent.

Why, how, and with what interpretation do such incidents happen?

The most creative area of media research in recent decades has been feminist criticism. It has built on a base of Black criticism from the civil rights movement and has statistically documented discriminatory non-employment, underemployment, and stereotyping throughout film and television, radio and recordings, magazines and newspapers, advertising, and the totality of super media industries. But feminist criticism has also gone well beyond traditional social science research methods and successfully incorporated the new insights of semiotics, structuralism, and psychoanalysis into media analysis, especially film criticism. As a major contributor to cultural studies, feminist criticism has created a profound new understanding of not only female but *all* representation in mass-mediated culture and imagery.

AUTHOR'S NOTE: *The research and writing of this chapter are very largely the work of Patsy Rae Winsor, to whom I am profoundly grateful, both for carrying out this study and for letting me incorporate it here.*

Employment and Portrayal of Women in Super Media

Progress in the equal employment and portrayal of women in media stems from centuries of struggle that reached watersheds in the 1960s and 1970s. In 1969 the United States Federal Communications Commission issued rules making it illegal for broadcasters to discriminate against women. Starting in 1971, broadcasters were required to file annual lists of female and minority employees and their job classifications. In 1972, Title VII protections of the Civil Rights Act were extended to private industry in the Equal Employment Opportunity Act, creating the first of a new group of broadcasting professionals, dubbed the "class of '72." This included Lesley Stahl, Jane Pauley, Marcie Carsey, Judy Woodruff, Suzanne de Passe, and others. Assessing the results of such measures, the U.S. Civil Rights Commission found that between 1971 and 1975 in the top four job categories at stations— officials and managers, professionals, technicians, and salespersons— minority male employment increased by 42.6 percent, minority female employment increased by 80.3 percent, and White female employment increased by 89.4 percent (U.S. Civil Rights Commission, 1977). By 1985 women held 26.7 percent of the jobs in the top four categories at commercial television stations, up from 21.5 percent in 1980 (Castro, 1988). However, some 80 percent of all jobs are listed in the top four categories. The FCC and the Civil Rights Commission agreed that during that period "minorities and women have not necessarily made significant employment gains," because many jobs were simply re-labeled to move them up into the top four job categories (U.S. Civil Rights Commission, 1977, pp. 126–127).

Entering the 1990s, there remain clear inequities in media employment patterns as for example in the case of female professionals in broadcasting. Women TV news directors earn 34 percent less, on average, than males, according to the Radio and Television News Directors Association. Women make up just 6.1 percent of all television station presidents, according to a study by American Women in Radio and TV, Inc., which called that figure "grossly deficient" considering that women constitute 52 percent of the population and 44 percent of all employed persons in the United States. The Directors Guild of America (DGA) found that, of the 65,000 prime-time hours aired between 1959 and 1980, women directed just 115. In 1986, women directed 348 of the 3,180 television programs produced in the United States; it is note-worthy that, from this 11 percent, women garnered 24 percent of the nominations for DGA directing awards. In 1988, 384 of the 4,684 members of the DGA were women, approximately 8 percent of the total (Castro, 1988). Similar underrepresentation occurs in most developed countries but is often even worse in the less developed countries, according to frequent United Nations and UNESCO conferences (Fullerton, 1984).

The restricted portrayal of women and minorities has been identified by scores of content analyses in recent decades. Both women and minorities have been underrepresented in proportion to their numbers in the total society. They also play a much smaller proportion of leading roles. Furthermore, when women have been presented, they are in a narrower range of occupations than men and usually exercise less authority. More specifically, a sample of 1,365 programs over the ten years from 1969 through 1978 found men outnumbering women 3 to 1 on prime time (Gerbner & Signorielli, 1979). Overall trends in media portrayals still fit the Civil Rights Commission's summary of the content of five years of programming in the 1970s:

> The television world presents a social structure in which males are very much in control of their own lives and are in a position to control the lives of others. Regardless of race, male characters were older, more independent, more frequently portrayed in serious roles, and they held more diverse and prestigious occupations than did female characters. Females were younger, more often unemployed and family bound, and more frequently seen in comic roles. Those who were employed were in stereotyped and sometimes subservient occupations.
>
> . . . The major difference between males and females was the degree to which men were involved in violent action, either as law enforcers or as criminals. Further, women were far more likely to be victims of violence rather than the perpetrators of it.
>
> Female weakness is the complement of masculine control on television, and it is seen in an exaggerated form in the portrayal of the nonwhite female. Most nonwhite females were in their twenties, unemployed, and the most likely of all groups to be the victims of violence. The frequent portrayal of the black female as a prostitute illustrates her vulnerability in television's violent world [U.S. Civil Rights Commission, 1977, p. 40].

Some of these issues appeared in Levy's (1987) analysis of Academy Award–winning roles reported in Chapter Three; many of the issues reappear below in our case study of male- and female-directed Hollywood films.

Differences in Popular Films Directed by Males and Females

Commercial films, as a medium of artistic and cultural expression, fluctuate in popularity from year to year but always remain a highly influential form of entertainment. Cable movie channels and home videos have expanded the marketing of movies and, entering the 1990s, theater attendance was reported to be the highest in years. Simultaneous with film's ongoing popularity is another interesting trend: an increasing number of films *directed by women* are seeing commercial release and popular acceptance. This phenomenon may seem incidental to the average filmgoer, but to the close observer of super media it opens up a new field of inquiry. Central to this are two points of consideration: the *place* of women's films in an enterprise that has been male-dominated from its inception, and the *difference,* if any, between films made by women and those made by men.

This place and difference can be examined by comparing and contrasting popular films made by male and female directors. The comparison serves several purposes: it calls attention to the variety and the nature of gender-specific differences in film-making; it assesses the centrality of the director's point of view, however unconscious that may be; and it elicits intertextual conclusions based on the collective comparison of films with roughly equivalent contexts and constraints. The comparison also allows us to position women's films on a continuum of Hollywood-generated products in order to provide a preview of the long-term influence of women directors on commercial cinema.

Unlike television directors, directors of contemporary films occupy the central creative position behind their product. Television is considered a producer's medium (Newcomb & Alley, 1983; Cantor, 1971, 1980). Of course, producers and stars also play a crucial role in films, especially in their marketing and to a lesser degree their creation. Likewise, writers are involved creatively, especially in the concept or idea stage. But whether one favors the purist "auteur" theories of film or not, no one else pulls the entire production together as decisively in its final creative expression as does the director. In addition, film has been regarded historically as an art, in the domain of humanities and fine arts, rather than as a social force measurable through behavioral science as television has been; as a consequence, film reaches us more as the individual creative expression of its director.

In order to provide somewhat equivalent comparisons—not an easy task with film—the films selected for study were the ten most financially successful films directed by males and the ten most financially successful films directed by females. (One each of the top ten men's and women's films—*E.T.*, directed by Steven Spielberg, and *Moment by Moment,* directed by Jane Wagner—were excluded because they were then unavailable for video review. The final sample therefore comprised two groups, each consisting of nine of the top ten films, one group directed by women and one group by men.)[1]

Selecting films that received the greatest degree of popular acceptance allows for serious comparisons to be made. Harold Hinds (1988) argues convincingly that "popularity," narrowly defined and quantitatively justified, should be the *sine qua non* of popular culture studies. If this principle is adapted, Hinds reasons, "then ideas, products, or whatever of similar popularity can be compared." The 18 films all have the common denominator of having been viewed by a great number of people. Viewers did not turn out for the films because they were "women's films" or "men's films," but because they were films that seemed to appeal to a wide cross-section of people. Useful as comparisons of mainstream Hollywood films with self-consciously feminist films may be for other purposes (see, for example, Kaplan, 1983), they are unmatched samples—one mass, the other elite—for making generalizations about comparable group quality and trends. The 18 "popular" films also have in common the use of stars, a more or less conventional, or "classical," approach to narrative and style, and a similar Hollywood machinery behind them in terms of production and release. With these variables thus held somewhat constant, the actual differences between the men's and women's films can be ascribed more directly to the influence of the male or female director and not to uncontrolled differences in production environment, targeted audiences, or other contextual variables. Hence, it becomes easier to isolate the differences as well as to draw tentative conclusions about the nature and future of women's films both within the Hollywood "mainstream" and outside it. This, in turn, opens up a discussion of gender and esthetics. In popular culture, is there a discernible women's or feminist esthetic? What role does it play in popular art?

Films are more than individual artistic expressions. They are cultural and ideological constructs; they transmit and reflect prevailing cultural values. Bill Nichols (1981) defines ideology as "the image a society gives of itself in order to perpetuate itself." Within those ideological constructs are myths. Myths, in the interpretation of Roland Barthes (1972), are sign systems drained of their original denotative meanings and infused with substitute meanings. These new meanings then operate on a second level, the connotative level provided by culture, and serve to fit the ideologies of that culture. E. Ann Kaplan (1983) provides an example:

> The image of a woman undressing cannot remain at the denotative level of factual information, but immediately is raised to the level of connotations—her sexuality, her desirability, her nakedness; she is immediately objectified in such a discourse, placed in terms of how she can be *used* for gratification. That is how our culture *reads* such sentences and images, although these meanings are presented as *natural,* as denotative, because the layering of cultural connotation is masked, hidden [p. 18].

As ideological constructs, not only do films develop culturally prescribed meanings for images, but the mere *presence* of those images as symbolic representations can reveal what a culture values. George Gerbner (1978, p. 44) notes that "ideal" symbolic representations in the fictional world or the mass media announce to audience members that the "real" particular social characteristic in question is valued and approved. These images tend to function conservatively, in Gerbner's view, because cultural dynamics are, by nature, resistant to change and tend to maintain the status quo. Conversely, in the popular media, "condemnation, trivialization, or absence means symbolic annihilation" (Gerbner, 1978, p. 44). John Fiske and John Hartley (1978, p. 24) note a similar pattern in television: "We can now see that the over-portrayal of white-collar jobs on television is simply a metaphor of their place in our culture's hierarchy of esteem. Here the transposition is from one plane, that of social values, to another, that of frequency of representation." These phrases echo Lazarsfeld and Merton's emphasis on media functions of status conferral and enforcement of social norms.

In considering the attributes of particular films, we must keep in mind the implicit values being set forth as "reality" and the audience reading of those values. As Mary Gentile (1985) reminds us, "No film is an island, to which the viewer responds in a vacuum. We all bring our experience and our contexts with us" (p. 154). John Berger (1980) calls this our "ways of seeing." These ways of seeing are subjective but are also "intersubjective" when shared by many, creating what Jerry Farber (1982) calls an "experiential unity." Keeping this in mind helps us understand to what audiences films seem to be appealing, which particular constructs they are presenting, and what relationship they may have to the viewer. Film has a unique esthetic (Munsterberg, 1916/1970) that provides a gestalt perception of unity (Arnheim, 1933) triggered especially by the montage technique (Eisenstein, 1942) of juxtaposing two shots to create a third reality. Whether one favors formalist (Balazs, 1952) or realist (Kracauer, 1947) theory of film, the director as "auteur" (Sarris, 1966) uses signs and codes (Metz, 1974) to create a phenomenologically powerful experience (Bazin, 1967). In "reading" the film text, the film viewer enters into an experience of the film esthetic unique to the 20th century.

Character and Stereotype in Film Discourse

For many of the reasons above, the particular variables chosen for examination in the sample of 18 films were those that concerned what a *character* is, does, and stands for within the context of the film. This assumes that character may serve as a primary means of representation of values and, implicitly, the values and views of the director and the "meaning" of the film. The variables are grouped here into four categories.

1. *Character inclusion and groupings* measures the amount of screen time for each character and whether that screen time was shared with men or women or both.
2. *Character demographics and activity* identifies the character's marital status, occupation, and major activity.
3. *Character interactions* measures instances of active or passive behavior toward others and of physical aggression.
4. *Character and discourse* examines the character's overall positioning in the film's narrative discourse.

By comparing the variables and attributes of individual films as well as of the aggregate of male-directed or female-directed films, we can look for a film's direct and implied meaning as well as ways to "read" or "reread" men's and women's films.

The study also examines the role that stereotypes play in character portrayals. "Stereotype" is a slippery concept to grasp. What is a stereotype? Stereotypes in film, and sexual stereotypes in particular, serve definite purposes. Pam Cook (1979) suggests that, in the early days of cinema, stereotypes were used as genre conventions to aid audiences in understanding the narrative of films. However she adds, "As cinema developed, we can see from the fact that male stereotypes changed more rapidly than female stereotypes that the use of stereotypes has a specific ideological function: to represent man as inside history, and woman as eternal and unchanging, outside history" (p. 231). What seemed to evolve was an image of woman that became more and more confining and negative, as indicated by Levy's (1987) study of male and female Academy Awardwinning roles. This is compounded by the "realism" of film and television moving images; a filmic metaphor does not merely point to but becomes the referent. As explained by Mary Ann Doane (Doane, Mellencamp, & Williams, 1984): "In film even the most blatant stereotype is naturalized by a medium that presents a convincing illusion of flesh and blood woman" (p. 6). Because of this more vivid imaging, the perceived gap between what a character is and what she or he stands for is smaller in cinema than, say, in literature. In other words, the film image has a more seamless "reality." Film builds stereotypes effectively and then enables stereotypes to build on stereotypes.

In calling for a "critical subjectivity" in the analysis of film roles of women, Mary C. Gentile (1985, p. 64) suggests part of the problem of stereotyping lies in the way the average moviegoer "reads" a film: "Women are either expected to live within predetermined and conflicting roles, or they are excluded altogether and displaced. The difficulty with which we recognize these contradictions and gaps reveals the extent to which we live within a world ordered by language and the ideology language represents." In other words, dominant ideology presents the female stereotype and masks the mechanisms of its presentation. Gerbner (1978, p. 46) places this issue in the context of the dynamics of cultural management, stating that the stereotyping of certain groups of people "has the social function of coping with threats, for it justifies both dismissing and brutalizing these groups." Gaye Tuchman (Tuchman, Daniels, & Benet, 1978) defines the stereotype and its effect:

> Sex-role stereotypes are set portrayals of sex-appropriate appearance, interests, skills, behaviors, and self-perceptions. This makes them stand out as such within the context of a film. Additionally, they are more stringent than guidelines in suggesting persons *not* conforming to the specified way of appearing, feeling, and behaving are *inadequate* as males and females [p. 5].

Sex-role stereotypes confer status and establish norms, both positive and negative, and then maintain themselves by enforcing these norms.

A further aid to recognizing stereotypes may be to differentiate between *types* and *stereotypes*. Orrin Klapp (1963) states that social types are shared, recognized, easily grasped norms of how people are expected to behave while playing certain roles, but stereotypes are based on much more stringent and confining guidelines. Emanuel Levy (1987), in his review of Oscar-winning film roles, notes how male roles throughout the years have allowed a great deal of flexibility for their characters—they are involved in a variety of occupations, they perform serious functions, they are of all ages and appearances; in other words, they are a variety of *types*. Women's roles, in contrast, are much more homogeneous and restricting; they are, in effect, stereotypes. These stereotypes, moreover, may have long histories reinforcing them. Kathryn Weibel in *Mirror, Mirror* (1978) traces the 200-year American history of the female stereotype and summarizes it with four adjectives: housewifely, passive, wholesome, and pretty.

Counterstereotypical behavior is of significance as well. In this study, what appear to be nonstereotypical behaviors will be noted, as when women give orders and initiate action or when men are vulnerable or uninterested in dominating a scene or a character. However, the risk of nonstereotypical behavior to men is less, for they have more choices. Simone de Beauvoir (quoted in Haskell, 1979, p. 62) put well the implications of counterstereotyping by a woman: "She knows the constant danger of unsupported freedom; it puts her in constant danger: she can win or lose all in an instant. It is the anxious assumption of this risk that gives her story the colors of a heroic adventure. And the stakes are the highest there are: the very meaning of existence."

Top Box-Office Hits by Male and Female Directors

The films analyzed here are listed in Table 5.1, together with the name of the director, year of release, and income from theatrical rentals as of 1988.

These 18 films are a remarkable record of a time and culture. They are filled with fantasies and fears, vivid heroes and villains. Together

TABLE 5.1 Largest Revenue-Generating Films by Men and Women Directors[a]

Title	Director	Date	Rentals
Directed by men			
Star Wars	George Lucas	1977	$193,500,000
Return of the Jedi	Richard Marquand	1983	168,002,414
The Empire Strikes Back	Irvin Kershner	1980	141,600,000
Jaws	Steven Spielberg	1975	129,549,242
Ghostbusters	Ivan Reitman	1984	128,264,005
Raiders of the Lost Ark	Steven Spielberg	1981	115,598,000
Indiana Jones and the Temple of Doom	Steven Spielberg	1984	109,000,000
Beverly Hills Cop	Martin Brest	1984	108,000,000
Back to the Future	Robert Zemeckis	1985	104,237,346
Directed by women			
National Lampoon's European Vacation	Amy Heckerling	1985	30,300,000
Yentl	Barbra Streisand	1983	19,669,000
Fast Times at Ridgemont High	Amy Heckerling	1982	15,781,942
Children of a Lesser God	Randa Haines	1986	12,056,608
Jumpin' Jack Flash	Penny Marshall	1986	11,000,000
Desperately Seeking Susan	Susan Seidelman	1985	10,937,200
Johnny Dangerously	Amy Heckerling	1984	9,100,000
Valley Girl	Martha Coolidge	1983	6,613,355
Grease 2	Patricia Birch	1982	6,500,000

[a]Excluding *E.T.* and *Moment by Moment.*

they are a colorful record of mythology and ideology. Many of the stories and characters are known in thorough detail by hundreds of millions of people throughout the world.

Differences of scale between the two groups of films are obvious. The top films directed by men include all of the highest moneymakers of all time. Those directed by women were considerably farther down on the list. In fact, the most financially successful female-directed film appears 171st on the list of the approximately 1,000 films that brought in $4 million or more. The total revenues for all nine women's films combined—$118,601, 497—barely exceeded that for the single lowest revenue producer on the men's list (*Back to the Future,* with $104,237,346). Total revenues for men's films were over $1 billion; for women's, approximately $120 million.

Certain individuals played especially prominent roles in the list of films. Two men, George Lucas and Steven Spielberg, had a hand in seven of the nine men's films, serving as executive producer, producer, director, and/or writer. In fact, they worked together on two of the films, the Indiana Jones sagas. On the women's side, only one woman appears more than once in these categories, and that is Amy Heckerling, director of *National Lampoon's European Vacation, Fast Times at Ridgemont High,* and *Johnny Dangerously.* Additionally, only one woman, Barbra Streisand in *Yentl,* served a multiple role, as executive producer, producer, and writer. She also has the distinction, shared on this list only by Dan Ackroyd and Harold Ramis in *Ghostbusters,* of starring in a film she cowrote.

In positions other than directing, men generally dominate the films on both the male and female lists. Of 49 producers and executive producers attached to the films reviewed, only 3 are women, all of whom worked on women's films. Of the total of 35 writers, 6 are women, and all but 2 of those (Leigh Bracktt in *The Empire Strikes Back* and Gloria Katz in *Indiana Jones and the Temple of Doom*) were involved in women's films. Male producers and writers predominated in all films reviewed.

In terms of genre, five of the nine men's films contained elements of fantasy, five were also adventures in part, and some were both. In contrast, all but two of the women's films were comedies. The majority of all directors, and especially those in the men's films, used existing stars. The male directors generally had bigger budgets to work with, giving them expanded opportunities to utilize special effects and exotic locations. They could pay higher salaries and demand the most widespread marketing and distribution. Six of the nine men's film were released before 1982. Taking all these matters into consideration, the nine films directed by women, all of which were released after 1982 by relatively new directors, did quite well for themselves.

Analysis of the films employed standard procedures and definitions. The 18 films were viewed on videotape.[2] Each film was timed, as well as every scene of 30 seconds or more duration. The character composition of each of those scenes was noted. "Major characters" were those that appeared in ten minutes or more of a film, and they are included in our character analyses. In male-directed films, 44 men and 9 women were major characters. In female-directed films, 19 men and 18 women had major roles. Included as "men" were the androids and humanoids in the Star Wars trilogy that had male voices and/or were referred to as "he." Major child characters were also included.

Character Inclusion and Groupings

Do the films of Steven Spielberg, George Lucas, and Robert Zemeckis give more screen time to men than the films of Amy Heckerling, Penny Marshall, and Barbra Streisand? Which give the most screen time to women? How are scenes shared by male and female characters?

The first category, "character inclusion and groupings," documents the *amount of screen time,* measured in minutes, that any character appears in a scene. A "scene" denotes any unit of 30 seconds or more duration; a scene ends when either the composition of characters changes or the time and locale change. Characters are judged to be in a scene if they are known to be part of a scene, although they may not appear in every shot of the scene. Also documented in this category is *groupings by gender* among major characters: (1) scenes of women without men present (one woman alone, with only minor characters, or with another woman), (2) scenes of men without women (one man alone, with only minor characters, or with another man), and (3) mixed-gender scenes (one or more men and one or more women together). Scene appearance ratios are also established, based on the total number of scenes per film.

Do male directors give considerably less screen time to female characters? The answer is a resounding yes. In films directed by men, major female characters occupied 336 minutes of screen time, and major male characters totaled 1,868 minutes of screen time. Thus, *roughly 5½ times as much screen time was allotted to men as to women in these male-directed films.* In contrast, in films directed by women, major female characters were seen on the screen for 853 minutes, and major male characters for 766 minutes. Thus, *in female-directed films there was only a 12 percent difference between genders.* As background, length of scene appears to be relatively well standardized across all films. Men's films totaled 566 scenes, for an average of

63 scenes per film. Women's films totaled 496 scenes, with an average of 55 scenes per film.

Is gender mix in scenes different in men's and women's films? Table 5.2 graphically illustrates the difference. Female directors created almost the same number of scenes with men-only and with women-only characters. Male directors created more than 16 times as many men-only scenes as women-only scenes. In only 4 percent of the scenes in male films did women appear without men, either alone or with other minor characters; and in only 28 percent of the scenes were women included with men, thus being totally excluded from 67 percent of the scenes. In contrast, men are excluded from only 25 percent of the scenes of women's films; they appear alone or with minor characters in 24 percent of those scenes, and with women in 47 percent of the scenes. So mixed-gender scenes are more than half again as frequent in female-directed films as in those directed by men, and overall, female directors are between two and three times as generous in their inclusion of the opposite sex in all scenes.

These differences raise the question whether, and to what degree, male directors believe that a woman alone, or two or more women, can sustain film scenes or the majority of a film. Interestingly, actresses are "billed" in male-directed films generally far out of proportion to their actual time on screen. It is as if film-makers want to draw the female viewer, or the male viewer looking for titillation or love interest for the hero, but not to the point of actually giving over a significant portion of the film to women. Although this condition appeared to improve somewhat starting about 1977, the biggest box-office hits still appear to have little room for women.

Character Demographics and Activity

In *Children of a Lesser God, Desperately Seeking Susan,* or *Valley Girl* are characters more likely to be married, in school, or in a profession than in *Ghostbusters, Star Wars,* or *Beverly Hills Cop?*

The second category for analysis, "character demographics and activity," notes each major character's marital status, occupation, and major activity. The major activity may or may not be related to occupation or marital status. A character's emphasis on friendship and relations was also examined. To quote Jean C. McNeil (1975, p. 267), "It is, after all, the focus of a character's activities which, more than any other

TABLE 5.2 Gender Composition in Film Scenes

Gender Composition	Number of Scenes					Percentage
	0	100	200	300	400	
Women without men						
Directed by women	124 ▬▬▬▬▬					25
Directed by men	22 ▬					4
Men without women						
Directed by women	118 ▬▬▬▬					24
Directed by men	381 ▬▬▬▬▬▬▬▬▬▬▬▬▬					67
Mixed gender						
Directed by women	233 ▬▬▬▬▬▬▬▬					47
Directed by men	161 ▬▬▬▬▬					28

NOTE: Percentages are of total scenes directed by women (top line of each pair) and total scenes directed by men (bottom line of each pair). A few scenes include no major character, making the total percentage for each group slightly less than 100 percent.

single content element, serves to define for the viewer the character's essential function within the story."

Tables 5.3 and 5.4 show characters' marital and occupational status. The most obvious generalizations about these tables are that most characters are single and that in men's films they have occupations while in women's films they are students.

In the male-directed films, of the nine major women characters, eight are single and one is married. One of the "single" women, the character played by Lea Thompson in *Back to the Future,* actually has a dual role: she appears as a woman married in the present, but also, for the majority of her screen time, plays the same woman 20 years earlier, when she was single. Two of the nine women have no discernible occupation and serve either as a man's helpmate (the Roy Scheider character's wife, played by Lorraine Gary, in *Jaws*) or as the "prize" sought by a man (Lea Thompson's role, when single, in *Back to the Future*). Of the remaining seven, the occupations of four have little or no relevance to the story; we see them at their occupations for fewer than seven minutes in any film and not at all in the case of Sigourney Weaver's cellist in *Ghostbusters.* Instead, they serve either as "sidekicks" for the male characters, assisting them in their major activities, or, as in the Weaver character, an excuse to put the men's occupations into higher gear and

TABLE 5.3 Marital Status of Characters

	Remain Single	Remain Married	Status Changes
Films by women			
Female characters	12	2	4
Male characters	15	2	2
Films by men			
Female characters	7	1	1
Male characters	41	1	1

TABLE 5.4 Occupational Status of Characters

	Occupation Identified	No Occupation
Films by women		
Female characters	3	15[a]
Male characters	8	11[a]
Films by men		
Female characters	7	2
Male characters	41	2

[a]The majority of these are students.

do battle with ghosts. Only Princess Leia as the commander in the three *Star Wars* films has an occupation that is directly relevant to her on-screen activity in helping her fellow rebels and home planet.

In contrast, of the 41 single and 2 married male characters *in men's films, all but the two high school students have occupations, and their occupations are, with one exception* (the Rick Moranis "nerd" character in *Ghostbusters*), *central to their character and to the story.* In fact, it is their occupations that define them and around which most of their actions occur. Besides occupation, friendship and assistance play a role for male characters, primarily in the *Star Wars* trilogy, but these values are realized mainly in the course of their jobs, and any friendship that develops is a by-product. A few other male characters have concerns beyond their occupations, such as the Roy Scheider character in *Jaws,* who must both save the town from the shark and prove to himself once and for all that he can face fear. Likewise, the Crispin Glover father-of-the-family character in *Back to the Future* is driven by a desire to be competent as well as to get the girl he wants.

In female-directed films, marital status and relationships play more central roles than in men's films. Of the 18 women's characters, 14 are single, but 2 of these get married in the course of the film, and 4 are married but 1 becomes a widow and 1 divorces during the film. This flux in marital status may point to a higher preoccupation with it, although the marital status of both men and women in all the films surveyed is preponderantly single. This differs significantly from marital status found in roles on television, where various studies have demonstrated that between half and two thirds of all females are married (Gerbner, 1972; McNeil, 1975; Tedesco, 1974). Of the 14 single women in female-directed films, 10 are students with no jobs and 9 of them want either a boyfriend or a husband. But friendship and doing the right thing morally also figure significantly in their activities, notably in *Fast Times at Ridgemont High, Valley Girl,* and *Grease 2.* None of the married women has an occupation, and here too they serve mostly as helpers of men. Of the single nonstudents, of which there are five, only three have occupations. The two who are without occupations appear in the same film, the Rosanna Arquette and Madonna characters in *Desperately Seeking Susan.* Their major activities, however, do not revolve around men—other than the difficulties they encounter with them—but instead are infused with an iconoclastic desire for fun and adventure in life and, in the case of the Arquette character, a more meaningful life, with or without men. In only one role, that of Whoopi Goldberg's computer operator in *Jumpin' Jack Flash,* does occupation figure prominently in the story, and her character exhibits a certain dedication to it.

In female-directed films, the 19 male roles include 2 married characters and 17 single ones, 2 of whom get married. Eight of the 19 are students, 2 with part-time jobs, but they are also interested in friendship and in finding a girlfriend or, in the case of the Mandy Patinkin character in *Yentl,* a wife. Eight of the remaining 11 have occupations, at which we see all of them during at least part of the film, sometimes almost exclusively, as with the men in *Johnny Dangerously;* their work sometimes figures importantly in the story, as with the William Hurt character in *Children of a Lesser God.* Many of these too, however, also place a value on love, friendship, and doing the right thing, including Hurt, Stephen Collins's computer operator in *Jumpin' Jack Flash*, Aidan Quinn's film projectionist in *Desperately Seeking Susan, and, to a lesser extent, the mob characters in Johnny Dangerously*. Of the three men who do not have discernible occupations in women's films, two are in *Valley Girl* as amiable "hoods" whose primary interest is in finding a girl, and one, Chevy Chase in *National Lampoon's European Vacation,* is a family man on vacation.

There are a greater number of female roles in women's films, and they occupy a greater amount of screen time. But we still do not find a great variety of female occupations or an importance placed upon occupation in relation to the story. Both male and female directors appear most comfortable showing men in strong occupational roles. Further, there are actually more occupationally tied female roles in male-directed films, as well as proportionately more "mature" women characters, primarily because 10 of the 18 female roles in women's films are students. Part of this relates to subject matter: five of the nine women's films take place in a school setting. This may reflect a timidity in women directors' approaches to strong female-oriented roles and occupations, or it may reflect the kinds of stories with which women directors feel most comfortable and which they believe are important.

Other attributes run a closer second to occupation in women's films than men's, and we see *the characters exhibiting these other attributes for more of the film—attributes including love, friendship, morals, and personal identity.* These alternative goals are perhaps most poignantly revealed in the activities of the lead characters in the two women's films that are dramas: Barbra Streisand's role in *Yentl* and Marlee Matlin's in *Children of a Lesser God.* Streisand plays a character struggling with her right to an education in an all-male school setting, and it is this desire, along with that for acceptance and love from a fellow male student, which is the focus of her major activity. And Matlin, who plays a former student working at a maintenance job in a deaf-school setting, also grapples with a simultaneous desire for an identity that will take her beyond her deafness and will enable her to believe in, and trust, love. This greater emphasis on relationships, integrity, and identity, as they emerge from the context of characters' major activities, should give us a clue about part of that elusive "women's esthetic."

Character Interactions

Are the films featuring Luke Skywalker and Indiana Jones more violent than those with a Yentl, a valley girl, and a deaf mute? In which films are male or female characters more assertive and directive?

The third category for analysis is "character interactions." The way in which film characters go about interacting with other characters and solving problems within the course of the narrative lends additional insight into directors' perceptions concerning appropriate character behavior. Characters may engage in two primary activities: *instrumental behavior* (active or passive) and *physical aggression*. Active instrumental behavior is that which initiates action, gives directives or instructions, "wins" a scene with another character, leaves another character, or helps another character. Passive instrumental behavior is that which "loses" a scene with another character by submitting after a struggle, takes directions from another, or invokes help from another character. An example of being helped occurs when the Rosanna Arquette character is taken by the Aidan Quinn character to his apartment after she develops amnesia in *Desperately Seeking Susan*. An example of "losing" a scene with other characters occurs when the Harrison Ford character gets captured in *Raiders of the Lost Ark*.

The second element of the interactions subcategory, physical aggression, occurs when one character exerts physical force upon another character or threatens that character verbally or visually with physical force. This includes any action in which a character's "private space" is aggressively invaded by another character, the minimum of which may be "collaring" or a raised hand, the maximum of which may be physical injury and death. No differentiation is made in the degree to which the viewer sees the result of the physical force.

How frequently do male and female characters in male- and female-directed films engage in instrumental behavior? Table 5.5 presents the data.

In men's films both women and men average one instrumental act for every 4.3 minutes of screen time. In other words, men are no more active per minute on screen than women. *But* almost half of all female instrumental behavior in men's films is on the part of one continuing character, Princess Leia in the *Star Wars* trilogy. In total instances of both active and passive behavior, men in male-directed films outnumber women in female-directed films by almost 2 to 1, but this merely

TABLE 5.5 Ratio of Instrumental Acts to Minutes of Screen Time

	Ratio *Acts per Minute of Screen Time*
Active behavior	
Films by women	
Female characters	1:4
Male characters	1:7
Films by men	
Female characters	1:4
Male characters	1:4
Passive behavior	
Films by women	
Female characters	1:9
Male characters	1:16
Films by men	
Female characters	1:7
Male characters	1:10

reflects the numbers: male characters in men's films are twice as numerous as female characters in women's films.

In women's films, women characters average one instrumental act every four minutes of screen time, whereas men average one every seven minutes. Women here are given almost twice as much active behavior as their male counterparts, a disparity made significant by the fact that men and women are on the screen in women's films for almost exactly the same amount of time.

"Passive" behavior provides perhaps the most interesting results. Though just as active, proportionate to screen time, as men in men's films, the women characters in men's films are one and one-half times as passive as men per screen minute. And in women's films they are almost *twice* as passive as men. It appears that women directors feel confident in having their female characters act with a certain amount of authority, being twice as active as men in proportion to screen time, but that they also feel it is okay for female characters to be *acted upon* by characters or events, with the result that they are also twice as passive as men. However, in male-directed films, women are both more active and less passive, in relation to the male characters, than they are in women's films. Male directors may be hesitant about letting females *appear* in their films, but once there, especially in the case of Princess Leia as noted, they allow females to be active.

As might be expected, it is in the occurrence of *physical aggression* that we see the widest divergence by gender (Table 5.6).

Male-directed films are clearly more violent. There were 305 instances of physical aggression in male films, 91 percent of them attributable to men. In female films, 82 acts of physical aggression were noted, 83 percent by men. Moreover one woman-directed film alone, *Johnny Dangerously,* is responsible for 46 percent of all physical aggression in the women's films, whereas in the men's films it is fairly evenly spread out, with an average of 34 aggressive acts per film. In stark contrast, seven of the nine women's films each contained 6 or fewer aggressive acts. *In total, men's films contained 3.7 times as much physical aggression as women's films.* A comparative graph (Table 5.7) may help in visualizing the difference.

How frequently do directors resort to physical aggression, compared with other forms of instrumental behavior? When aggression is compared with instrumentality, interesting results occur. In the women's films, women averaged 18 instrumental acts for every physically aggressive act, and men averaged 2 instrumental acts per aggressive act. In men's films, in contrast, women averaged only 3 instrumental acts per aggressive act, and men 1.5 instrumental acts per aggressive act. *Male directors accept physical aggression over other instrumental behavior for all their characters much more readily than their female counterparts.* Women directors appear to view aggression as a less appropriate form of problem solving than more socially approved forms of instrumentality.

It is debatable whether or not the ability to perform violence is a positive attribute in a film character. Women have traditionally had an aversion to violence, from being both victims of it and untrained for it. That this sensibility is reflected in films by women comes as no surprise. But the question that must be asked is, if "violence is, after all, the continuation of language by other means" (Fiske & Hartley, 1978, p. 25), just whose language is it that is being spoken? The vast discrepancy between violent acts in men's and women's films tells us that although men may be conditioned to accept violence as an acceptable expression of film language, there are other methods to be explored,

TABLE 5.6 Instances of Physical Aggression

	Aggressive Acts by Women	Aggressive Acts by Men
Films by women		
National Lampoon's European Vacation	1	3
Yentl	0	1
Fast Times at Ridgemont High	0	3
Children of a Lesser God	0	0
Jumpin' Jack Flash	7	14
Desperately Seeking Susan	0	6
Johnny Dangerously	4	34
Valley Girl	1	2
Grease 2	1	5
Total	14	68
Films by men		
Star Wars	3	32
Return of the Jedi	5	36
The Empire Strikes Back	2	23
Jaws	1	20
Ghostbusters	2	12
Raiders of the Lost Ark	8	42
Indiana Jones and the Temple of Doom	5	53
Beverly Hills Cop	1	36
Back to the Future	1	23
Total	28	277

other voices to be heard, other valid points of view. Feminist practice as well as critique may help us all learn to speak and understand a better language in this regard.

TABLE 5.7 Physical Aggression in Male- and Female-Directed Films

	Acts of Physical Aggression						
	0	50	100	150	200	250	300
Films by women	XXXXXXXXX						
Films by men	XXXXXXXXXXXXXXXXXXXXXXXXXXXXXXXXXXXXXXX						

Character and Discourse

Are the characters played by Whoopi Goldberg, Madonna, and Marlee Matlin as central to the story line and outcome as those played by Dan Ackroyd, Harrison Ford, Eddie Murphy, and Michael J. Fox? How are male and female characters positioned in the discourse of these films?

The fourth category, "character and discourse," refers to the character's overall positioning in the film's narrative structure and the consequent meaning that the character signifies within the terms of the film. Included in this are stereotyping and nonstereotyping, the overall effect of the accumulation of image and activity, and through these the nature of the dominant discourse within the film. By focusing a film's ultimate meaning on discourse, we can shift our interpretation away from the mere presentation of image, and its "truth" or "falsity," and instead draw our attention to the prevailing *voice* within the film. As Christine Gledhill (1980, p. 13) stated it, the question to be asked of a particular conjuncture of plot device, character, dialogue, or visual style is not "Does this image of woman please me or not, do I identify with it or not, but rather: *what is being said about women here, who is speaking, for whom?*"

Character and discourse concern central issues of plot and relationship, issues where gender is often prominent. Examination of character and discourse turns up interesting patterns and personalities at the same time as it suggests tentative conclusions about the overall thrust of the characters and their meaning within the films. With the exception of the *Star Wars* trilogy, these are discussed here in descending order of financial success.

Character and Discourse in Male-Directed Films

The three *Star Wars* films are unique in that the actions of an ensemble of characters can be followed through the course of three films. Three of the major characters, those of Mark Hamill, Harrison Ford, and Carrie Fisher, change in varying degrees from sequel to sequel. Especially significant is that Fisher's Princess Leia is allotted increasing screen time in the sequels, almost doubling the length of her screen appearances from the first to the third installment.

However, it is Hamill's Luke Skywalker who perhaps changes the most. For him, the saga is a coming-of-age tale; he makes both moral and emotional progress. Ford's notably mercenary character, Han Solo, goes through a kind of redemption through ordeal, having received his "comeuppance" by being the victim of carbon-freezing, to be rescued by Luke in the third film. Han Solo also learns to care for Princess Leia and actually sheds tears in her behalf.

Princess Leia probably changes least of the characters, but her activities are forceful. It is her goal to save her planet and its people that sets the whole saga in motion. Though a "princess" and almost exclusively dressed in white, she wears her brown hair tight to her head, her collars are mostly high, she never screams and rarely expresses fear, and she can carry and use a laser gun. Further, she is often seen giving orders— as a commander—or talking back to those who would silence her, whether it is the condescending Han Solo or the evil Imperials. She appears as the steadiest of the characters, which helps counteract her dearth of screen time, and she is even allowed to feel affection for two men at the same time without either causing them to come to blows or being somehow punished for this emotional license. One could wish that male screen appearances by major characters in the *Star Wars* trilogy did not outnumber those by females (the only female being Princess Leia) by a ratio of 6 to 1. But, even if the *Star Wars* world is a mostly male and violent one, the characters, their troubles and personalities and, most of all, their spirit of cooperation provide a balance to the films and help expand the concept of the "human" in our shared human condition.

Jaws tells us in even more explicit detail that it is a man's world, that men are in control and are the only ones capable of solving *the* problem—an effectively rendered horror unleased on a seaside community. In *Jaws* women are less instrumental in their lives, are mostly sexual beings, are prone to hysteria, and, as unforgettably demonstrated in the first four minutes of the film, will be violently killed if they step out of line by going swimming at night in the nude. All but one of the major and minor characters and occupations are played by men. The one major female role—the Lorraine Gary character who is police chief Roy

Scheider's wife—is a homemaker who appears in the film for 16 minutes. Further, in five of her six scenes she is wearing either a provocative nightgown or a revealing swimsuit (even when she is in the hospital visiting her son, a near-victim of the shark). She also cries and becomes almost hysterical at one point. Most of the other women we see are wearing either swimsuits or low-cut dresses and, on at least seven different occasions, are screaming on the beach. Each of the major male characters screams once, but this is only near the end, when they are in immediate danger of being eaten by the shark. We do see a vulnerable side to Scheider, as he both fears the water and is unable to stand up to the mayor (weaknesses that he overcomes), and, inversely, we do see the death of the highly condescending and dominating character of Robert Shaw's macho sharker. *But little room is made for women, and what room is permitted takes the forms of a mold—a stereotype—that says women are to be looked at, are emotionally unstable, and do not have occupations.* There are other ideological interpretations of *Jaws,* as, for example, a parable on Watergate political corruption or on America's last year of "sharking" in Vietnam. But as Stephen Heath (1981, p. 203) argues, one might say the gender movement of the film is "to get rid of women."

Ghostbusters also presents a man's view of the world, but in somewhat altered ways. Bill Murray's leading character role is of a somewhat macho type, a beer-drinking womanizer and a "buddy" man, and he makes derogatory remarks about women on at least five occasions. He is highly instrumental in both solving the ghost problems and rescuing the Sigourney Weaver character from "herself." Weaver is the victim of several stereotypes. Although she has a job as a cellist, we never see her at it; instead we see her carrying groceries, cooking, and sewing. But, most significantly, she is transformed into a ghost vampire who tries to seduce men with her legs spread apart and her skirt high up to her thighs and is further transformed into a seething dog-ghost. She becomes purposeful only by becoming "evil" and must be rescued from this evil in order to become "herself" again.[3] In all, Weaver appears in 27 minutes of the film, compared with 185 minutes by the male characters. Although there are some very funny moments in this film, the message it gives the viewer about male-female roles is that men can get away with just about anything and get the girl besides; but women cannot be a part of these all-male activities—women are not in control of themselves, they must be helped by men, and they are permitted to be purposeful and/or seductive only if such activity can be blamed on an exterior, and in this case evil, source.

Harrison Ford in *Raiders of the Lost Ark* is a love-'em-and-leave-'em swashbuckling archeologist pitted against a smoking, drinking, gambling female bar owner (Karen Allen) who loses nearly all of these attributes 30 minutes into the film. What Allen does manage to maintain is a spunky resistance to male domination, and she is the most physically aggressive of all female characters in the films reviewed. But ultimately, she becomes only a high-spirited helpmate going along for the ride with Ford. This is a man's story, a man's adventure—fun as it is—and women play no intrinsic part in it.

In Eddie Murphy's police character, *Beverly Hills Cop* has a genuinely comical antiestablishment hero. Murphy has a female friend who appears occasionally and is somewhat competent in her assistance of him. In contrast to the two local policemen in the film, Lisa Eilbacher's character is quieter and more mature and refined, and she enjoys and likes Murphy. In a sense, she may be dispensable, but she is a positive and nonstereotypical presence in the film. It is rare that we see an interracial film friendship between a man and a woman that is exactly that, a friendship.

Character and Discourse in Female-Directed Films

Turning to women's films, *Yentl* may not have been the dramatic or financial success producer-writer-star Barbra Streisand had hoped for, but it does succeed in confronting some issues more directly than any of the other films reviewed. *It is one of the most significant feminine discourses in major studio films.* It took the full force of Streisand's star appeal and financial clout even to get the film produced. The narrative takes a sheltered but rebellious teenage girl through serious change and challenge. As a young Jewish female, Yentl succeeds in getting an education in an all-male Hebrew school in tradition-bound turn-of-the-century Eastern Europe by disguising herself as a young man. Education is her primary dream, and she opts for it over marriage. She is secondarily influenced by her desire to be a good friend to men as well as women. Although she starts to fall in love, she remains steadfast in her goal.

Yentl contains the most scenes of interaction between two women of any film reviewed. The fact that one woman was disguised as a man complicates the representational implications. It may be, from evidence of box-office hits, that Hollywood does not trust scenes without male characters, unless perhaps one of the two women is disguised as a man. Here in *Yentl* the women are not objects under the control of others, but are subjects in their own right. Streisand teaches the Talmud to Irving, a taboo for women then. She explains to Amy Irving that women are equal in the Bible and that it is all right for women to "refuse" their husbands, telling her, "I'm proud of you and I want you to be proud of yourself." In song she asks Irving, "Why have a mind if not to question?" and then inquires of Patinkin, "Don't you ever wonder what she's thinking?" The discourse here is primarily female, about female concerns and struggles, and we get the feeling at the end, when Streisand leaves Patinkin and Europe for America, that it is his loss. She is hurt, but she has learned and will continue to learn. All in all, it is rather profound subject matter for a popular film, and it is to Streisand's credit that she broached it whether it was a box-office smash or not.

In *Children of a Lesser God* director Randa Haines presents us with two dynamic characters who are exceptional both separately and together. *The film is notable in being the only one of those reviewed to contain absolutely no physical aggression, as well as tying with* Indiana Jones *for containing the highest number of "mixed gender" scenes of any film in this study.*

William Hurt portrays a well-rounded, fairly well-adjusted teacher around whose occupation the story revolves. He is highly instrumental in terms of what he ultimately accomplishes—both with his hearing impaired class and with Marlee Matlin's character, and he is also extremely empathetic with almost everyone he knows. He takes this a little too far with Matlin, wanting to take care of her, and has her move in with him: "Screw your job," he tells her, "I have mine." But he is risking his professional reputation by doing this, and in several scenes he comes across as almost painfully sensitive; and he is not afraid to cry when he thinks he has lost Matlin.

Matlin, in contrast, is from a different social class, works at a menial job, and is deaf, stubborn, unsympathetic, and combative. Her deafness almost puts her into an a priori position of passivity, but it also leads her to a certain empowerment, for it is this that she must rise above— and does, thanks to her strong-willed nature and her inherent desire to make something of herself. Although she is sexually aggressive, her active past leads her to distrust the intentions of men. So part of her struggle is coming to trust that Hurt loves her. But she must also make a claim for herself in the world, and this she does in a highly instrumental sequence where she reconciles with her mother, gets a better job in another city, and begins to save money toward college. Finally she can meet Hurt on equal terms. Much has happened to both of them, but more to her. In the last line of the film, she asks him: "Can we meet somewhere not in silence or sound?" He assents, and their separate journeys can now be rejoined.

It is apparent, in many of these female directed films, that there is no lack of powerful, inspiring role models. Unleashed by female direction, the women leads in *Yentl* and *Children of a Lesser God,* as in *Jumpin' Jack Flash* and *Desperately Seeking Susan,* discussed below, are thought-provoking, fully realized characters.

Penny Marshall's directing of Whoopi Goldberg in *Jumpin' Jack Flash* added to this growing pantheon an assertive, successful, single, urban woman. Here is a woman who is highly instrumental, who lives alone and likes it, who is not preoccupied with her looks or with men, who dresses unconventionally and in a way that avoids female stereotyping, who has a good job and likes it (and around which the entire story revolves), who has women friends who mean something to her, and who, on top of it all, is very funny and very expressive both verbally and visually. *She is in every scene of the film and has the most scenes of any film surveyed featuring one woman alone or with minor characters.* In fact, 12 of these 25 scenes she shares with supporting female characters. She also performs the highest number of acts of physical aggression by a woman in a woman's film (only Karen Allen in *Raiders* surpasses her in our 18-film sample). She uses foul language but is notably sympathetic with other women. She also takes digs at racism, sexism, and women's preoccupation with their appearance, and she off-handedly comments in ways that women can understand—for instance, stating during a particularly stressful time that "I feel like I got my period every day." She puts compassion for others before personal feelings as a matter of course, and in that we find the strength of her character, a "type" that is rare among women—or men—in popular films.

Desperately Seeking Susan is unique among the 18 films surveyed in featuring two female leads who are not "buddies" and share only one scene together in the entire film. Each of them separately is responsible for more instances of female instrumentality than female characters in any other film: together they total 68 instrumental acts. The film is also second only to *Jumpin' Jack Flash* in featuring the greatest number of scenes sustained solely by one woman. Director Susan Seidelman has clearly put two women in the spotlight who make things happen.

How do these ambiguous and active characters perform in the narrative underlying this female discourse? Rosanna Arquette's character, in subconsciously longing for a respite from a dreary suburban life and an unfaithful husband, finds her alter ego in personal ads addressed to someone named Susan. Being a romantic, she is initially drawn to the love affair going on in the ads, but soon she is thrust into life on the streets when she develops amnesia and mistakenly "becomes" Susan. What ultimately drives her to change her lifestyle is not, however, the meeting of any one man, but her *identification* with Madonna's free-spirited Susan and the new insights gained from her new experience. Her husband, by turns, believes that she has become a hooker, is on drugs, or needs professional help. Instead, she has got what may be her first job, has developed self-confidence, and has found a better man to boot.

Madonna's Susan offers an interesting array of contradictions. Her dress is often risqué, yet it is for her own pleasure. She goes her own way, takes money from men without asking, smokes like a man, has obviously been lifting weights, and is happy and carefree with or without a man. She has a boyfriend, but he seems incidental to her, and the "desperately" of the title, in the ads written by her boyfriend, refers to his condition, not hers. Arquette knows she will never be like Madonna, having had too proper an upbringing, yet the lesson she learns is that if you follow your instincts, it will be good for you.

What is at work in this film is an almost entirely female discourse. Some of the choices available to women in contemporary society are laid out in a whimsical, ultimately touching way. The narrative may be a little idealistic, but the story is about dreams and real fantasies women have. In this respect, the film succeeds exceptionally well.

Gender, Esthetics and Ideology

In collectively viewing the overall discourses within these films, it is no surprise to find that it is still a man's world. In men's films, women appear far less frequently overall than men, and they appear in a narrower range of occupations and activities and with far less impact on the narrative discourse of the films.

In all 18 films, the female characters who stand out are seen as "exceptions" and are put in a context of having to oppose men to make their individual claims, such as the characters played by Marlee Matlin in *Children of a Lesser God,* Barbra Streisand in *Yentl,* Karen Allen in *Raiders of the Lost Ark,* and Rosanna Arquette in *Desperately Seeking*

Susan. Less frequently, they merely stand out because they are lone "strong women," best exemplified by Carrie Fisher's Princess Leia in the *Star Wars* trilogy.

Never broached is the concept of strength in numbers for women, yet this is a common use of male characters in many male-directed films, such as *Ghostbusters* and *Jaws,* as well as the *Star Wars* trilogy. Gerbner (1978) places this in the context of maintenance of the status quo and calls it a "double-barreled cultural tactic":

> When women or other groups that have been denied full access to power are shown as independent, adventurous, or powerful, they are portrayed as *enforcing* rather than challenging the laws that oppress them. They become policewomen, detectives, or soldiers. In other words, they are accepted into the ranks of power provided they act on behalf of the rules designed to protect the interest of the majority groups. And even then they usually need to be rescued by male partners [pp. 49–50].

The prominent female characters in the films studied are permitted instrumentality—if not prominence—by virtue of being the "lone woman," as Princess Leia, or else they are reacting against men, thereby either trying to "be" one (Streisand in *Yentl,* Allen in *Raiders*) or trying to "be something else" (Arquette in *Desperately,* Matlin in *Children*).

The only character who seems to be an exception to this pattern is that played by Whoopi Goldberg in *Jumpin' Jack Flash.* This role reportedly was originally written for a man. That might help explain Goldberg's centeredness in her character and her centrality in the film. Although the film as completed was tailored to her gender, her gender is not relevant to the narrative; in other words, she *transcends* gender, but without losing sight of her roots. She is also notably the only female character in all the films surveyed who is not "beautiful" in the conventional, idealized sense. As Julia Lesage points out (1979, p. 45): "Makeup, the selection of women with certain size breasts, halo lighting, the whole visual iconography of women characters . . . can be analyzed in detail to write the story of sexism in film." Yet Goldberg's character is also that of a struggling worker firmly placed in a world beset with the usual problems. She even takes jibes at racism, as when she tells a police detective that the only reason he thinks she is a hooker is that she is a Black woman. In total, it is as if her character carries a secret: this is how to value yourself and make the most of your life as a woman and a Black woman, in a (White) man's world.

The role played by Madonna in *Desperately Seeking Susan* also transcends gender to some extent, but her narrative positioning within the film is a more problematic one. She is not really situated in the film and, in fact, is almost outside its context. Her role makes little comment on gender relationships; here she is also like the "lone woman," yet is without the benefit of any men to speak of—or anyone, for that matter—surrounding her. Her character also makes little comment on the *meaning* of her role in the world of film. It is as if she is a creature who is "above it all," living out some idealized reverie that has no relation to the real world. If Madonna's character were self-consciously aware of options and her chosen self-definition and were more central to the plot, perhaps changing along with the Arquette character rather than merely serving as a foil to her, the role would carry more import ideologically.

But all is not lost in *Desperately Seeking Susan,* for Madonna's alter ego, played by Rosanna Arquette, does struggle with her identity in a male-dominated world. So credit must be given to those films, notably *Jumpin' Jack Flash, Yentl,* and *Children of a Lesser God,* as well as *Desperately Seeking Susan,* all of which were also written or cowritten by women, where female characters are at least placed within a historical/cultural context and in their own ways try to come to grips with it.

This is not necessarily to say that women's films are freer from stereotypes than those directed by men. The three films by Amy Heckerling alone, especially *Johnny Dangerously* and *National Lampoon's European Vacation,* present women primarily as sexual beings and appendages to men. These are women whose main interest in life is to be sexy, to be a good "helpmate" to a man, and/or to "get a man"—in other words, women who more closely approximate the stereotypes routinely presented in men's films. Patricia Birch's *Grease 2* is also questionable on these same terms. But unlike almost all the films by men, women's films, even some of those named just above, do manage to present women with a kind of *multiplicity* of activity. One's occupation may not be the primary motivating force, either personally or dramatically, of the characters in films by women, but this may not be all bad. Value is placed on, and proportionately more screen time devoted to, friendship with other women, finding an identity that may encompass more than one's career, being open and vulnerable to life, exploring the meaning and implications of love, verbalizing gender-related issues, resolving conflict without resorting to violence, and being morally responsible. To a lesser extent, many of the male characters in women's films also place value on some of these issues, especially friendship and vulnerability. It could be said that many of the male characters in films directed by men are morally motivated, but their actions, like most of their other activity, are almost exclusively related to their occupation. So it remains unclear to what extent they would still act morally if the impetus of job duty were removed.

What may be starting to surface here is some sense of a women's esthetic in filmmaking—a point of view, an ideology, an approach—which more often than not is tied to gender but which is nevertheless finding its more encompassing *voice,* intentional or not. Peter Wollen (1973, p. 136) states that it is through the force of the director's preoccupations "that an unconscious, unintended meaning can be decoded in the film, usually to the surprise of the individual concerned." These resultant meanings may be more of a surprise to male than to female directors, since women directors are acutely aware of their position as outside the moviemaking mainstream, as "marginal" filmmakers. By the same token, women are also in a unique position, both as directors and as viewers, to focus on the contradictions between women on film and women in real life. This becomes the contradiction between being objects in film and being subjects in their own right in reality. Feminist film theorist Julia Kristeva states that women "must begin to see themselves as in a network of multiple possibilities, multiple perspectives, multiple identities, where there is no clear split between 'I' and 'not-I,' but rather a range or continuum of existence. Women must function as a 'subject-in-the-making'" (Gentile, 1985, p. 19). Women likewise have the opportunity both to "read" films for new meanings and to carve out a space for themselves as the makers of new meanings. This is admittedly an uphill battle in a male-dominated business, but women directors have a hidden resource with potentially far-reaching significance: half the moviegoing audience is female.

Women filmmakers also have another potential ally, the same tool that male directors have utilized as a matter of course, and that is the role film plays in society as a mode of subjective expression. Jerry Farber (1982) states that "insofar as social institutions are antagonistic to the subjective existence of individuals, art plays what is potentially a political role by validating and supporting subjectivity, and, also, perhaps, by suggesting the possibility of a more congenial objective world" (p. 186). What women filmmakers are finding is that they can be coparticipants in this search for a more congenial objective world, a world that moves beyond oppositions and fear of the other and beyond rigidly defined sex roles, so that, in the words of E. Ann Kaplan (1983, p. 206), we can explore and think about "ways of transcending a polarity that has only brought us all pain."

Questions

1. What is the history of the employment and portrayal of women in the super media industries such as television?

2. What are the differences in films directed by males and females in reference to:

   • the amount of screen time given to male and female characters?
   • the ratio of active and passive instrumental behavior to screen time?
   • the number of acts of physical aggression?

3. Which of the 18 films sampled had strong independent female characters whose activities were central to the narrative plot line?

4. Is there a "feminine esthetic" discernible in the narrative discourse of any of the films?

Notes

1. The source for the list of film box office successes is the January 20, 1988, issue of *Variety*. *Variety* annually updates its roster of All-Time Rental Champion Films, pictures that have paid $4 million or more in domestic U.S. film rentals to the distributor (of which there were just under 1,000 as of 1988). Film rentals are that portion of box-office ticket sale grosses remitted by exhibitors to the film's distributor. The figures are absolute dollar figures for each film, reflecting annual amounts received by the distributors, not adjusted to reflect inflation.

2. The coding process was undertaken with the use of a video cassette recorder, which could be stopped at will, and a stopwatch. "Scene composition by gender" was timed in this way. References to "marital status" were noted, and characters were presumed single if no reference was made to marital status. "Occupations" were designated by either seeing the character in action or noting references made to that character's occupation. "Major activity" was designated by noting all the major activities of a character and then summing up the preponderance of those activities. Instances of "instrumentality" and "physical aggression" were noted as they occurred. The overall "character discourse" within a film included an examination of the attributes above, as well as notations of apparent stereotypical and nonstereotypical behavior, the film's narrative, and outstanding character iconography, including physical appearance, visual symbols, and composition.

3. Gerard Lenne (1979) explains that "vampirism is the product of a deliberate crossbreeding between the fantastic and the erotic" (p. 34). He notes that the sexual desire of vampire women in horror films "is not the pretext for action, but the very condition on which the action depends for it existence" (p. 34). As both victim and aggressor, such a character "satisfies the sado-masochistic phantasmagoria that is part and parcel of all fantastic films" (p. 35). The Sigourney Weaver character in *Ghostbusters* evokes this tradition.

6

Critical Analysis 1:
The Cold War in Film and Television
or, Take *That,* You Dirty Commie!

Uncle Sam and the Russian Bear stand toe to toe, eyeball to eyeball, threatening and waving lethal weapons. They order about their client states as underlings. They marshal every resource in their deadly duel, sometimes smiling, sometimes poker-faced.

In Leningrad and New York City, two students watch this posturing. Each of the two thinks, one in English and one in Russian:

"How lucky I am to live in safety and freedom! How tragic it is that others must live under that evil empire, suppressed and exploited! Sports, movies, politics—everywhere I see evidence of their greed and our altruism.

"Perhaps I should volunteer to defend my country, to save others from their invasions, to keep them from starting the nuclear holocaust.

"Still, for all that . . . is this whole struggle necessary?"

One task of cultural studies is to search out in media the predominant underlying meanings that operate beneath the level of overt primary messages. Political and ideological meanings run throughout the offerings of popular entertainment as well as news and public affairs reporting. No problematic better illustrates this unique task of cultural studies—and the undeniable presence of an ideological level in super media discourse—than the part played by the Cold War in super media.

Since World War II, no single issue has so consistently distorted super media messages and effects as the so-called Cold War between the Soviet Union and the United States. The ideologies of anticommunism on one side and anticapitalism on the other have been both causes and effects of this Cold War. Antagonistic pictures are painted, these pictures lead to other pictures, and the cycle continues. In the longer view, the ideologies of private-enterprise capitalism and egalitarian communism have been constructed in opposition to each other for more than a century. But since the breakup of the temporary World War II anti-Nazi alliance between the Soviet Union and the United States, the poles of international conflict have become frozen, with the extremes represented, both symbolically and militarily, by the two superpowers.

How does the Cold War inform and distort the operations and effects of super media today around the world? Accuracy of information and clarity of judgment are essential to the optimum functioning of a cultural system, whatever the system's ideological orientation. Clearly, Cold War battle lines have distorted information and clouded judgment *and not only in political matters.* The entire range of cultural signs, symbols, and codes has become polarized as the Cold War has served as a cultural-political Continental Divide, on each side of which resources coalesce and multiply but can never pass over to the other side.

Before we examine cases, some clarification of the bedeviling term *ideology* is necessary. We take it here to mean *any collective set of beliefs,* regardless of their truth or falsity. Our use here is in the general rather than the special sense. The concept of ideology derives from the philosophy of mind (*The Compact Edition of the Oxford Dictionary,* 1971, p. 1368) and a concern with the origin and nature of ideas. But in a more confined sense, *ideology* is sometimes used to refer only to false beliefs arising from distorting social structures. In contrast, the more general sense of *ideology* refers to any set of group values and beliefs, regardless of its social causation or its truth or falsity. Precise definitions of *ideology* are extremely risky and controversial. In their widely debated work, *The Dominant Ideology Thesis,* Abercrombie, Hill, and Turner (1980, p. 87) examine the relationship between ideology and more material forces in economics and society. They note, "It is widely agreed that the notion of 'ideology' has given rise to more analytical and conceptual difficulties than almost any other term in the social sciences. The term has suffered many demolitions and reconstructions."

Dictionary definitions emphasize ideology as "the body of ideas reflecting the social conditions and aspirations of a group, class, or culture." In this general sense, an ideology is somewhat similar to a world view or political value system. It may be explicitly articulated, as in a political pamphlet, or only subconsciously felt, as in a fear of certain ideas or groups. To further clarify terms, a "cold war" is a strategy of international relations and psychological warfare fought through charges and countercharges in a combat of words, posturing, pressure, and any other means short of direct armed conflict. "Hot wars" are fought with military force, cold wars with economic, diplomatic, and psychological force. Ideology, like territory, drives both kinds of wars.

In what sense is there a "dominant ideology" infusing media and public alike? Behaviorists and pluralists, prominent in American media research, have spoken little of ideology since Daniel Bell's premature proclamation *The End of Ideology* (1961). However, across the Atlantic, Raymond Williams, Stuart Hall, the Glasgow University Media Group, Peter Golding and Graham Murdock (1979), John Fiske and John Hartley (1978), and others in the United Kingdom have brought the ideological debates of Louis Althusser, Jurgen Habermas, Antonio Gramsci, and other Continental thinkers over into debates on the place of media in preserving power and shaping thinking. The dominant-ideology thesis charges that media convey an underlying ideology that serves the interests of the dominant classes by incorporating subordinate classes and making them quiescent, concealing social relations, and overcoming social contradictions. Critics of the dominant-ideology thesis argue that television (Lodziak, 1986) and ideology (Abercrombie, Hill, & Turner, 1980) in themselves may support but not be the principal causes of such conformity. Instead, other material forces in the form of economic coercion through employment patterns, working conditions, living situations, and the absence of alternative outlets force subordinate groups to conform to conditions that serve dominant interests rather than their own. However, both these critics and proponents of the dominant-ideology thesis reject the pluralist "consumer-sovereignty" thesis, which argues that media give the people what they want without exception. This latter conflict, between the theses of dominant ideology and consumer sovereignty, is the more fundamental question examined here. In the context of American media research, the question has not been whether ideology is "absolutely" dominating, but whether *there are* forms of domination and ideological bias expressed in media.

Cold War–Mindedness and Hollywood Films

> Cold War mindedness . . . short-circuits rational, intellectual discourse [and] becomes paralyzing . . . facts, logic, reason have no impact.
> —Smythe and Wilson (1968, p. 59)

In our popular media, a mythology of distortion created by and about the superpowers reduces the complex equation of U.S. Soviet relations to American hero versus Russian Villain. Pop cult stereotypes and fantasies often replace realistic analysis. In turn, the press of many U.S.-aligned countries has tended to become obsessed with Cold War issues, contributing to a global myopia that distracts from real problems of nutrition, literacy, medical care, shelter, kinship, and self-determination. The tangible issues of physical well-being and survival are central players in the life drama of the majority of the world's population but for the most part play only background roles in super media today, primarily because of super media's preoccupation with entertainment, mass sales, and profit, and because of superpower Cold War preoccupations. Here we can see a pervasive ideology at work.

The Hollywood media industry, often accused of leftism (Rusher, 1988, Stein, 1979; Efron, 1971, and others), has in fact consistently supported conservative American Cold War positions in major films, just as Hollywood rallied behind the war against Hitler. This anti-communism in Hollywood film and television has occasionally taken virulent form when, in the words of Michael Parenti (1986), "the media fight the Red Menace." However, a more pervasive form is the subtle but consistent portrayal of all things communist or Soviet as sinister and dangerous.

In the 1980s many products of Hollywood seemed to represent a return to a 1950s Cold War polarization and reductionism in the popular culture.[1] The Geneva and Helsinki accords called for positive cultural relations among signatory nations, which included both the United States and the Soviet Union. However, as Olympic boycott reporting illustrates (see Chapter Seven), neither country takes special care to present the other in a fair light. Each side alleges that "they" make propaganda but "we" communicate with diversity and balance. In fact, both sides use standard propaganda techniques, the kind listed in many World War II–era propaganda manuals:

- Over-simplifying issues
- Stereotyping the enemy
- Aiming at the lowest common denominator
- Overgeneralizing through "glittering generalities"
- Creating "bandwagon" peer pressure
- Using psychosocial techniques

These habitual techniques explain well the distortions in American, Soviet, and other media allied to the superpowers. But propaganda and ideology are phenomenologically much broader than a mere grocery list of techniques. They operate also metaphorically, allegorically, and contextually. As Ellul (1966) warns, the image of the propagandist as an agitator for political change working vertically downward on the masses is a caricature that can blind us to more powerful propaganda. Propaganda can also work, in Ellul's terms, as integration into the sociological status quo through horizontal peer influence. This latter experience of propaganda is the more common one in the technological societies of super media.

Both American and Soviet press theorists claim that their own system is free and trustworthy but that the enemy's system is manipulated and distorted. Near the height of the 1950s Cold War, mainstream media researcher Wilbur Schramm (Siebert, Peterson, & Schramm, 1956) noted that Soviets consider American media the puppets of commercialism, while Americans believe the Soviet press to be rigidly restricted. The same stereotyped and self-serving imagery operates today. While American news stories loudly decry Soviet suppression of internal anti-Soviet or Jewish dissent, the Soviet press scornfully reports American crime rates and mass violence.

For some years now, spokespersons in the Soviet Union have expressed concern over anti-Soviet stereotyping in popular films from the United States. Labeling as "warnography" such films as *Rambo* and *Red Dawn,* a Soviet cultural panel that included poet Yevgeny Yevtushenko asked, "How can we resolve this flow of anti-Soviet films with the spirit of Geneva?" From the same position, Georgi Ivanov, Soviet deputy minister of culture, condemned the "so-called freedom of expression" behind *Rambo, Red Dawn,* and the ABC miniseries "The American," all of which portrayed brutal Soviet and Soviet-backed troops. He charged that through these films "a new generation of Americans is being brought up that will consider murder natural, even necessary."

To examine this charge and to assess the potential bias of Hollywood films, we can employ a fundamental semiotic technique, *inversion.* This technique simply reverses the binary oppositions and the implicit value judgments presented in a cultural product. If we invert the sides presented in a few Cold War Hollywood films typical of the 1980s, how do they look? Imagine, for a moment, how it would appear if the Soviet Union were to produce the following series of mass appeal films.

Cold War Films Turned on Their Heads

• *Yankee Nights,* featuring a dancer, Jimmy, who has defected to Russia from the United States. On a routine flight from the USSR to Cuba, his plane must suddenly make an emergency landing in enemy territory, Florida. There sinister CIA agents force him to make a series of videotapes on aerobics with his opposite number, Sammy, a Soviet Jewish defector. They become buddies. Sammy, the Soviet defector, begins to realize the error of his ways and to long for his native Russia. Both yearn to flee from repressive Miami. Finally, a daring escape and a spy-exchange deal release the two to creative and political freedom in Cuba. (*White Nights,* 1985, directed by Taylor Hackford and starring Mikhail Baryshnikov and Gregory Hines)

• *Ivan IV,* continuing the athletic saga of a heroic, self-sacrificing former Muscovite foundry worker. It opens with the irresistible pounding beat of its famous theme song. Ivan, now the Soviet Union's number-one professional wrestler, travels to Washington, D.C., to confront America's horrible bionic behemoth, Rocko Whitedawn. In the final climatic, tear-stained scene, Ivan stands above the quivering remains of his courageously felled opponent, the red flag draped across his shoulders. (*Rocky IV,* 1985, starring Sylvester Stallone)

• *Black Dawn,* opening the eyes of a complacent Soviet public to the danger of a Yankee military invasion. Carried out by American mercenaries from Central America, the Middle East, and Afghanistan under the command of Pentagon imperialists, the conquest is brutally effective. But the heroic resistance of a gang of rebellious Soviet teenagers cannot be suppressed. (*Red Dawn,* 1984, directed by John Milius and starring Patrick Swayze; also later released as *Steel Dawn*)

• *The Enlightening Bareness of Being,* unveiling the sufferings of a Caribbean ménage-à-trois during and after the 1983 invasion of their island by American ships, planes, tanks, and troops. Feeling fearful of the American soldiers, the sensual threesome sail off to Cuba. There they attempt to reconstruct their lives. Serena, one of the exiles, goes off to the Soviet Union, where she paints in a lovely cottage by the Black Sea; the other two, Tomás and Lolita, return glumly to American Grenada. They retreat to the tropical forest and live simply until a freak banana boat accident kills them. In the final scene, on the other side of the world, Serena tearfully reads a letter telling of their death as the sun gently sinks into the pastel-shaded Black Sea. (*The Unbearable Lightness of Being,* 1988, based on the Milan Kundera Novel.)

The style and sign systems of these films would be as important as their plot lines. For example, lighting, lens filters, and soundtrack would be used to "color-code" each side. Every time a street scene in the United States appears, such as in Miami or Washington, the lighting, lens, and camera angles would convey a flat, cold, harsh feeling. The soundtrack for United States scenes would always be somber and foreboding. One would consistently feel fear, tensions, and discomfort in American scenes. In sharp contrast, whenever anything Soviet or communist was portrayed, it would be in lush colors with pleasant, positive music and sounds. Similarly, there would be an unmistakable feeling of ease, and satisfaction, and hope present in all Soviet scenes.

We would have to imagine, alongside these hypothetical pro-Soviet films, numerous films of similar tendencies: the inverse versions of *Russkies, Little Nikita, Missing in Action, Invasion USA, Firefox, Gotcha, Tamarind Seed, Top Gun,* and so on. Moreover, these films would have been preceded by four decades of similar one-sidedness. And, added to the films stigmatizing the United States and extolling Soviet virtue, would be equally procommunist cultural products in television, newsweeklies, comic books, radio, wire services, sports pages, paperback spy novels—everywhere the average consumer turns to obtain information and form impressions. Many of the resulting images would be subtle, but some, especially in films, would be terrifying portrayals of lip-curling CIA agents, pillaging corporate executives, self-serving United States politicians, and their brainwashed lackeys.

Now let us step back and look at this exercise in inversion. The sense of ridicule it provokes indicates the nature of its mirror image, to which we are continually exposed.

The extent of anticommunism in Hollywood film and television is well documented. During the peak of McCarthyite anticommunism, Hollywood cranked out such Cold War classics as *I Was a Communist for the FBI* (1951); *Big Jim McLain* (1952), in which, according to the film's publicity, "Big John Wayne as 'Big Jim' smokes out the Reds in Hawaii"; *My Son John* (1952), with Helen Hayes turning in her offspring for subversion; *Pickup on South Street* (1953), portraying the Soviet stealing of secrets; and *Night People* (1954), about Russian kidnapping. All depicted communists as conspiratorial Soviet-backed gangsters; all were major releases; and all were produced by a Hollywood industry accused, ironically, of being liberal. Michael Ryan and Douglas Kellner's *Camera Politica* (1987), and John Lenihan's chapter on the Cold War in *Showdown: Confronting Modern America in the Western Film* (1985) both recount the consistent anticommunism of Hollywood films. Television presented similar simplistic anticommunist stereotypes, well documented by J. Fred Macdonald in *Television and the Red Menace: The Video Road to Vietnam* (1985).

But virulent anticommunism in film extends beyond direct portrayals and takes allegorical and metaphorical form as well. Peter Biskind has added this dimension in *Seeing Is Believing: How Hollywood Taught Us to Stop Worrying and Love the Fifties* (1983). Biskind casually notes that there were "two hundred or so anticommunist films produced by Hollywood between 1948 and 1953" (p. 162). But what were the ideological implications of nonpolitical films of popular fantasy, science fiction, and horror films of the period?

It has "never been much of a secret," Biskind observes, "that movies influence manners, attitudes, and behavior" (p. 2). We may not especially enjoy the movies or be aware of their influence, but we tend to accept the "frames of reference" they supply. This is cinema's ideological role, according to Biskind: "If we add up all that movies say and show about how we are supposed to be, we find that they present a 'world-view,' an 'ideology,' that conveys an attitude toward everything from the trivial to the profound, from what we eat for breakfast to whether we should go to war" (p. 2). What Biskind finds most interesting is not the phenomenon of the many, many films in the fifties whose ideology was overt, the anticommunist films like *Iron Curtain* and *My Son John*. More fascinating are the more popular films of the fifties, ones that seemed merely to present reality as it was, the natural, common-sense point of view: "And yet," Biskind observes, "when we come to these films from another time, another place, their ideology suddenly becomes dramatically clear" (p. 3). Biskind's form of cultural criticism describes "what we see when ideology becomes visible" (p. 6).

Them! (1954) portrays a national emergency handled well by civic officials, the military, and scientists from Washington. Such Yankee competence and force could repel foreign attack, one senses, but in this case the emergency is an invasion of red ants, who begin by killing an FBI agent and then kill entire cities. Biskind points out, "In 1954, when *Them!* was made, those humans that Americans regarded as antlike, which is to say, behaved like a mass, loved war, and made slaves, were, of course, Communists, both the Yellow Hordes that had just swamped GIs with their human waves in Korea, and the Soviets, with their notorious slave-labor camps" (p. 132). Comparing *The Thing* (1951) and *Them!*, Biskind finds Russians identified with the dangerous Freudian id: "Each implied that not only did the Soviets pose an external threat and, worse, an internal one through unreliable, wrong-thinking elements . . . but worst of all, they penetrated our very selves" (p. 136).

Invasion of the Body Snatchers (1956) has a similar anticommunist metaphorical power. The alien pods possessed people by stealing their minds, eating their brains, snatching their bodies, and leaving no visible evidence. This, in the words of Biskind, was "an overt metaphor for communist brainwashing, which had just turned GIs into Reds in Korea" (p. 140). The pod society, a familiar mechanistic utopia, is taken as a metaphor for communism.

Even Elia Kazan's magnificent film *On the Waterfront* (1954) had, underlying its excellent drama and powerful performances, a timely, topical, and autobiographically self-serving Cold War element. Kazan himself had turned informer, testifying twice in 1952 to the notoriously red-baiting House Un-American Activities Committee (HUAC). He was one of the few major directors to accede to the witch hunt by repudiating their past, abasing themselves before the committee, and, most important, naming former friends and colleagues as alleged communists. As a reward, his career thrived, while the accused were hounded out of the industry. *On the Waterfront* creates a story in which the only defensible action for a just man is to turn informer against a totally corrupt and exploitive organization. The organization in the film is a waterfront union, but its metaphorical extension is made explicit in the on-screen preface to the film: "The incidents portrayed in this picture . . . exemplify the way self-appointed tyrants can be fought and defeated by right-thinking men in a vital democracy" (Biskind, 1983, p. 172).

How do gluts of films inspired by the Cold War come about? American media are not subject to a system of public bureaucratic control that might be used to explain uniformity in Soviet filmmaking to an American public. Hollywood's bureaucracy is private: power resides among studio executives, agents, independent producers, and the financial community. These are the persons who finally determine which movies get made and which do not. They are not motivated by a self-conscious ideology, but that does not mean that their decisions do not reflect or create ideology. In fact, they do both.

Profit, caution, and precedent dominate Hollywood gatekeeping. Best-selling author and Oscar-winning screenwriter William Goldman

(1983) notes that nobody really knows beforehand what is going to be a hit. What studio executives do know is what *has been* a hit. As Goldman points out, "Movies are always a search for past magic." That may have a lot to do with the Cold War production of *Rambo*s and *Rocky*s: If it worked once, it is a safe gamble. If it worked twice, then why not again? Riding that wave, Sylvester Stallone became a new John Wayne, hero and icon of American ideology. The products of Hollywood are the safest, surest bets on what the public may want, taking into account trends and pressures from politics to puberty.

Popular entertainment almost inevitably draws on stereotypes and exploits popular prejudices. The anticommunist gospel reassures us that there is only one enemy and one problem in the world, and we can overcome it by sheer strength and guts. Knowing this, what commercial film executive can resist the security of Cold War formulas? The simplicity of such formulas results in what a detailed study of James Bond calls the "ideological preoccupations of the imperialist spy-thriller" (Bennett & Woollacott, 1986).

Political Economy and Ideology in American Film and Television

While American media research has been dominated by behaviorist "administrative" research, a countertrend of critical research has suggested insight into why Hollywood films and other American super media accept and exploit the Cold War. Administrative research helps private and public agencies answer "little problems, generally of a business character" (Lazarsfeld, 1941, p. 3). Critical research steps back and considers the general role of media in the present social system. It considers prevailing social trends by examining media control, concentration of ownership, standardization, promotional manipulation, social problems, and threats to basic human values.

Hollywood exists within a world of transnational corporations, many of them American-based, operating cultural industries that produce super media products for mass consumption. Powerful Japanese and European transnational corporations—Sony, Phillips, Thompson, Murdock, Mitsubishi, and others—play formative roles alongside AT&T, RCA, Warner, Turner, IBM, Kodak, AP, and the rest of the *Fortune* 500. These corporations provide international culture and information. They set the pattern of private commercial practices and influence public policy. In the search for competitive advantage and increased profit, they do not act as a monolith but tend to splinter society. Furthermore, their activities cross national boundaries as if they did not exist, with the results that individual nations are often unable to counter their power. The expanded "privatization" of control during the Reagan-Thatcher era strengthened their autonomy through increased deregulation and commoditization, trends that allowed them to depart further from the ideals of traditional liberal democracy, with its emphasis on public election and accountability.

Cultural priorities and ideology are directed by political-economic forces under the influence of transnational corporations. These forces are marked by a "shift away from involving people in society as political citizens of nation states towards involving them as consumption units in a corporate world" (Elliot, 1986, p. 106). Schiller (1984, p. 122) sees this as the reversal of democracy, since it gives power not to the voting individual but to the purchasing dollar and replaces rational politics with irrational consumption. Moreover, proliferating computer networks centralize "the producing, processing, storing, and distributing of information" and operate with an inequality of access and control that "hinders the establishment of democratic communication processes" (Hamelink, 1983b, p. 12). Inevitably, the super corporations of the *Fortune* 500 appropriate new communication technologies and dominate transborder data flows as part of the global integration of world business systems. Operating within this larger structure, controllers of super media technology ultimately defer to the influence of capital and the use of the state as it serves corporate ends (Schiller, 1981). They also become part of the general shift in responsibility from *individual* decision making to *institutional* structures, which dictate an emphasis on corporate profit and stock dividends. For example, stock-exchange rules prohibit boards of directors from sacrificing profit for social welfare, thus limiting altruistic corporate policy and activity. The infamous "military-industrial complex," warned of by President Eisenhower, plays a distorting role in this system and increases the power of the dominant over the subordinate groups, classes, and countries (Smythe, 1981).

The present Western system of political economy results in a number of controversial outcomes. Capital accumulation and market considerations influence the way new technologies are introduced, overriding the role of equity or education or public service. Corporate power and control are dominated by networks of cross-directorates wherein one individual sits on many decision-making corporate boards. The result is that extensive information control is centered in a small network of interlocking directorates, the priority of which is to make money and assume the public good is served by that (see Guback, 1969, 1974, 1979; Wasko, 1982). Illustrating the effects of this system on Hollywood filmmaking, Steven Bach's story of the demise of United Artists, *Final Cut* (1985), tells of Michael Cimino's megalomaniacal follies but also of the obstructiveness of a corporate bureaucracy threatened by job insecurity. Bach accepts responsibility for his role in losing $40 million on a motion picture and destroying one of Hollywood's most distinguished studios, but he also charges that decision making in movies has become the job of "pencil pushers," the accountants, and is dispersed in such a way as to ensure that no single good judgment can hold sway. Why do Hollywood films have problems? Bach's insider account as the vice-president in charge of production points to the political economy of filmmaking for an answer. Similarly, Eric Barnouw (1978) suggests that American television has been negatively served by commercial sponsorship. These historical narratives by Bach and Barnouw also tend to confirm Phelan's argument (1980) that corporations have become depersonalized and seemingly beyond moral considerations.

We should remember, however, that there are no subterranean conspiracies directing this concentrated power, and the effect of the political economy of super media is not uniform. The earlier Frankfurt School formulations tended to picture media as a single cultural industry automatically immobilizing the masses and misleading them into passive and dehumanizing submission and diversion. Adorno, Horkheimer, Lowenthal, Benjamin, Fromm, and Marcuse, among others, were the first to sense the central role of mass culture. In their view the popular forms of culture—music, radio, newspapers, cinema—were being used to pacify individuals experiencing the decline of family and community. This, in turn, created anomie and inauthenticity within the exploitive institutions and practices of consumer culture. More recent critical theorists—Jameson, Ewen, Aronowitz, Kellner, and Wander—have looked not at the mechanical uniformity, but at a more subtle and complex set of cultural industries and outcomes. At the center of this, Gramsci's notion of hegemony through consent rather than coercion, and the shift from thinking of "cultural industry" to "cultural industries," have brought an increased sophistication to critical analysis.

The entire structure of transnational communications, therefore, favors the system of capitalism in which it operates so successfully and self-servingly. It opposes communism because that system would eliminate precisely the institutional arrangements, incentives, and profits that direct the transnationals. It is in the best interests of transnational media giants not only to oppose communism as such, but also to ensure that the masses of the public oppose it also. Favorable portrayals of communism would violate the self-preserving instincts of the corporations. Top-level management and decision makers accept this and, by and large, agree with it. That ideological frame of reference is shared down the line through the corporate structures. There is simply no reason to portray communism as anything but negative and capitalism as anything but positive—the political economy of private-enterprise transnational super media dictates this. The policy does not have to be formulated and talked about, and individuals do not have to assume responsibility for it. The Cold War ideology and policy simply underlie and override anything else. Even theories of "freedom of the press" do not extend to incorporating points of view as deviant as communism, an ideology subscribed to by half the world but impermissible in commercial super media.

More than any other factor, it is the political economy of Hollywood and similar super media that creates and supports the aggressive anti-communism of Cold War ideology. This political economy accounts for the persistence of Cold War ideology, even through periods of political moderation. It accounts for it in the Cold War movies described above and in the Cold War television described below.

Distortions of super media due to the Cold War occur on both sides of what Cold War ideology likes to call the "Iron Curtain." Even before March 5, 1946, when Winston Churchill created that rhetorical label for the division between East and West, communist and capitalist, American politicians and media were reversing the Soviet stereotype back to the prewar negatives that were temporarily suspended during World War II (LaFeber, 1971). Since that time, American transnational super media have generally portrayed the world as divided between the "Free World" and the "Soviet bloc." How deeply this dualism has pervaded American media and culture is seldom acknowledged. Occasionally the Cold War mind-set emerges in stark and vivid form in super media, as in the infamous cases of Senator Joseph McCarthy and his communist witch-hunting, the blacklisting of writers and filmmakers called the Hollywood Ten, the accusations of anti-Americanism leveled against critics of American involvement in Vietnam, and the Iran-*contra* hearings, in which Marine Lieutenant Colonel Oliver L. North was the star witness.

Colonel North and the Contragate Hearings

The curious media phenomenon of "Ollie mania" illustrates the workings of Cold War ideology in mass-mediated culture. In midsummer of 1987 the Select Committee on Secret Military Assistance to Iran and the Nicaraguan Opposition conducted hearings. When such a formal congressional hearing receives the publicity that those hearings did, it becomes a super media event. The Iran-*contra* hearings were dubbed "Contragate" (and "Iranamok"), recalling the Watergate hearings that led to the resignation of President Nixon. Such hearings carry important ritual meanings as well as political substance (Alexander, 1986) because they present the deliberations of the American government before the people. They provide a forum and spectacle of great prominence. What gets presented and not presented entails a cooperation between government and media on a unique level in America. What did get presented?

The star witness was the chief officer operating the conduit between the White House, Iran, and Nicaragua. Earlier investigations and press reports had established that the White House, contrary to stated policy, had sold arms to Iran in the hope of freeing hostages and had used the arms profits secretly to provide military aid to antigovernment *contra* rebels operating along the border of Nicaragua. Government military aid to the *contras* had been prohibited by Congress and made illegal by the Boland Amendment.

When he took the witness stand, the star, Colonel Oliver North, was given the opportunity to defend his actions and, as it turned out, a pulpit from which to articulate the ideological center of American Cold War anticommunism. When the television networks preempted daytime programming to carry his testimony live, and when the press profusely reported his statements, they validated by that very coverage the legitimacy of his beliefs. North's six days of testimony to the Select Committee of the United States Congress received the widest possible press coverage and instantly catapulted North to folk hero and superstar.

North chose to sit at the witness table in his green Marine uniform, facing the congressmen and the cameras, with his six rows of medals and two large medallions highly visible. The uniform and medals were carefully selected to serve as a sign, since they represented more than just clothing and decoration. In fact they were *indexical* signs, in that a military uniform and medals bear a necessary relationship to military service, the nation, and patriotism. They signify much as a national flag signifies. The symbols created a redundancy with the content and style of North's testimony, both of which portrayed him as a devoted soldier and patriot. His fervent patriotism and choirboy sincerity, expressed with articulate, emotional pride and injured innocence, instantly touched off a firestorm of popular reaction in the country and the press. His good-Marine style of obedient commitment and self-sacrifice came out in his careful answers to questions, elaborated with extensive explanations of his motives and political opinions.

Signs and symbols reduce complexity to a few representations (Fiske, 1982). This is both their strength and their weakness. The reading of North's signs and text by the public was ambiguous but overwhelmingly positive from the start. To those who believed that the Soviet Union was indeed the "evil empire" of which President Reagan had warned (March 8, 1983), North's verbal and visual signs were true and reassuring. To those skeptical of the Cold War view of the Reagan administration, North's world view and tales of intrigue were disturbing. Surveys found that the public, by a spread of 10 to 1, found North more a "hero" than a "criminal." But North's popularity was not based on superficial visual signs alone.

The first condition of North's instant popularity was the conformity of his message to what Hall calls the "dominant code," or dominant ideology of the society. President Reagan's seven years in office had shifted public opinion away from the antiwar mood of the post-Vietnam era. Official mainstream America stood for strong military rhetoric against deserving enemies. The line of heroic accountability ran from John Wayne and Clint Eastwood directly to Oliver North. Any subordinate or oppositional codes were clearly secondary to the "preferred reading" of the international Cold War scene, in which all evil stemmed from communism. The dominant ideology is not necessarily the only ideology, and as is obvious, many variations of ideology coexist in the United States. Yet, the dominant ideology clearly "sets limits and exerts pressure," as Williams and Hall phrase it. For a large segment of traditional America, North was articulating the dominant ideology.

A second condition of North's popularity was the manner in which he presented the "whole" Oliver North, uniting the often separated spheres of public and private life. This recalls Raymond Williams's insistence that culture is best studied not in isolated spheres of art or literature or politics or folklore, but by seeking a characteristic structure of feeling spanning the patterns and general organization of the culture. North managed to sketch in details of his personal life and military history in a much more complete portrait than is usual in public political forums. Never veering from a recitation of his central commitments to serve his country and combat communism, North nevertheless managed to work in details of his multiple roles as family man, religious believer, public servant, fervent patriot, secret agent, international negotiator, military officer, faithful husband, and more. The length and personal elaboration of his testimony portrayed in close-up detail an idealistic, heroic servant who favorably "personalized" the militant Cold War code that he was promoting.

The close relationship of ideology, politics, and religion emerged in North's testimony. One of his fellow church members observed how North's religious convictions blended with his political convictions: "He had a born-again experience in 1978, and he's integrated his religious life with his political life. It adds an element of righteousness to his cause. Religion is very important to him" ("North's Story," 1987.) This religious-political union came at a time when the religious right was powerful on television and espoused the same ideology as North.

The third condition of his super media success was that North defended his actions with the most traditional and powerful stereotypes of the Cold War. Semiotically, the signs and codes chosen to explain his actions and himself were self-consciously identified with generations of powerful anticommunist imagery and mythology. In his prepared statement, North spoke of "Moscow's surrogates in Havana and Managua" (*Taking the Stand*, 1987, p. 266). He warned, "This nation cannot abide the communization of Central America. We cannot have Soviet bases on the mainland of this hemisphere" (p. 270). What is the difference between Nicaragua and Vietnam? North responded, "You're talking about the efforts of the Soviet Union, not on the other side of the Pacific Ocean, but right here in this hemisphere" (p. 271). He vividly portrayed the communist plot to infiltrate and dominate the world and resurrected the much-criticized "domino theory" of states falling to communism (p. 269). In brief, to North everything international is explainable through the fundamental binary opposition of communism and the Free World.

In the context of a national consciousness shaped by decades of anticommunism, this rhetoric is "anamnesic"; that is, it functions to bring to mind what the audience already knows. The anamnesic function also tends to switch off our ability to read in terms of any other interpretations (Fiske & Hartley, 1978, p. 178). All the events and conflicts discussed in North's testimony, therefore, become inextricable from the Cold War context in which he places them. Moreover, the Cold War context is not the "human rights" emphasis of the Carter years but the "international terrorism" emphasis of the Reagan administration and the CIA director William Casey. This shift in emphasis had been accompanied by a systematic removal of the association of terrorism with issues of "national liberation and social justice" and the substitution of a linkage with "the Soviet war against the West" (Paull, 1987, p. 30). The resulting doublespeak, of which Orwell warned, enables North to present his clandestine arms deals and attacks on Nicaragua as opposition to terrorism when, under a different set of definitions and associations, North himself would be classified a terrorist.

A fourth condition of North's success was that he articulated his experiences and convictions with all the style and principles of effective *propaganda* techniques. The sharpest expression of this was in North's narration of the administration's fund-raising slide show on Nicaragua, the Sandinistas, and the *contras.* The congressional committee, aware of the powerful propaganda potential of the slide show, refused to let the slides be shown. Instead it permitted North to describe each slide and present the narrative of the show. The style and sequence of the slides recall many classics of modern propaganda: the World War II Frank Capra "Why We Fight" series, the less successful Johnson administration *Why Vietnam?* film, and such anticommunist milestones of the 1950s as *Communist Blueprint for Conquest, Red Nightmare,* which is the fantasy of a communist takeover of the United States narrated by Jack Webb, and NBC's history of the Soviet Union tellingly labeled "Nightmare in Red." (For details on this last, see Rollins, 1983.) What these films have in common is a portrayal of the "enemy" as the culmination of all totalitarian evil in the world, bent on domination of a Free World defended by America.

North opens the slide narration with standard propagandistic techniques of labeling and association. Soviet communism is labeled as *the* global military threat to freedom; the Soviets are then immediately associated with Cuba and Nicaragua. The communist "enemy" is then vividly depicted through massive weaponry, threats by communist officials, and the grouping of the Nicaraguan Sandinista government with terrorists of every stripe, including Muammar Qaddafi of Libya. North proceeds to describe traditional "bleeding maps" and domino scenarios that identify the seemingly diabolical infiltration and strategies of the enemy. Finally, set sharply against these horrors, he describes photographs that bring out the bravery and altruism of the Nicaraguan *contras,* which North calls the "freedom fighters" and the "democratic resistance," a private army created by the CIA under Casey and North (Woodward, 1987). In the slide narrative their cause is the noblest, and their need for support the greatest. North in the end proclaims, "The conclusion of the briefing is, gentlemen, that we've got to offer them something more than the chance to die for their country and the freedoms we believe in. Thank you, sir" (*Taking the Stand,* p. 680). It was this slide show and narrative presented by the Reagan administration to select private groups that had raised millions of dollars from wealthy Texans and others to arm the *contras.* It is a forceful expression of centrist Cold War anticommunism.

Omissions From the Text

An important exercise in critically interpreting any text is to apply the semiotic *principle of omission,* which asks what is *not* said by being omitted from or suppressed in the text. When media presented North, it meant not presenting, for example, a representative of the Sandinista government or any other alternative to North's position. Within North's presentation and in the Cold War ideology of the National Security Council (NSC), the White House branch that employed him, the problems of Nicaragua and Central America, as of the Third World in general, are reduced to problems of communist aggression, a force so illegitimate that every form of opposition is justified, including lying, stealing, and killing. Not only does this remove all constraints on modes of influencing others, it also omits and suppresses the possibility that problems being addressed may have arisen from causes entirely unrelated to the Cold War. Poverty, exploitation, unemployment, bad working conditions, and resulting unrest, are, in Cold War ideology, attributable only to exogenous causes outside a noncommunist country, never to internal domestic inequalities. This means that although the freedoms and living standards of neighboring Guatemalans and Salvadorans may be demonstrably as bad as any Nicaraguan's, this is not a real or serious problem because these sufferers are on the correct side in the Cold War. Their condition will become bad enough to warrant intervention only if communists try to exploit it. Documented Sandinista advances in education, literacy, and health care are simply erased by Cold War ideology. For example, when a congressman asked the CIA director William Casey, during his heavily documented testimony to Congress on Nicaragua, what information the CIA had on how much the Sandinistas were spending on schools, roads, and hospitals, Casey snapped back, "I don't know" (Woodward, 1987, p. 242).

Not only Reagan administration ideologues but also the American press tended to carry on these omissions, consistent with Cold War propaganda. A content analysis of editorials and columns in the *Washington Post* and the *New York Times* in the three months preceding a major congressional vote on *contra* aid found 85 pieces on the Sandinistas; *all* were negative. There was no mention, for example, that in both services to the poor and not slaughtering its own citizens, the Nicaraguan government had a better record than Guatemala and El Salvador (Chomsky, 1987). What is excluded by Cold War ideology may be even more important than what is included. The literary technique of metonymy selects part of a thing and makes it stand for the whole, as when the plight of Hester Prynne wearing her scarlet letter in Hawthorne's novel symbolizes the fate of all who suffered from New England puritanism. Cold War ideology does this by taking a part of Nicaragua or Central America and insisting that it is the whole.

The dominant ideology and code, as present in the Cold War rhetoric of Oliver North, reveal themselves to be little more than a hegemonic set of cultural values in which demonstrably narrow moral and ideological opinions overwhelm contrary values, opinions, and even facts.

North's employer and staunchest supporter, President Reagan, supported Cold War ideology to such an extent that it distorted his understanding. For example, most of his quotations from Lenin where inaccurate and misleading; but among Cold War true believers that mattered not at all. Reagan charged (January 20, 1983) that the statement "Promises are like pie crusts, made to be broken" was from "the ten commandments of Nikolai Lenin." Lenin made the pie crust reference as a criticism of the tactics of his opponents, not as his own credo, and in fact, there are no "ten commandments" of Lenin or of communism. President Reagan also said (May 3, 1987), "There was a line attributed to Nikolai Lenin, 'The road to America leads through Mexico.'" No such statement exists in Lenin's collected works. On another occasion (September 9, 1985) Reagan said, "Lenin made an eloquent statement. He said, 'We must take Eastern Europe. . . . We will organize the hordes of Asia. . . . We will move into Latin America. . . . We will not have to take the last bastion of capitalism, the United States. It will fall into our outstretched hands like an overripe fruit.'" Neither the Library of Congress nor the White House Press Office could substantiate this alleged statement. The fabrication did appear, however, in *The Blue Book of the John Birch Society,* written in 1958 by the militant anticommunist founder of the society, Robert Welch (Green & McColl, 1987).

President Reagan's attitude on communism had, of course, been clear for decades and was stated in his first presidential press conference, when he charged that the Soviets "reserve unto themselves the right to commit any crime, to lie, to cheat." That Reagan believed the press should consciously support the American side in the Cold War was very clear (March 8, 1983):

> So in your discussions of the nuclear freeze proposals, I urge you to beware the temptation of pride—the temptation blithely to declare yourselves above it all and label both sides equally at fault, to ignore the facts of history and the aggressive impulses of an evil empire, to simply call the arms race a giant misunderstanding and thereby remove yourself from the struggle between right and wrong, good and evil [Green & MacColl, 1987, p. 43].

Clearly Reagan was at home with North's Cold War ideology. The formulators of policy in the Reagan CIA and NSC seemed to agree that the world was engaged in a struggle between right and wrong, good and evil, and that America's enemy was "the evil empire," however much Reagan may have qualified his opinion at his final Moscow summit.

North's congressional testimony conveyed the heart of Reagan's mainstream Cold War ideology and anticommunist policies to the American people in a highly visible and sympathetic way. The boy next door was suddenly presenting the Cold War to 55 million viewers a day. Movie critic David Denby found echoes of the "rich ambiguity" of Gary Cooper and Paul Newman, the attentive listening of Joan Crawford, the joking politeness of Clint Eastwood, and the teary idealism of Jimmy Steward in North's presentational style. But, most of all, Denby found actor Ronald Reagan's own style: "The superbly timed catch in the voice, the mixture of truculence and maudlin self-pity, the anecdotal view of world politics; the habit of referring to himself, with rueful affection, in the third person, as if he, too, were a fan of Ollie North's, . . . it is Ronnie all over" (Denby, 1987, p. 43). Alexander

Cockburn (1987, p. ix) saw another similarity between Reagan and North, who by his own admission was a professional in the deceit required by covert operations: "North has Reagan's own capacity for the vibrant lie, uttered with such conviction that it is evident how formidable psychic mechanisms of self-validation, in the very instant of the lie's utterance, convince the liar—Reagan, North—that what he is saying is true." The result for North and Reagan, according to Cockburn, was "absolute moral assurance that his lawlessness was lawful . . . that all impediments in his path, legal or moral, were obstructions created by a hostile conspiracy." In the words of James David Barber (quoted in *U.S. News & World Report,* July 27,1987), North "arouses the *feeling* of candor" on camera, reducing questions of fact to sentiment, and this "represents a fundamental deterioration of political discourse" (p. 18). *U.S. News & World Report* (July 27, 1987) headlined its coverage of North "Television's Blinding Power."

Polysemy in Ideological Texts

The polysemy of North's text, however, must be taken into account. The text had several layers of meaning and offered different interpretations to different people. Initially, the reaction appeared overwhelming. Polls showed that approval for *contra* aid jumped from 30 percent in June to 48 percent after North's testimony in July. Fully 64 percent saw North as a "victim" of Congress. Still, only 19 percent saw North as a "hero," and many wondered, in the long run, "Will he play in Peoria?"

What interpretations were given to North's text? To the conservative right, North's text confirmed and strengthened their Cold War beliefs. To the critical left, the text was irritating, biased, and ultimately rejected. To the uncommitted middle, the text seemed to find early strong and positive agreement but less over time. Temporarily North had shifted opinion in his direction, but as months passed, his import diminished. What remained symbolically, however, was that a strong Cold War text had been presented by him through the many channels of super media. Alternative texts were also proposed in the hearings, such as that of Chairman Inouye, who rejected North's absoluteness on Central America and refused to condone the CIA/NSC bypassing of Congress and violation of the intent of the Boland Amendment to prevent direct aid to the *contras*. But none of the alternative texts were truly *oppositional* texts to the Cold War content of what North presented. The impressions of communism and Soviet strategy proposed by North were not countered but, rather, sidestepped. For later use and exploitation, those stereotypes and conditioned reflexes were largely left intact.

Only when Reagan personally led the super media tour to Moscow for the 1988 summit were "subordinate" readings of the Cold War facilitated by his administration. It is one of political history's ironies that among Reagan's final acts as President was his leading of 5,365 super media reporters and technicians from sixty-two countries, including 1,060 Americans, to enjoy the sunshine and hospitality of the sometime evil empire itself. And even then, Soviet society was presented favorably primarily in the ways in which it was imitating the United States in allowing dissent and restructuring through *glasnost* and *perestroika,* not in the ways in which it remained uniquely different. Russians may be getting better, but *communism* is not, seemed the message. In fact, in the same historic week that the summit was beamed to the world, *Rambo III* opened to huge crowds with its cartoonish stereotypes of cruel and inhuman Soviet officers in Afghanistan.

The public may interpret the Cold War texts of super media in many conflicting ways, but the dominant Cold War ideology continues to "set limits and exert pressure," in the classic phrase of Hall and Williams. Subordinate codes compete with its dominance, but directly oppositional codes exist only in obscure corners of Western super media, primarily in less accessible publications of the print media. Whether one decries it or celebrates it, the presence of the Cold War as an influence in super media illustrates the undeniable reality and importance of ideology in the shaping of modern culture.

The three ideological forms mentioned by Giddens (1979) all appear in the Iran-*contra* hearings. Colonel North's case for the *contras* is, in Giddens's phrase, "the representation of sectional interests as universal ones." North American interests are substituted for any representation of Nicaraguan interests as if the two are the same. There is also in North's testimony what Giddens calls "the denial or transmutation of contradictions." The omissions described above in North's testimony avoid contradictory information. There is, finally, what Giddens calls "the naturalisation of the present: reification" in North's insistence that his ideological analysis is all of reality. What Congress or the United Nations or the World Court may say about Nicaragua is of no importance because Cold War battle lines are the most real present reality. These ideological forms are seldom as clear as in the Iran-*contra* hearings.

Hollywood films illustrate the metaphorically expressed biases of the Cold War, while congressional hearings illustrate the direct articulation of Cold War ideology. These are ideological emanations from the material base of capitalist political economy. Through the middle third of the 20th century, media research slighted the fact that media are not autonomous institutions, because of "restricted and inadequate conceptualizations of media effects" (Curran, Smith, & Wingate, 1987, p. 2). At present there are contending research positions and models, but there is a consensus in empirical, structuralist, ritual, and critical analysis that media are not autonomous. Super media have been relocated in the context of competing social forces. The interplay of these forces shapes media organizations, technologies, and content, and they structure the values that audiences bring to media and take away from media. The distorting role of Cold War ideology in American film and television varies from subtle to obvious but for many decades has never been completely absent. We will examine it again from both sides of the Cold War, in a discussion of superpower Olympic maneuvering in the following chapter.

Questions

1. How did Hollywood films of the 1980s portray communism and the Soviet Union?

2. How do these portrayals compare with earlier anticommunist portrayals in films of the 1950s?

3. How does the semiotic technique of inversion help to reveal the biases and distortions of Hollywood films?

4. What is the political economy of Hollywood and other super media as structured in transnational corporations?

5. How does Cold War ideology in super media serve the interests of private transnational corporations?

6. What role does anticommunism play in American congressional hearings and foreign-policy debates?

7. How did Colonel North's presentation utilize dominant codes, culture, and ideology?

8. What do the semiotic principles of omission and metonymy indicate about Colonel North's analysis of problems of Central America?

9. How does dominant ideology set limits and exert pressure?

Note

1. The analysis of anticommunism in Hollywood films of the 1980s was developed in collaboration with Jonathan Jerald.

7

Critical Analysis 2:
Media Bias and Olympic Boycotts

What worries me is the athletes of the world are being used for political purposes. We're in the trough of the Cold War.

—Lord Killanin, past president of the
International Olympic Committee[1]

The Olympic Games provide an international stage for Soviet-American power struggles. In the two superpower countries, press coverage of the Olympic boycotts of 1980 and 1984 was a microcosm of conflicting Cold War ideologies and rhetorical posturing. The two boycotts present a striking symmetry: each superpower hosted one of the two successive Summer Olympiads, each boycotted the opponent's Olympics, each lobbied Cold War allies to join in the boycott, and each boycott received worldwide press coverage through newspapers, magazines, radio, and television. How, why, and to what extent do Cold War terms, concepts, and frames of reference appear in Soviet and American Olympic boycott reports and comments?

The relationship between this continuing Cold War and the news media was examined in some detail by Dallas Smythe and H. H. Wilson (1968). They found "Cold War–mindedness" permeating the practices, structures, and implicit ideologies of media within each of the superpowers, the United States and the Soviet Union. Increased bias and antagonisms are the result. "In the super-powers and in nations under their control . . . , the information effectively available to the public from the mass media has been managed in the interest of the respective super-power" (p. 61). Smythe and Wilson conclude their sobering analysis with a warning that Cold War–mindedness in media "serves to short circuit rational, intellectual discussion of issues, policies, philosophical differences. In practice it becomes paralyzing" (p. 62). Do the respective national presses of the United States and the Soviet Union rise above partisan narrowness and provide two-sided balance and comprehensiveness, or are the presses also caught up in the myopia of Cold War–mindedness? Does Cold War ideology serve as a distorting lens working in both directions between the superpowers?

Answers to these questions can be found in a comparison of U.S. newspaper editorials, articles, and letters to the editor, as represented by the *Los Angeles Times,* set up against Soviet press articles, editorials, and letters to the editor, as reprinted in the *Current Digest of the Soviet Press* (Goldstein, Mechikoff, & Real, in UNESCO, 1986).[2]

Previous studies find inconsistencies in press judgments on Olympic boycotts. In 1976 both *Time* and the *New York Times* opposed the boycott by Black African nations and argued idealistically that sports should rise above politics. However, in 1980 both publications staunchly supported the U.S. boycott and argued pragmatically that politics have always been mixed in with the Olympics. Chorbajian and Mosco (1981) trace this change of policy to the sense of ideological leadership within Western capitalism which both *Time* and the *New York Times* assume and which led the two publications to speak from the perspective of the interests of the power centers that they represent. Corcoran (in UNESCO, 1986) finds similarities to this in his examination of the coverage of the 1984 Soviet boycott by the three largest U.S. newsmagazines—*Time, Newsweek,* and *U.S. News & World Report.* Barton (1982) examined the American television perspective on the 1980 Olympic boycott, and Frey (1984) examined the British response. Whannel (1984) found Cold War interpretations of the Moscow games in "The Television Spectacular" provided by British television. International political allegiances and ideology conflict with press objectivity in coverage of Olympic boycotts.

Events other than the Olympics also shed light on the role of Cold War ideology in super media. For example, Cirlin (1983) analyzed U.S. and Soviet responses to the downing of the Korean Airline Flight 007 in August 1983, in which 269 persons were killed. He concluded, "The rhetoric of both superpowers was highly biased . . . was politically oriented . . . [and] created rhetorical links to use the KAL downing to further other political aims." He suggested that a more "respectful rhetorical policy toward the Soviet Union would be . . . a step in the right direction" (p. 32).

Alternative Systems of Media Control and Ownership

Differences between American and Soviet coverage arise not only directly from Cold War coverage but also from differing conceptions of the role of the press and differing structures for controlling the press. Soviet theory and structure place the media as servant of the people and of the party and state, which represent the people. American theory and structure place the media as independent of the state and as servant of the people through the private-enterprise press institutions.

The usual American characterization of differences between the presses of different nations is "libertarian versus authoritarian" or "social responsibility versus communist." Such polarized oversimplifications seriously distort the variety of systems in the world today. From Venezuela has come a useful scheme for characterizing media ownership structures worldwide. J. Asdrupal Contreras Arellano (1987) avoids the bias in the American schema by identifying six basic forms of television ownership.

1. A government monopoly. The state is the sole owner and direct operator of the country's media systems. The USSR and the People's Republic of China are examples, but many noncommunist countries also run their television system by government monopoly. These include Denmark, South Africa, Colombia, Egypt, India, Kenya, and Turkey.

2. A monopoly by a partnership of government and private or nongovernment groups, as in Belgium, Finland, France, and Holland.

3. A monopoly by a private corporation, obtained by concession from the state, for a determined period of time and with payment of a fee. Luxembourg, Monaco, Taiwan, and Morocco are examples.

4. A federalist or state monopoly, in which all the states of a nation form a cooperative broadcasting organization. West Germany is an excellent example, as well as Nigeria and Saudi Arabia.

5. A pluralized system, in which government and private television co-exist and match in importance. This is the case in Great Britain, Canada, Australia, Japan, and Peru.

6. A private-enterprise system, of which the United States is the most prominent example. Government, public, and private ownership all exist but do not match evenly. The profit motive is dominant, as in Argentina, Brazil, Chile, Indonesia, Mexico, the Philippines, Thailand, and Venezuela.

In this range of options, the Soviet and American systems occupy opposite ends. As UNESCO debates have illustrated, the view of the

American system in many parts of the world is not enthusiastic. For example, questions of control and responsiveness to aspirations of people and needs of social reform have been a special focus of Latin American media research for many years (Atwood & McAnany, 1986). The view from the South has been more critical than that from the United States (Bordenave, 1988, p. 146).

How do differently structured media systems report Olympic boycotts?

The U.S. Boycott of the 1980 Moscow Olympic Games

Olympic boycotts are nothing new to the modern Olympic Games, although they are prohibited by the Olympic charter and therefore are officially labeled "nonparticipation" or a similar euphemism. Each Olympiad is boycotted by someone. For example, in 1956 Spain, Switzerland, and the Netherlands boycotted the Melbourne Games in protest of the Soviet invasion of Hungary. In the same year, Egypt, Iraq, and Lebanon boycotted to protest the Israeli takeover of the Suez Canal. The 1976 boycott by Black African nations was especially significant, but never until 1980 had one of the superpowers attempted to organize a multicountry boycott and remove large numbers of likely medal winners from competition.

The 1980 boycott was a Carter administration response to the Soviet intervention in Afghanistan in December 1979. At the time, President Carter faced a sagging economy at home, a reelection campaign with Edward Kennedy challenging from the left and Ronald Reagan from the right, and Iran escalating as the news event of the year. The Carter strategy was to use the Olympics as an instrument of foreign policy to oppose Soviet aggression in a peaceful but highly visible manner. An effective Olympic boycott and grain and technology sanctions against the Soviets were Carter's diplomatic measures to "contain Soviet aggression."

The Carter White House hoped in ensuing months to marshal American opinion and international decision makers in support of a widespread Moscow boycott. However, to create an official U.S. boycott, the administration had to win the support of the United States Olympic Committee (USOC), an autonomous decision-making body. Initial reaction to a boycott plan by USOC officials and potential competitors was one of resistance. A final decision was due by May 24, 1980. The

White House effort to persuade the USOC and the American public, as well as foreign governments and sports officials, in the words of Laurence Barton (1982, p. 9), provided "a fascinating instance of mobilization and manipulation."

U.S. Coverage of the 1980 Moscow Boycott

The *Los Angeles Times* joined the boycott effort in the very beginning with an editorial on January 18, 1980.

> The United States cannot erase the consequences of what the Soviets have done in Afghanistan. But it can exact a stiff price for that behavior, at the same time that it serves notice that any future aggressiveness will be met with effective responses. We think a U.S. boycott of the Moscow Olympics would be effective. We believe that action should be taken now.

Several key points should be noted. First, the *Times* immediately backed the administration's call for a boycott. In fact, at this time, President Carter had discussed a boycott, but he did not officially call for one until January 19. Second, the *Times* endorsement makes repeated references, five in all, to the "aggressiveness" of the Soviet Union. The editorial warns, "The United States must protest aggression, it must act on principle, 'self-respect' is the issue at stake." In the 12 editorials that were to follow in the first quarter of 1980, the *Times* never deviated in its pro-boycott position. If the United States were to go to Moscow, the *Times* argued, it would be an endorsement of unacceptable Kremlin politics.

Even before its editorial endorsement, the *Los Angeles Times* had prepared the way for boycott support. On January 12, a front-page article in the *Times* quoted a U.S. government analyst who stated, "A boycott would be a tremendous blow to Soviet prestige—crushing and humiliating—and you would find great howls of pain and indignation from them." The same *Times* article quoted President Carter: "The Soviet Union must realize that its continued aggressive actions will endanger both the participation of athletes and the travel to Moscow by spectators who would normally wish to attend the Olympic Games." Then, in its January 18 boycott endorsement, the *Times* bought this reasoning, stating, "Even if the United States must go it alone, the effect would be considerable."

Despite its editorial allegiance to the Carter administration position, the *Times*'s overall news coverage of the boycott was in most respects balanced. This is most noticeable in the *Times'* letters to the editor section and the independent columns presented on the op-ed page. In late January 1980, the *Times* acknowledged that it had received 39 letters in favor of a boycott and 18 letters opposed. The letters to the editor published in subsequent months were split 50/50 for and against the boycott. A similar distribution is found in related columns on the boycott issue.

It was apparent to the *Times* in March, as Soviet troops remained in Afghanistan, that to many American allies an Olympic boycott decision was a controversial and painful choice. West European governments vacillated on the boycott idea. On March 27, the *Times* noted,

> This indecisiveness, along with the widespread reluctance of Olympic athletes to support a boycott, has the White House worried. In the end, the United States might conceivably find itself alone in the boycott, faced with the painful choice of applying government pressures to prevent American athletes, most of whom were anti-boycott, from journeying to Moscow.

The United States used muscle as well as media to ensure that it would not be the only country to boycott Moscow. A British Olympic Association secretary recalls boycott lobbying during the February Winter Olympics: "All the National Olympic Committees who were thought to be potentially sympathetic to a boycott were at some time or other approached by the CIA to ascertain their attitudes to, and support for, a boycott during the Lake Placid Games" (Riordan, 1982, p. 151). Foreign public opinion posed a problem. Only 12 percent of the public in Japan, 13 percent in Canada, and 28 percent in Britain supported the boycott idea (Frey, 1984).

On April 9 the *Times* ran a strong editorial criticizing the USOC's delaying tactics.

> The President of the United States and his appointed representatives have for some weeks now been engaged in an embarrassing campaign of pleading, cajolery and threats aimed at getting the USOC to support an American boycott of this summer's Olympic Games in Moscow. The embarrassment of this effort arises from its very necessity. The pressures being put on the USOC could and should have been avoidable, if only that body had acted promptly to do what respect for national honor and an enlightened regard for its own self-interest required it to do.

With public opinion stirred up and pressure from the White House, in mid-April the USOC capitulated and officially voted to boycott the Moscow Games.

The *Times'* support for the boycott was not confined to the Afghanistan issue but grew eventually to include a general opposition to the Moscow Games as such. In June a *Times* editorial expressed relief that the West German decision to boycott Moscow ensured the boycott effort "will not suffer from a humiliating collapse." Curiously, the *Times* now seemed eager to see the Moscow Games undercut, whether the boycott raised the issue of Afghanistan or not.

> With so many potential medalists from the United States and now West Germany out of the Olympics, the quality of competition at the games promises to be inevitably diminished, to the point perhaps where the Olympics will hardly be of world-class stature. It is that fact, rather than moral disgust at Soviet aggression, that may be the decisive consideration in enlarging the scope of the boycott.

As the Moscow Olympics neared, general Cold War rhetoric became more explicit in *Times* editorials. For example, an April editorial drew some tenuous conclusions from a report that the Soviets planned to remove from Moscow "300,000 Russian political dissidents, common drunks and other undersirables" and that "average Russians are being warned to beware the smiles and guile of visiting foreigners" who may be "subversives and spies." The *Times* editorial even quoted Sempon Isvigun, first deputy chief of the KGB: "Ideological subversion is . . . to smuggle a bourgeois world view." Ignoring the fact that U.S. rhetoric often warns against the contaminating effect of foreign ideology, the *Times* concluded its editorial in classic Cold War style:

> What is remarkable about Isvigun's warning is its implicit admission that Soviet ideology may at best have no more than a tenuous standing among the Russian people. The vulnerability of the system, the weakness of its doctrine in the arena of free discussion, is being acknowledged.
>
> After more than 60 years of Communist rule and indoctrination, Russians still can't be trusted to reject a "bourgeois world view." That being the case, they must be kept insulated from purveyors of that view. Whatever happens in sports arenas, the Soviet system can't take the competition outside.

A *Times* editorial on July 15 awarded a gold medal to the Soviet Union for "flagrant obstructionism" when the Soviets refused to transmit from Soviet facilities a West German documentary, *Olympics and Propaganda,* which was critical of the Soviet Union. The editorial said the Soviets were "harrumphing about the beastliness" of the United States and "had two-facedly been on both sides of the same issues." Acknowledging that the West Germans were free to fly the film back to Germany for showing, the *Times* editorial concluded: "That's the only bright spot in this dismal but not unexpected reversion to type by Soviet authorities. Other opportunities to interfere with free reporting from Moscow no doubt will arise, and no doubt will be seized upon."

In general, the 1980 *Times* boycott position reflects American Cold War interpretations. On one side is the Russian Bear, invading a defenseless nation, spreading communism, and utilizing the Olympics as a showcase of totalitarian politics. On the other side is the altruistic and high-flying American Eagle, ready to confront the Bear, acting on ethical principles, willing if necessary to stand alone in the world as the defender of good against evil. Moscow boycott coverage by the *Los Angeles Times* and other mainstream United States media both reflected and reinforced this ideological position.

Other U.S. Newspaper and Television Coverage of the Moscow Boycott

In its coverage and editorializing, the *Los Angeles Times* was consistent with other American media, including the newsmagazines. On January 28, *Time* magazine reported that "there is probably no single action short of war that would punish Moscow more than to have the Olympics taken away or spoiled." *Time* argued editorially on February 11 that not to boycott "would be an act of diplomatic negligence." The *Time* editorial further stated: "To say that the Olympic Games have nothing to do with politics is the equivalent of saying that disco dancing has nothing to do with sex."

Overwhelming support of the boycott was also evident in the *New York Times* and the *Wall Street Journal.* According to Chorbajian and Mosco (1981, p. 5), *New York Times* boycott coverage included "over two dozen editorials and columns, close to 40 letters to the editor and over 300 news stories." Of 29 editorials and columns, only 3 opposed a boycott. An op-ed *New York Times* editorial on January 8 noted that "taking the politics out of the Moscow Olympics is about as feasible as taking the alcohol out of vodka." In a typical remark, columnist

Anthony Lewis observed: "The boycott could not be the only answer to Afghanistan, but it could be a clear political and moral symbol. And symbols matter." The *Wall Street Journal* also backed the boycott with such pessimistic columns as "No Tears for the Demise of the Olympic Games" on June 22 by Frederick C. Klein, author of the *Journal*'s regular "On Sports" column. He argued that since "the Olympics have turned into an orgy of nationalism marred by cheating . . . it is a spectacle we well can do without."

Interestingly, U.S. press endorsements of the 1980 Olympic boycott were a total reversal of positions taken by the same publications opposing the 1976 African boycott in protest of South African apartheid. In their study of *Time* and the *New York Times,* Chorbajian and Mosco (1981) found that "while both publications took strong positions against governments employing the Olympics to pursue political goals in 1976, both publications in 1980 sought to provide justification and legitimization for the U.S. boycott of the Moscow Games" (p. 12).

A detailed examination of American network television coverage of the boycott movement reveals homogeneity in coverage. According to Barton (1983), each network emphasized a slightly different perspective: CBS was skeptical of a boycott, NBC focused on the athletes, and ABC stressed international reactions. But, he concludes, "all three networks gave the Olympic boycott roughly the same amount of attention in early 1980, and all three had fairly similar approaches to the the topic." The networks presented striking interviews with frustrated American athletes, images counter to the boycott, but, according to Barton, "Such reporting was usually juxtaposed with newsfilm of developments in Afghanistan." In fact, Barton concludes that "television news acted as a collective conscience, showing Soviet tanks rolling over the fields of Afghanistan in the process of subjugating a poor remote land."

The effect of administration and media persuasion on American public opinion was dramatic. According to an NBC Associated Press poll, in mid-January 49 percent of the public favored the boycott and 41 percent opposed it. By early February, 73 percent supported the boycott and only 19 percent favored U.S. participation. In short, almost one quarter of the American people reversed their position from opposition to support within a few weeks. That shift, and the subsequent continued high support for the boycott throughout the spring, is not surprising, given the media messages available to the American public as described above.

The tangible result of the American boycott campaign was the absence of some three to five dozen nations from the Moscow Games of 1980. Frey (984) makes the number 58, while Barton (1983) reports it as 36. The withdrawal of three nations alone, the United States, Japan, and West Germany, was credited with having a significant impact on the final medal tally.

Soviet Coverage of the 1980 U.S. Boycott

Moving now to the other side of the Cold War continental divide, from the beginning the Soviet Union proclaimed the 1980 Summer Games a "showcase for socialism" (Hazan, 1982). These were the first Olympic Games ever held in a socialist country. In Soviet ideology and social planning, sports play a significant role. The West tends to separate sports from politics, but Marxism places greater stress on the interplay of politics and economics and other spheres. Sports are given the responsibility for stimulating physical health, inspiring social cohesion, and symbolizing the progress of socialist development. Since its entrance into Olympic competition in 1952, the Soviet Union has taken the Olympics very seriously. Finally in 1980 came the opportunity to take center stage before the attentive masses as the mass-mediated host of the number-one spectacle in the world.

The Soviet press comments on the boycott simply reversed the hero and villain roles in Afghanistan. In May 1980, A. Petrov wrote a typical analysis in *Pravda* on the occasion of the announcement of the West German boycott.

> In-as-much as the American statements and now the statement of the Federal Republic of Germany (FRG) government use the Afghan theme as a pretext for justifying anti-Olympic actions, it must be said that it is the U.S. imperialist circles and their accomplices who bear primary responsibility for the development of events around Afghanistan. They are continuing to interfere in the internal affairs of the Afghan people. . . . This interference not only is not lessening, it is increasing in scope and has assumed the form of outright aggression against the sovereign, independent state of Afghanistan and its legitimate government [*Current Digest*, May 28, 1980].

A June 1980 *Tass* report accused the White House of using countries as pawns in a political game, as Moscow lashed out at U.S. pressures to make the boycott worldwide:

> Washington has been unable to hide its impotent rage every time the Olympic committee of another state, especially a West European state, refuses to obediently play the role of pawn that has been assigned it from overseas in the White House's political game and, reaffirming its loyalty to the ideals of the Olympic movement, decides to send a sports team to Moscow [*Current Digest,* June 25, 1980].

V. Goncharov, a political commentator for *Tass,* brought up the Cold War to explain anti-boycott sentiment among potential Olympic athletes from the United States:

> [American] athletes reject official Washington's attempts to use international sport as an instrument of political pressure. They understand that the demand for a boycott of the Olympic Games is intended to galvanize a policy of reviving the Cold War—a policy subservient to President Carter's re-election considerations [*Current Digest,* May 7, 1980].

Soviet coverage tended to picture the United States as *the* opponent, an imperialistic force pressuring allies around the world to follow an American party line.

The boycott of the Moscow Olympics deeply affected parts of the world besides the United States and the Soviet Union. To cite but one example, the British fought vigorously over whether to send a team, the government eventually losing out to the British Olympic Committee. Even though British athletes competed, the public and privately owned British networks agreed to cut their planned coverage from 180 hours to 40 hours. Then, in the words of Whannel (1984, p. 37), "the Moscow Olympics became the site of an enthralling television battle—a struggle between Soviet television and the British channels to define the meaning of the Games." It was a symbolic Olympic television Cold War. Whannel recalls.

> British commentaries made frequent use of Cold War language and stock Iron Curtain cliches. The Kremlin was "one of the most feared buildings in the world"; . . . one boxer was in danger of a "salt-mine job"; there was a small British contingent in the "giant Communist crowd." . . . There were references . . . to the "shadow of Afghanistan," and to people being

trampled underfoot. Mika, the mascot, "shed a cardboard tear" in the great mosaic, and we were instantly offered a "moment to remember the real grief elsewhere" [p. 38].

World Press Comments on the U.S. Boycott of the Moscow Games

To place American and Soviet reports in context, a few comments from press editorials around the world (*World Press Review,* April 1980) are helpful as epistemological framing devices. *El Comercio* of Quito, Ecuador, placed the problem squarely in the context of the Cold War: "The real mistake was in scheduling the Games in one of the superpower countries—which are, by definition, conflict-prone. In the eyes of the world, this was rekindling the Cold War." The independent *Verdens Gans* of Oslo, Norway, noted the divisiveness of the issue: "Participation in the Games will be interpreted as support for the Soviet Union. Boycotting the Games will be another kind of political act. There is no middle ground; an in-between attitude is impossible."

Conservative papers in the West tended to support the U.S. boycott. The *Sydney Morning Herald* based its stand on historical reasoning: "Those who advocate a withdrawal can cite the example of the Berlin Olympics of 1936, which gave respectability to a detestable regime. With hindsight, it is possible to say a boycott then could have done heavy—perhaps irreparable damage to the Nazi movement and possibly have saved the world much bloodshed." *L'Aurore* in Paris advocated canceling the Games because of the presence of the Cold War: "The time has come to cancel a sports competition which the Soviets have stripped of all meaning. . . . Although no one wants to admit it, we are once again in a Cold War period. And in times of war, simple decency has always prompted nations not to hold the Games."

Independent and liberal papers in the West were skeptical of the 1980 boycott. For example, the *Corrierre della Sera* of Milan, Italy, worried about the polarization increased by the boycott: "History has taught us that when the flow of dialogue ceases and the Olympic Games are disrupted, the shooting begins." *Le Soir* of Brussels, Belgium, supported the positive potential of sports in international relations: "Boycotting Moscow means destroying what international sports have built up over the past thirty years. We must not forget that sports have sometimes served to bring countries together. The Ping-Pong match in

Peking, for example, marked the first step in the U.S.-China rapproachment which radically changed international relations." In contrast to such high-minded reasoning, the *Guardian* of London took a more cynical "Realpolitik" stance on politics and the Olympics:

> It would be wrong to pretend there is something uniquely appalling about the 1980 Olympics. From Hitler's Olympics [and] Arab-Israeli shootouts, African boycotts, assorted Chinese exclusions, to Black Power salutes and steroid injections to improve "shamateur" performances, the Games have come a long way from innocent attempts at the celebration of international sportsmanship.

Considering that South African apartheid was the target of various sports boycotts, it is not surprising that the *Daily News* of Durban, South Africa, also opposed the 1980 boycott: "The West should go to the Games, even in totalitarian Moscow . . . Lord Killanin, the IOC chief, is right—politics should be kept out of sports."

Viewed in retrospect, American and Soviet press coverage of the 1980 Olympic boycott accepted basic Cold War positions and rhetoric. Indeed, an awareness of Cold War positions is necessary as a larger frame of reference in order to understand, as well as explain, media coverage of the 1980 boycott. The controversy is not confined to the single issue at hand, an Olympic boycott, or to the single boycott motive, one country's alleged violation of another country. Immediately old grudges and polarizations are dredged up.

"Cold War–mindedness," as Smythe and Wilson define it, provides the fundamental binary opposition that is the deep structure which both gave rise to the 1980 boycott and provides the necessary rhetorical and epistemological framework for explaining its representation in the press. American press accounts portray the United States as accepting its responsibility as "leader of the Free World" to boycott Moscow's "showcase Olympics" in protest against "Soviet aggression" in Afghanistan. The United States finds ready support in the U.S. press and then lobbies its Cold War allies to join in this boycott. Moscow, in turn, countercharges the United States with imperialism, accuses it of diplomatic arm twisting, suggests that the boycott is only a reelection ploy, and mounts its own Cold War campaign against the boycott.

What happens when, four years later, the sides in this Olympic boycott battle are reversed?

The 1984 Soviet Boycott of the Los Angeles Olympic Games

The Soviet "nonparticipation" in the Los Angeles Summer Games was announced on May 9, 1984. Early warning signs had been given by the Russians as early as 1980 that a pullout was possible. Moscow explained the nonparticipation as the direct result of violations of the Olympic charter by the Los Angeles Olympic Organizing Committee (LAOOC). Moscow charged that the safety of Soviet athletes could not be guaranteed in Los Angeles, owing to the anti-Soviet hysteria whipped up and endorsed by the Reagan administration. The question of athlete safety was used by other Soviet allies as they joined the USSR pullout. In the end, the absence of 14 countries from the 1984 Summer Games was conceded to have diminished the value of a medal at Los Angeles, particularly in the swimming, strength, and track and field events. How did the U.S. and Soviet presses report this Olympic boycott?

Soviet Coverage of the Los Angeles Boycott

The sharpest warning signs of an impending boycott appeared in April in the Soviet press when a statement by the USSR national Olympic committee and a press conference by its chair, Marat V. Gramov, received extensive coverage in the Soviet Press. These stories stated the "serious concern" of Soviet authorities about conditions in Los Angeles. *Sovetsky Sport* reported "a number of persuasive instances" cited by Gramov as "flagrant violation of the rules and traditions of the Olympic Games" (*Current Digest,* May 9, 1984).

Eight of the nine problems cited were specific and somewhat technical. Gramov charged that the U.S. government was four years tardy in assuring in writing that "Olympic rules, regulations and traditions would be observed." Planning three Olympic villages instead of one violated rule 40 of the Olympic charter. Athletes were to be accepted only two instead of three weeks prior to the Games. A large cash fee was being demanded from countries *prior* to March 1, 1984. Services, including those for journalists, were too costly, a telephone installation costing 100 times what it did in Moscow. The "special procedure" announced by the U.S. Embassy in Moscow for issuing Olympic visas violated rule 50 of the Olympic charter. The U.S. State Department acted contrary to the Olympic charter in rejecting a signed Soviet agreement with the LAOOC on access to Los Angeles by Soviet ships, planes, and journalists. Radio Liberty and Radio Free Europe should not have been accredited for the Olympics because they "conduct subversive activities against other countries."

The further source of serious concern was "the anti-Soviet, anti-socialist campaign that is under way on a wide scale in the US." Gramov stressed, "Various terrorist organizations and groups are threatening physical violence against our athletes, coaches and journalists, and provocations are being openly planned. . . . What sort of hospitality, traditional for all Olympics, can one talk about in this case?" Gramov dismissed U.S. administration disclaimers of responsibility for this "rampage of anti-Soviet hysteria" by citing U.S. press reports that leaders of the effort "have been gladly received in the White House" and "found complete mutual understanding in the U.S. administration." The *Tass* report on April 25 on the special International Olympic Committee (IOC) Executive Committee meeting to resolve these issues concluded by warning: "Certain questions still remain to be resolved. For example, the problem of security for those participating in the Olympics must be decided at the state level" (*Current Digest,* May 23, 1984).

On May 9, 1984, the Soviet Union officially launched its symbolic Cold War missile, Olympic nonparticipation, against the United States, retaliating in kind four years and four months later against the first U.S. preemptive strike. The Soviet Union on that date announced its decision not to participate in the 1984 Los Angeles Games. The Official statement in *Pravda* and *Izvestia* by the National Olympic Committee (NOC) of the USSR emphasized:

> Political demonstrations hostile to the U.S.S.R. are being prepared, and undisguised threats of physical violence are being addressed to the U.S.S.R. NOC and to Soviet athletes and officials. The ringleaders of anti-Soviet, anti-socialist organizations are being received by representatives of the U.S. administration, and their activities are being widely publicized by the mass news media [*Current Digest,* June 6, 1984].

This decision caught many by surprise, including American Olympic and ABC officials; they were prepared for it but not quite expecting it to happen.

On May 15, *Sovetsky Sport* published a long 2,900-word report of a press conference held by Gramov to further elaborate Soviet reasons for not participating in the Los Angeles Games. The emphasis was again on the stepped-up anti-Soviet and antisocialist activities in the United States.

Gramov denied that the Soviet decision was revenge for the 1980 U.S. boycott but did use the opportunity to criticize the U.S. boycott for its political and heavy-handed quality, in contrast to the Soviets' pragmatically based nonparticipation:

> As far as the Olympic boycott that former US President Carter called for, and which the current President supported, is concerned, it included demands that the Games be moved out of the USSR or that the Olympic Games be cancelled altogether, political pressure on the governments of a number of countries and a whole set of economic sanctions aimed at wrecking the organization of the Games in Moscow: Television broadcasts were banned, firms bound by contracts were forbidden to deliver equipment, and so forth. That's what the boycott by the United States of America was like! [*Current Digest,* June 6, 1984]

To counter the suggestion in the Western press that Soviet officials were fearful of athlete defections, Gramov, as head of the Soviet Olympic Committee responded:

> We have been to Hollywood, we have been to Los Angeles. Our athletes have been there and have seen all those bright lights. . . . To put it bluntly, on returning from Los Angeles many of our athletes said they were glad to be back in the Soviet Union where the air is freer and there is no need to fear everything of which Hollywood and Los Angeles boast [*Soviet World Outlook,* May 15, 1984].

Besides reporting official justifications and explanations for the boycott, the Soviet press quoted extensively from world press reports in support of the boycott, emphasizing the subsequent participation of other countries in joining the boycott and printing numerous letters to the editor in support. The letters were from average citizens as well as previous Olympic greats. "The Games cannot be a sports festival if their participants do not have a guarantee of their safety, acceptable conditions for competition or a friendly reception," wrote N. Sergeyev from the village of Ileikino. "They have made intensive preparations to create an uncomfortable and dangerous atmosphere for the Soviet Olympians during the Games. Therefore, I resolutely support the decision on the non-participation of Soviet athletes in these Olympics," read a letter signed by the star of the 1972 Summer Games, Olga Korbut (*Current Digest,* June 6, 1984).

Subsequent reports on the Los Angeles preparations reinforced the negative image in the Soviet press. The killing of 22 persons at the San Ysidro McDonald's Restaurant, south of Los Angeles, and the automobile assault on 50 persons on a Los Angeles sidewalk, both shortly before the Olympics, were commented on in the Soviet press as confirmation of Soviet fears for safety. ABC was called "clairvoyant" for including a clause in its LAOOC contract reducing its payments if socialist countries boycotted; *Izvestia* even suggested ABC was "well informed about the plans and intentions of the Reagan administration" to create intolerable conditions (*Current Digest,* June 20, 1984). Convening the Friendship Games in August was explained as a result of the "antisocialist hysteria" preventing countries from participating in Los Angeles (*Current Digest,* August 1, 1984).

As a whole, Soviet coverage of the 1984 boycott unanimously supported the decision of the Soviet National Olympic Committee. The decision was reported as based on technical violations of the Olympic charter, but explanations of the decision included negative characterizations of American political leaders and social conditions. Soviet boycott reports regularly reverted to a variety of traditional Cold War charges against American political, economic, and chauvinistic priorities.

Perhaps most strikingly, the 1984 Soviet press portrayal of the United States almost perfectly mirrors the 1980 American press portrayal of the Soviet Union. Both based the boycott decision in the reprehensible and negative character of their opposite, the host. The Soviets invade defenseless neighbors; the Americans exploit and endanger everyone, including their own citizens. In each case, government leaders make a decision, the national press reports and supports it, and within national boundaries the impression is clear: this is the only honorable action to take. The many differences between the Soviet and American systems intriguingly disappear when Washington or Moscow decides, the press follows, and public opinion falls in line.

U.S. Coverage of the Los Angeles Boycott

The *Los Angeles Times,* like many of its counterparts in other cities, took an early and strong anti-boycott position. In contrast to 1980, the insistence of the *Times* was that the show must go on. A *Times* editorial (May 15, 1984) faced the fact that the Russians were not coming: "The focus ought to be on getting on with the best possible Games. The Olympics have been diminished, but they remain the Olympics—a showplace for the best in athletic talent, a gathering of nations, a spectacle that in scope and color has no rival."

The *Times* heavily reported the Soviet boycott, with extensive speculation by American officials on motives and consequences of the Soviet action but only a few quotations from Soviet officials. Of the approximately 25 letters to the editor published on the Russian pullout, only 2 backed the Soviets' claim of not coming to Los Angeles for safety reasons. Over 20 letters published were either critical of the Olympic ideal or negative toward the Soviet Union. Not one independent column published on the op-ed page was in support of the Russian move and the Soviets' reasons for not participating. There were two columns critical of the Olympic ideal and four columns opposed to the Soviet move.

The *Times'* judgment of the Soviet boycott stood in stark contrast to its stance on the previous American boycott. In 1984 there were no calls to move the Games from Los Angeles because a major power had chosen to stay home. In contrast, in 1980, on four separate occasions (January 12, 13, and 16 and February 9), the *Times* called for moving the Games from Moscow. In the *Times,* moral imperatives dictated a 1980 U.S. boycott. In 1984, by contrast, Soviet bias and nitpicking were seen as violations of Olympic unity. The overt position of the *Times* was simple: in the 1980 U.S. boycott, political principles overrode the usual separation of sport and politics, while in 1984 the autonomy and semisacredness of the Olympics stood above other considerations. But there may have been a subtext beneath this surface.

The *Los Angeles Times* and its parent Times-Mirror Company, together with its many subsidiaries and other Chandler family holdings, had an economic self-interest in seeing that the Los Angeles Olympics reached as grand a level as possible. The Summer Olympic Games were to bring $3 billion into the Los Angeles economy, and no one was more closely associated with the Los Angeles economy than the *Times.* The newspaper's economic ties to the Olympics were self-consciously clear. In 1983 the *Times* published a lavish full-color 40-page booklet, *Los Angeles, the Olympic City: The Market and the Media.* The booklet explained aspects of the Los Angeles economy and emphasized the circulation and advertising reach of the paper in the context of the 1984

Summer Olympic Games. The *Times* also contributed some $4 million as official sponsor of the Olympic Arts Festival, and Dorothy Chandler, wife and mother of the past and present *Times* publishers, was installed as honorary chairwoman of the cultural and Fine Arts Advisory Commission for the Olympics.

The relationship between Times-Mirror and the Olympics was broad and deep because of the extensive Los Angeles based *Times*-Chandler empire (Halberstam, 1979; Gottlieb & Wolt, 1977). The Times-Mirror Company is one of the five largest publishing concerns in the country. In addition to the *Los Angeles Times,* it owns other major newspapers as well as numerous magazine and book publishing companies, televisions stations, and cable systems. Its yearly revenues are $3 billion and climbing, placing it well within the *Fortune* 500. Besides the Times-Mirror Company, the Chandler family owns banks, real estate companies, oil, agriculture, and shipping businesses. The Olympics were expected to be a boon for airlines, banks, and insurance companies, as well as other service industries to which Times-Mirror and the Chandlers were economically tied.

In this context, "going for the gold" meant for the *Los Angeles Times,* as for ABC Television, more than athletic victories; it meant vast financial profits. The Eastern-bloc pullout was expected to diminish profit expectations for the Olympics, but as long as the Summer Games went on, with or without the Soviets, the *Times* could expect substantial one-time-only revenues. At the same time, the Games would make the *Los Angeles Times* *the* print authority for the world press and public gathered in Los Angeles.

World Press Comments on the Soviet Boycott of the Los Angeles Games

In 1984, *Granma Weekly Review* of Havana, Cuba (May 13) echoed the Soviet press: "It is well known that from the start of preparations for the upcoming Games, the U.S. administration decided to use the Games for political ends; chauvinist feelings and anti-Soviet hysteria are being fanned in the U.S." The majority of world press comments, however, opposed the 1984 boycott (*World Press Review,* July 1984). That politicians are aware of the public importance of the Olympics was a point stressed and regretted by the *Indian Express* of New Delhi: "the modern Olympic Games are the politician's delight, because no sporting event attracts more global attention. The recent history of the Olympics shows that politics has long been a cause of trouble."

A funereal quality crept into some accounts. The *Globe and Mail* of Toronto, Ontario, interred the Olympics with the pronouncement: "The Games have assumed an importance far beyond what they deserve, and now they are sinking because of their own bulk. They will open in Los Angeles with fanfare on July 28. The last rites will be on August 12." *Die Zeit* of Hamburg, Germany, was even more macabre: "Every four years the world stands bewildered beside the grave of the Olympic ideal. The noble corpse, buried many times, will be exhumed once again. Following the Soviet decision not to go to Los Angeles, the public, faced with a grotesque mixture of superpower politics and sport, does not know whether to laugh or cry."

Summary and Conclusions

Although American coverage contained more variety of comments, the sequence of political decision making, press reporting, and public support for the two Olympic boycotts was virtually identical on both sides, as Table 7.1 summarizes.

The media performances appear in many ways as *mirror images* of each other. Similarities are more apparent than differences. Each country had a long-standing tradition of Olympic participation. Each boycott decision was apparently made at the top of the political power structure, although in the United States the independence of the National Olympic Committee delayed compliance. Press reporting and editorializing and letters to the editor supported the boycott, overwhelmingly in the American case and unanimously in the Soviet. American public opinion shifted from 41 percent opposed in mid-January to only 17 percent opposed by mid-February, a strikingly rapid shift. American allies and Soviet allies were rallied to join the boycott with mixed success in each case. Cold War opponents decried the boycott by each superpower. When the Olympics finally were held, each boycotting country provided little or no press coverage of the Games.

As in the sequence of events in Table 7.1, so in the dichotomous reasoning in Table 7.2 there is abundant evidence of Cold War factors in U.S. and U.S.S.R. press reports on the 1980 and 1984 Olympic boycotts. Table 7.2 summarizes some of the more frequent and obvious evidence of the Cold War as it appeared in press accounts.

TABLE 7.1 Sequence of Boycott Actions

Boycotter's Activity	*United States 1980*	*Soviet Union 1984*
Previous record	Olympics since 1896	Olympics since 1952
Boycott decision	President	Olympic head
Press positions	Support boycott	Support boycott
Public reactions	Mixed (yes = 49% Jan., 73% Feb.)	Unknown
Reaction of allies	36 countries boycott	14 countries boycott
Reaction of Opponents	Oppose boycott	Oppose boycott
Media noncoverage	No TV, little press	No TV, no press

TABLE 7.2 Cold War Terminology and Concepts in Boycott Reports

U.S. Boycott Rhetoric	*Soviet Boycott Rhetoric*
Soviet aggression	Violation of Olympic charter
Totalitarianism	Anti-Soviet hysteria
Repression	Antisocialist campaign
Isolation	Lack of security
Expansionism	Violence
Blow to Soviet prestige	Commercialism
National honor	Imperialism
Moral imperatives	Votegetting
National security needs	Socialist ideals

Writers in the American and Soviet press reflect Cold War differences in their terminology and also in their choice of sources, quotations, and explanations. The Soviet press quotes heavily from the USSR National Olympic Committee and its head, Marat Gramov. The United States press relies on American explanations from administration and Olympic officials even for understanding Soviet decisions. Each press tends to present the other side only in minimal quotations and then largely to criticize such comments rather than to accept them as explanations.

There are differences between American and Soviet press coverage that must be noted. The American coverage is noticeably more "leaky." More varied positions and opinions are presented. Soviet reporting reflects more uniform positions with fewer exceptions. These are genuine differences reflecting different ideologies and press practices in general. But the differences are less striking in this case study than the similarities.

One lesson of the boycott is a call to journalists on both sides of the Cold War to better understand and represent the other side. The American and Soviet press coverage of the boycotts seems clearly to confirm the assertion by Wilson and Smythe, cited earlier, that the Cold War in the mass media acts to short-circuit rational considerations. Precious little effort is made to place oneself in the other's shoes and see the issue from the opposite perspective. The citizens of the Soviet Union and the United States are not presented comprehensible presentations in depth of the alternative point of view in press reports. Objective, impartial reporting is not the norm in the Cold War. As a result, such press coverage can only foster more antagonism and mistrust. Members of the press in the Soviet Union and in the United States are at once victims *and* perpetrators of the Cold War. Measured by the classic phrasing of Harold Lasswell (1948/1960), the press is neither adequately "surveying the environment" nor appropriately "correlating the parts." The sources of the failure are not merely individual; they are structured into the institutions, expectations, and ideology of each side.

For political leaders the challenge is to consider long-range international relations as well as short-term domestic consequences. In terms of struggles for tactical advantages, the decisions to boycott the Olympics offer rewards to the superpowers. The polarized press coverage does contribute to an internal national cohesion in each country, albeit a negatively motivated cohesion, and a certain kind of tactical achievement in frustrating the Cold War opponent on the world stage. But in a larger and more progressive frame of reference, such antagonisms and distancing are dangerous and dysfunctional. Of course, a Cold War is preferable to a hot war fought with material rather than symbolic weapons, but both are unmistakably inferior to international understanding, cooperation, and peace.

The success of the 1988 Seoul Olympic Games in bringing the Superpowers and their Cold War allies together for sporting competition is encouraging, as is the outlook for Barcelona and beyond. Of course, whether the Olympics survive intact is not the most important issue. More critical is the establishment and maintenance of a working dialogue between the superpowers; the Olympics, as the world's most encompassing shared event, can contribute profoundly to that dialogue. This global spectacle can serve human needs and international cooperation, but only if participating countries, including especially the superpowers, are also committed to those goals and can reach beyond the stereotypes of Cold War ideology.

Cold War Ideology and Media Bias

What emerges from a consistent investigation of the media presence of Cold War ideology is an unmistakable sense of a cultural system in which sports reporting, movies, congressional hearings, military heroes, and many other expressions combine to create a one-sided and self-serving distortion of the world. Of the many possible world views that super media might potentially support, the American version in particular and the Western one in general never understate the horrors of the Soviet and communist systems or the benefits of the Western and capitalist systems. This, like its Soviet counterpart, both reflects and strengthens dominant ideology.

How dominating is the Cold War in English-language super media? A distinction must be registered that the Cold War is not the *only* factor present in the dominant mediated ideology, nor is it always the *central* factor. News, entertainment, and artistic expressions, in fact, generally reflect ideological factors unrelated in any direct way to the Cold War. Further, the Cold War waxes and wanes in importance as Soviet-American relations periodically heat up and cool down.

But, as Raymond Williams and Stuart Hall emphasize, an ideology *sets limits and exerts influence*. American media expressions do not contradict the Cold War; Cold War ideology sets limits. Media also often use plot lines, character portrayals, terminology, settings, stylistic emphases, and other devices that subtly reflect and reinforce the Cold War even when the subject matter is supposedly apolitical, as in sports events and action adventure stories; the Cold War exerts influence.

The reality of Cold War ideology casts the frequent debates about bias in American media in a different light. The left bias, alleged by Spiro Agnew (speech to Midwest Republican Conference, 1969, in Porter, 1976), Edith Efron (1971), Joseph Keely (1971), Ernest Lefever (1974), Peter Braestrop (1983), and many since, has been countered by

Johnson (1970), Cirino (1972), Altheide (1976), Gitlin (1983), Parenti (1986), and others. Robert Lichter and Stanley Rothman (1981) interviewed 240 journalists and broadcasters working for the most influential news media and found a variety of viewpoints and even divisions on many questions. However, they found that 54 percent labeled themselves as "liberals" and only 19 percent as "conservatives." Yet because of the Cold War, it can be misleading to consider American "liberal" a left pole of debate. Ranney (1983) points out that *liberal* in this context tends to mean impartial or uncommitted. For example, Walter Cronkite labeled himself a "liberal," defined as "one who is not bound by doctrine or committed to a point of view in advance" (Epstein, 1974, p. 214). C. Richard Hofstetter (1976) originated the distinction between "political bias" and "structural bias," a distinction sometimes used to explain that, while partisan political party bias is avoided, the structural biases of perceived news interest, competition for ratings, and professional prestige are always at work. In these terms, media may successfully avoid overt party bias but not more subtle structural bias.

The most succinct summary of media bias is Daniel Hallin's phrase *reformist conservatism* (in Gitlin, 1986, p. 29). Media reformism descends from populist liberalism ready to expose violations of fair play, equal opportunity, and prosperity; it is suspicious of power and favors the common man. But this reformism is conservative because it coexists with "a strong belief in order, consensus, moderation, leadership, and the basic soundness of American institutions and benevolence of American world leadership" (Hallin, p. 29). Hallin amplifies this by considering how Reaganism exploited not only ideological conservatism but also a "We're Number One," "America Is Back" nationalism. One consequence was increasing stridency in coverage of consensus enemies from the Cold War. Hallin recounts a belligerent introduction by Dan Rather to an otherwise even-handed story on Soviet memories of World War II: "The militaristic and totalitarian Communist party that rules modern Russia constantly emphasizes its version of the war as a lesson for its people and a lesson for others" (p. 36). American television journalism was especially conservative in its role, in the words of Hallin,

> as the ideological arm of cold war foreign policy, presenting the world as a great and simple battleground between good and evil, with America as the unique embodiment of good. One would think the nation would have learned over the course of forty years of cold war the dangers of this kind

of perspective, which include not only the risk of war, both "limited" and cataclysmic, but also damage to democracy and complacency about festering problems within the United States [p. 41].

"The press over time tends to reflect official foreign policy positions" rather than critically evaluate them, in the words of William Dorman (1988, p. 71). Dorman notes that when an Israeli jet fighter downed a Libyan 727, killing 106 innocent men, women, and children, the headlines were cautious. "A Deadly Blunder Over Sinai," read *Newsweek's* cover. When a Soviet jet downed a Korean airliner, *Newsweek's* cover read "Murder in the Sky," and the inside story was titled "A Ruthless Ambush in the Sky." Dorman finds American coverage of the Soviet Union filled with suspicious interpretations and value-laden language that is not applied to American allies. The effect of this worries Dorman:

> The cold war has resulted in the same kind of willingness on the part of the media to suspend the critical function that hot wars have always elicited. The roots of the phenomenon can be found in the establishment of a permanent garrison state of the mind for Americans. This permanent state of psychological siege . . . has led to what I call a "journalism of deference" to the National Security State. Whatever its sources, such deference has put the journalistic watchdog, much celebrated in democratic theory, on a rather short tether with consequences that ought to be of serious concern [p. 71].

The press, by maintaining an autonomous perspective, could act as a reality check on policy makers, but instead, the Cold War has created a closed information loop for American policy makers: "The information they receive confirms the policy choices they already have made" (Dorman, p. 72).

The research literature on the Cold War is extensive. Even the titles evoke its dramatic entertainment potential: *Secret Contenders: The Myth of Cold War Counterintelligence* (Beck, 1984), *The Balance of Terror: Nuclear Weapons and the Illusion of Security, 1945–1985* (Bottome, 1986), *Endless Enemies: The Making of an Unfriendly World (Kwitney, 1986), The Twilight Struggle: Tales of the Cold War* (Attwood, 1987). It has been severely criticized for its origins (Walter LaFeber, 1971) and consequences (Chomsky, 1982; Schell, 1982; Kennan 1983). It combines stereotyping, as in *The Soviet Union In the Third World: Threat to World Peace?* (Whelan & Dixon, 1986), with inflammatory rhetoric (Brockriede, 1970; Corcoran, in UNESCO,

1986). Western mass media and popular culture have become inseparable from the Cold War. Why?

Smythe and Wilson (1968) explain how historically the mass media
in the United States, from the early 19th century on, increasingly
became commercial instruments selling to an audience and speaking for
the corporate system. In so doing, the media surrendered their independence and critical potential. They became virtually an arm of the state
selling ideas, official interpretations, and policies as well as goods and
services. Media became instruments rather than critics of a Cold War
motivated by determination to prevent social change unacceptable to
American interests anywhere in the world. The result was a set of
media-fostered and popularly accepted myths about capitalist virtue
and communist villainy, the inevitability of conflict, and the necessity
of military victory.

In order to sustain popular support for Cold War policies, in the view
of Smythe and Wilson, it was necessary to construct a dream world of
popular myths. These seven myths can work for either superpower.

1. *We are good: they are bad.* The reprehensible nature of the Cold
War enemy and our virtue define the sides and justify every form of
opposition. Olympic boycott coverage carries this theme, as do Hollywood films and testimony of such national security experts as Oliver
North.

2. *Our superpower enemy leads an international monolithic conspiracy against us.* The enemy's ideology makes it target us for destruction,
whether by direct conquest or subtle subversion. To Soviets, American
imperialism appears uniform and implacable; to Americans, Soviet
domination appears consistently voracious. The North testimony on
Central America showcased this domino, or contagion, theory of the
Cold War opponent. CIA and KGB espionage tales in film, video, or
literature help spread this myth.

3. *Foreign relations problems are caused by our enemy,* and, therefore, our engagement against it in every world trouble spot is justified
and deserves support. The belligerence and international guile of Soviets emerge from the text of many American media products; similar but
reversed categories dominate Soviet media.

A corollary of this myth is that *indigenous problems in countries can
be ignored* unless they are understood to emanate from the enemy or to
provide an opportunity to extend our sphere of influence against the
enemy. For the United States this means support of counterrevolution
and of any government, no matter how repressive, that claims to be

threatened by communist subversion or force. For the Soviet Union it means support of anticapitalist revolution in the West and the Third World and opposition to reform within the Eastern bloc.

4. *The only appropriate response to foreign problems is military.* We must be tough, for force is the only thing our enemy respects. The enemy portrayed in popular media as subverting and attacking innocent people obviously exists outside any bounds of civility and can be countered only with violence. From the six-gun to *Top Gun,* the militaristic solution has ideological priority because violence is super media's favorite solution to any conflict.

5. *The public must defer to foreign policy decisions of authorities.* Because foreign policy is believed to be too complex for citizens to understand, decisions must be made by the chief executive and his military advisers. Foreign news in super media often appears too remote, fast-changing, and complex to allow the lay public to assimilate it. Moreover, in popular fiction the array of supertechnology and complicated strategies employed by spies and international saboteurs, together with the need for coded secrecy and behind-the-scenes manipulation, creates a world in which an informed public plays no role. Authoritarianism is given free rein.

6. *Technology, know-how, and winning are the all important values.* As in hypercompetitive sports, the only value is in being number one and destroying the opponent. Clandestine operations and the unscrupulous can-do guy become the ideal of Cold War national security policy makers. Huge expenditures for such technologies as exotic remote sensing systems and secure communications linkages create the tools for aggressive teams and individuals to win "the big ball game" against the Cold War enemy.

7. *We are defenders of the free world, and we must take any risk to preserve and extend our system.* No film hero, sports competitor, or military combatant in the popular media can give less than his all to represent and defend his country and way of life. The only alternative is spineless cowardice or traitorous treason. Ironically, this myth brings us full circle. A capitalist or a communist defending and extending his or her system for high motives acts toward the other precisely in such a way as to confirm the other side's belief that it is threatened by an aggressive, international conspiracy against good in the world, that military action determined by its leaders is necessary, that it must win out over this enemy, and so on.

Whether consciously conceived or not, these myths are the popular media results of the Cold War–mindedness that Smythe and Wilson find permeating the mass media. Dorman (1988, p. 71) adds the point that this media behavior does not imply that reporters and producers are part of a planned conspiracy or that editors act on instructions received directly from the state department. The behavior is spontaneous and usually unconscious, reflexive rather than deliberate. Instead of serving as an autonomous reality check on official policy, the media become cheerleaders, in Dorman's words, as a result of "both the media system's ideological orientation and Cold War conditioning."

The "relativity" of terminology and classifications becomes most evident through a comparative chart of ideological positions (Table 7.3). As mentioned above in clarifying the liberal-bias thesis about American media, the American assumptions and categories may be significantly different from more global classifications. Table 7.3 illustrates graphically why there are confusions and inconsistencies in many debates, in particular those over the supposedly liberal or leftist bias of super media. What American commentators label left is closer to center in a worldwide perspective. The American center, in turn, is to much of the world a generally rightist position. In contrast, a rightist ideology in Cuba or China might coincide with the American liberal left. A centrist position in a communist country would be off scale by standards of capitalist ideology. Commonwealth countries largely resemble the United States on this scale, although leftist thought in the British Isles has generally been more vigorous than its English-language counterparts across the Atlantic.

Perhaps this can be illustrated by considering that curious blend of show biz and politics known as celebrity endorsements. Considering which candidates and causes they campaigned or raised money for, celebrity endorsements confirm the *Los Angeles Times'* assertion that "most of Hollywood, and its money, leans liberal" (June 7, 1988) *if* one uses the narrower American capitalist ideological spectrum as the frame of reference. Table 7.4 illustrates this by using more worldwide labels for the *Los Angeles Times' classifications of celebrity endorsements of Jesse Jackson, Michael Dukakis, and George Bush.*

It certainly seems appropriate to place Bill Cosby, Willie Nelson, and the other celebrities in the left column in Table 7.4 as "centrist" on the ideological spectrum, whether their endorsement of Jesse Jackson is the measure or not. The placement of Frank Sinatra, Clint Eastwood, and

TABLE 7.3 Comparative Chart of the Cold War Ideological Spectrum

Left	Center	Right		
	Communist Ideology			
		Left	Center	Right
			Capitalist Ideology	
Left		Center		Right
		Generic Worldwide Ideology		

TABLE 7.4 Celebrity Political Positions and Endorsements

Left	*Left/Center*	*Center*	*Center/Right*	*Right*
		Bill Cosby	Sally Field	Frank Sinatra
		Casey Kasem	Richard Gere	Cheryl Ladd
		Cicely Tyson	Cher	Tom Selleck
		Quincy Jones	Meryl Streep	Robert Stack
		Martin Sheen	Sissy Spacek	Clint Eastwood
		Louis Gossett	Woody Allen	Chuck Norris
		Willie Nelson	Paul Simon	Helen Hayes
		Al Jarreau	James Taylor	Rich Little

others in the right column should find little disagreement. The most debate might revolve around the "center/right" column of Sally Field, Woody Allen, and others, whose widely visible "liberalism" is often considered left but who accept private enterprise capitalism and who fit relatively well within Hallin's (1986) classification of "reformist conservatism."

The full *Times* list of celebrity endorsers totaled: Jackson 47, Dukakis 45, and Bush 11. This might be trumpeted by conservative columnists as leftist Hollywood bias, but here it can be seen to be what it is, centrist moderation. Hollywood has never been a hotbed of wild-eyed revolutionaries—is the good life too pleasurable for that?—and has been generally devoid of even communist sympathizers since the devastating

Red scare and blacklisting after World War II. Even the right's archenemy celebrity, "Hanoi Jane" Fonda, remains in the public eye primarily as an accomplished actress and an inexhaustible aerobics promoter. If this is "left" as charged by Ben Stein, Kevin Phillips, and others, then the scale is right-skewed, as Donald Lazere has argued in both his writing, "Conservative Media Criticism: Heads I Win, Tails You Lose" (in Lazere, 1987), and his editing, *American Media and Mass Culture: Left Perspectives* (Lazere, 1987).

The effect of the Cold War in America seems to indicate a dominant ideology. The dominant ideology thesis begins by taking ideology as any collective set of beliefs, regardless of their truth or falsity, and then identifies four constituents. First, there is a dominant ideology, the content of which is not always specified or consciously understood. Second, the dominant classes in society benefit from this ideology, though not necessarily through their deliberate activities. Third, the dominant ideology incorporates subordinate classes, making them politically quiescent and concealing social relations. Fourth, the mechanisms of the dominant ideology are powerful enough to overcome contradictions. The classic statement of the thesis is an old one: "The ideas of the ruling class are in every epoch the ruling ideas: i.e., the class which is the ruling *material* force of society, is at the same time its ruling *intellectual* force" (Marx & Engels, 1970, p. 61). The first two constituents seem borne out in our cases examined here, but the latter two constituents contain complications arising from the enthusiastic participation of Americans in the Cold War, a participation that takes us beyond evidence in these cases.

Hollywood films, congressional hearings, and Olympic boycott coverage indicate the unmistakable existence of a dominant ideology, whether it is from media alone or from other causes as well. The super media expressions of Cold War ideology contain ample evidence of bias in their representations, in their hegemonistic thrusts, and in the personal consciousness they reflect and appeal to. Cold War ideology sets limits on the dominant codes and culture. The notion of dominant ideology is not a universal law of all human experience in the way that gravity is. It does not mean the exclusive ideology but only the dominant. Nor is it a necessary institution of all societies, as family, economics, and politics are. But it is finally impossible to conceive of a society with a recognizable identity without an ideology, whether one calls it dominant or not. Ideology may be liberating or oppressive, but it cannot be denied or ignored, even in democratic societies. Cold War ideology has certainly played a prominent role in recent American public life.

The most comfortable and reassuring view of the ideological place of super media today would be to conclude that they are consistently independent and objective in their representation of global reality. Unfortunately, the reality of the Cold War and its presence in super media prevents such smug comfort. A long, complex series of influences works through owner bias, commercial incentives, careerist opportunism, information gaps, inherited stereotypes, institutional pressures, peer opinion, and other social-economic forces to systematically distort super media world views. Cultural studies and critical theory assists in uncovering both the effects and the causes of these distortions.

The idea of a free and impartial press on the international level exists more in rhetoric than in reality. Not only must media professionals seek to elevate their individual performances, but also the institutional and structural sources of bias and distortion must be increasingly articulated and countered. Super media in the English-speaking world are no more the flawless reflection of existent world conditions than they are the mindless pawns of a controlling few. Improvements are possible and needed. Perhaps the only function of media more urgent today than media's critical, independent role in public affairs, is media's own critical, independent confrontation with itself as gatekeeper and agenda setter for a public in need of leadership as well as celebrity, ideals as well as images, truth as well as information.

Like the youths in Leningrad or New York, the boys in the bar in Peoria feel the Cold War. Bar regulars mix with refugees from the sudden summer rainstorm. Bar signs identify liquor brands with outdoor American scenes and Olympic victories.

A couple of roofers are glad to stop working because of the rain. One shifts his Rambo hat up on his head, orders another beer, and hopes it will rain all afternoon.

Talk of Ollie North intermingles with crude jokes about the new wildlife preserve: "Peoria's night life sure improved with them animals around, heh, heh." "Hey, didn't Ollie make them politicians look silly!"

What do you really think about Ollie? It gets almost serious. Finally, Dan the bartender speaks quietly. "Well." Long Pause. "Some of us have a more intellectual reaction. We think he was a military zealot." The last two words are carefully enunciated, almost bitten off.

Despite anticommunism in America, the Cold War is not playing flawlessly, even in Peoria.[3]

Questions

1. How are Soviet and American media systems differently controlled in practice and differently justified in theory?

2. In Olympic boycott coverage, what impressions of Soviet life and policy do American media convey, and what impressions of American life do Soviet media convey?

3. In what ways are Soviet and American press coverage of the 1980 and 1984 boycotts alike and in what ways different? How objective and unbiased are they?

4. Do American and Soviet media carefully quote authorities from the other side and sympathetically explain their positions and reasons?

5. What myths are fostered by media bias to defend policies in the Cold War?

6. Is the ideological spectrum similar in all countries and systems? Are labels of left, center, and right uniform in use and meaning?

7. In ideological domination, what are some of the pressures and limits enforced by Cold War–mindedness?

8. Examine in detail another case in super media where Cold War ideology has a skewing effect: judgments of the value of advertising, arguments over realism and formalism in the arts, debates on deregulation of media, interpretations of the legitimacy of revolution, definitions of nonaligned countries, reasons for the arms race, the need for increased or decreased nuclear weapons, sources of terrorism, and similar cases.

Notes

1. *Los Angeles Times*, May 9, 1984.

2. This boycott research was developed in collaboration with David Goldstein and Robert Mechikoff. The U.S. material was drawn primarily from the *Los Angeles Times*, with additional examples from the *New York Times* and the *Wall Street Journal*. The *Los Angeles Times* was selected because it was the major daily newspaper of the host city for the 1984 games and it has the second-largest weekday and third-largest Sunday circulation among U.S. newspapers, surpassed only by the *New York Daily News* and the *New York Times*. The Soviet material originated from one principal source, *The Current Digest of the Soviet Press*, a weekly publication that translates a wide range of articles and editorials touching on all aspects of Soviet affairs. The *Digest* presents only direct quotations from the Soviet press, either the entire text of an article, editorial, or letter or, if excessive length dictates, verbatim excerpts. The boycott and related topics received substantial coverage in the Soviet Union, and the *Digest* provides a somewhat representative sample of coverage on the topic. Selected articles from various geographical regions outside the United States and the Soviet Union were also examined to represent international reaction to the two Olympic boycotts. Each Olympic reference in the *Los Angeles Times* and *The*

Current Digest of the Soviet Press was examined. Because the U.S. and Soviet press selections are not equivalent matched samples, qualitative rather than quantitative aspects of content were analyzed.

3. This scenario is based on ethnographic research conducted in Peoria, Illinois, in early August 1987.

8

Ritual Analysis:
The Global Olympic Event

It is early fall and still monsoon season in India. On the banks of Lake Nigal outside Shrinigar, Kashmir, several generations of the Baktoo family watch the Olympics.

The blue glow of the television fills the interior of the large two-story home, high in the Himalayan plains, as they follow the pageantry of the opening ceremony. They wait for their Indian Olympic team to be introduced. They speculate whether their countrymen will rise to the occasion and make a good run for the gold in field hockey this time.

They watch, they eat, they talk. A perfectly normal event, except . . .

Like extraterrestrial beings joined by a single exotic beam, the Baktoos are joined with millions of other Indians and literally billions of others around the world. They are sharing in what has become the world's number-one media event, the modern super-mediated Olympic Games. How? What does it do for people? What does it mean?

The modern Olympic games are, via media, the most widely shared regular event in human history. Super media press and broadcast coverage of the Summer and Winter Olympic Games bring people together in Europe, Asia, Africa, the Americas, and places in between, everywhere that modern means of communication are widely available. When the Olympic Games take place during each four-year Olympiad, people from countless countries and cultures *simultaneously* enter into

AUTHOR'S NOTE: *This chapter draws on a ground breaking report for UNESCO (1986),* Global Ritual: Olympic Media Coverage and International Understanding, *under Contract #341304, directed by the author. Fifteen studies by scholars on six continents examined press and broadcast reporting in 17 countries during the Winter and Summer Games. This chapter uses those and other studies but does not represent the opinion of UNESCO or any other organization. Breda Pavlic and Alan Hancock of UNESCO deserve thanks for their interest and support. Valerie Jacobs, Julie Guild, and Robert Mechikoff played important roles in compiling and editing the studies. The full 362-page UNESCO report is available for $25 U.S. from M. Real, Department of Telecommunications and Film, San Diego State University, San Diego, Calif. 92182, USA.*

this mass-mediated sports spectacle. No other event in human history can claim the 2 billion or more live viewers who tune in to the Olympics or the "Copa Mundial del Fútbol." The Baktoos, in entering into the Olympics via media, are doing something not only impossible throughout previous millennia of rich Indian history but inconceivable in most of the world as recently as a generation ago. Anywhere in the world a short century ago, the largest number of people that could share in a single event were those who could be gathered within hearing distance of the human voice. Now millions share daily in media events, such as sports, while they are happening. A "normal" event in modern super media exotically blends technology, entertainment, ritual, and competition on an astonishing scale. In fact, the *scale* of ritual participation in these events marks in some way a new stage in cultural history. For the first time, we can speak of a truly global ritual.

The Super Media Olympics as Global Mythic Ritual

The complexity of the Olympic media event comes together intelligibly when viewed as "ritual" in a cultural studies manner. The scale is new but the style ancient, as mythic-ritual analysis takes us into the many dimensions of technology, text, interpretation, and ideology at play here.

The power of the super media Olympics as a human experience stems from their compelling combination of drama, beauty, achievement, celebrity, and accessibility. The "text" of Olympic coverage reveals this, and the "interpretations" of readers, listeners, and especially viewers confirm it. Who could not be moved by the nearly unbelievable perfection of an Olympic gold-medal performance by an Olga Korbut, Nadia Comaneci, or Mary Lou Retton? Run it in slow motion. Bring up the soaring, pounding soundtrack. Feel those waves of emotion pour over us and through us. Tears well up at the grace, control, movement, reflexes, all welded into a startling achievement. It is visual, dramatic, visual, emotional, visual, accessible. It goes out to and conquers the whole world at once. Super media, what hath been wrought?

The Olympics and Olympic media coverage involve vast international resources and money. The organizational infrastructure and expenses of the mediated Olympics surpass those of many national governments. Terrorists and other factions struggle to make the Olympics serve their political, economic, and special interests. The Olympics hold center stage in the world on a regular basis on an absolutely unique scale.

The ritual force of the Olympics "centers" the attention of the world, however briefly. Mass media coverage makes the Olympic host city—Barcelona, Albertville, Seoul, Calgary, Los Angeles, Sarajevo, Moscow, Lake Placid—the center of the world during the Games. Every Olympic year the attention of the world draws toward one host city as that city, in a kind of Faustian bargain, trades its sports venues, housing, transportation, utilities, and soul to the world for a few weeks, in order to gain eternal Olympic fame and a vastly enhanced tourist and business income. To be the center of the universe, if only for a moment, is a goal difficult for urban promoters to resist.

All this is possible because of the progressive growth of media coverage of the modern Olympic games since their founding in 1896 by Baron Pierre de Coubertin. As early as the 1912 Stockholm Games some 500 accredited journalists attended. Press reporting on the Olympics increased between world wars, as *Chariots of Fire* illustrated in showing the active press and national attention given the 1924 Paris Games. With the addition of radio and film (and even a television demonstration) for the 1936 Berlin Games, newspapers became one among many Olympic media. After World War II, with the BBC coverage of the 1948 Olympic Games and the first sale of television rights for the 1956 Melbourne Games, the Olympics increasingly have become in many parts of the world a television event, with other media playing supporting roles. In 1972, sale of television rights surpassed ticket sales as the number one source of Olympic income. By 1984, the 8,250 accredited media representatives at Los Angeles—more than half of them television personnel—outnumbered the 7,800 athletes.

Mythic Theory and Olympic Functions

"Myth" is clearest in ancient and primitive cultures but is even more intriguing in modern society. Many of the crucial personal and social functions of the global Olympic celebration become clearest when the mediated Olympics are considered as mythic ritual. The primary, overarching function of myth is "to organize meaning in a culture" through vehicles such as the television discourse (Breen & Corcoran, 1982, p. 133). The four functions of myth that together organize meaning in a culture are (1) to provide a perceptual system, (2) to create exemplary models, (3) to mediate conflict, and (4) to make history intelligible. Never before in history has a mythic event been able to perform these functions on the global scale on which the Olympics operate.

First, Olympic myth provides a perceptual system by creating what Breen and Corcoran call the "common social understandings" of a culture, in this case of world culture. This follows Malinowski (1961), who defines myth as a body of narratives that dictate belief, define ritual, and chart the social order of a culture. Olympic media play an instrumental role in shaping mental pictures and global perceptions. The Summer Olympics present representatives of more than 150 countries, the winter Games more than 50 countries. National colors, flags, and costumes are featured. Where else do media audiences meet this diversity and join in celebrating it? For many in the world audience, the Olympics are the only exposure to actual persons and information from many countries of the world, especially those nonsuperpowers absent from the daily headlines.

When Olympic audience members try to think of "the world" or particular foreign countries, it is logical that the perceptual structure they use for doing that comes at least in part from the Olympic experience. Breen and Corcoran write, "As with spectacles, we see the world through the lens of myth, without consciously being aware of the distorting effect of those spectacles." Olympic super media do not provide equal access to the Olympics, nor do the Olympics equally present all countries and people. But the distortions are secondary in importance to the fact that the Olympics provide an unparalleled global breadth of exposure for our perceptual systems.

Second, Olympic myth provides heroic models for imitation. Myth functions, in the words of Breen and Corcoran (1982, p. 128), "to create exemplary models for a whole society in a process that translates a single life-history into an archetype, thereby setting up patterns for imitation." Exemplary models from Olympic media comprise a magnificent pantheon of historic, awe-inspiring gods. The legendary American Indian Jim Thorpe, for his performance in the 1912 Olympics, was proclaimed "the world's greatest living athlete" by the host, the king of Sweden. "Flying Finns" from distance runners Paavo Nurmi and Lasse Viren to ski-jumper Mati Nykanen symbolize a special quality for Finland. Jesse Owens, a Black runner, by winning four gold medals in the 1936 Berlin Olympics, became a heroic antidote to Nazi racial mythology. Daley Thompson and Carl Lewis symbolize heroic achievement, as did Mark Spitz, Jean-Claude Killy, Wilma Rudolph, Babe

Didrikson Zaharias, Cassius Clay (later Muhammad Ali), Sonja Henie, and innumerable others before them. Florence Griffith Joyner with or without her one-legged leotard, placed herself with the great women athletes of all time with her performance in Seoul. Who can forget seeing her break into a smile 30 meters *before* the tape as she set a record in the 100-meter dash? In figure skating in one year alone, the "Battle of the Brians" between Boitano and Orser and the "Challenge of the Carmens" between Katarina Witt and Debi Thomas provided heroic models of victory and effort.

Super media's power to motivate imitations of heroic models creates a level of "media effect" that behavioral empiricism has never been able to comprehend. Current Olympic athletes often have been motivated to direct virtually every detail of their life around a specific goal, largely because of their previous media exposure to role models. A youthful Mary Lou Retton sees an incredible Nadia Comaneci on Olympic television and decides to try to do the same. Without the media exposure to such role models and heroes, there would be virtually no next generation of stars. The effects of super media do not take place only during or immediately after viewing. They may be delayed and cumulative, and yet of immense power. The Olympics via media affect an enormous number of people slightly—those passive audience members around the world—but they also affect a small number of people very profoundly: the would-be Olympians who sacrifice years of their life to the dream of Olympic glory in front of the whole world. Olympic athletes generally know the importance of media in what they are doing. Why are the Olympics more important than the often better run and more thorough World Championships? Debbie Green, the charming setter on the silver-medal-winning United States women's volleyball team in 1984, answers simply, "Because of the media. The media attention is so much greater for the Olympics." The super media Olympics provide mythic heroes for imitation.

Third, Olympic myth can mediate conflict. Breen and Corcoran (p. 130) note that myth can be a language of argument as well as a chorus of harmony, in its handling of conflict both within a culture and between cultures. Relations between the United States and the Soviet Union have been negotiated since 1952 through fluctuating Olympic competitions and boycotts. The "two Chinas" problem between Taiwan and mainland China was mediated in the Olympics of the 1970s, just as the sports isolation of South Africa triggered a Black African boycott in 1976 and additional Olympic pressures at other times. The Olympics represent who is "in" and who is "out" and are a stage for mediating changes in such positioning. The 1972 massacre of Israeli athletes in Munich and the 1968 deaths of Mexican students just prior to the Games exemplify negative outcomes of the Olympic mediation of conflict. The famous and bloody Olympic water-polo confrontation between the Soviets and Hungarians following the 1956 Soviet invasion of Hungary typifies the Olympic role as surrogate warfare, replacing actual death and devastation. Media reporting of conflict between athletes, teams, and countries is part of the mythic negotiating process, sometimes resolving conflicts and at other times intensifying them.

Fourth, Olympic myths make history intelligible. Myths, ancient or televised, serve in "the reduction of the continuous randomness of historical experience to an intelligible pattern" (Breen & Corcoran, 1982, p. 131). The Olympics wrap history around themselves and, in so doing, create a particular sense of a historical past and its culture. Historical mythology surrounds the Games as a direct inheritance of the ancient Greek Olympic Games. Perhaps no other modern institution can claim roots as ancient as 776 B.C., when the Greek Olympics were founded. Those Games continued uninterrupted for a thousand years, until 394 A.D., and surround the modern Games with layers of classical mythology and historical precedent. For millions, untouched by the classics of ancient Greek sculpture, architecture, drama, and philosophy, the Olympic Games serve to bring them into the cultural tradition of classical Greece and its formative role in Western history. It is a history of conquest and exploitation as much as a history of beauty and achievement, but like it or not, the Olympics bring it ritually into the lives of more than half the modern world.

Myths are more uniform than the history on which they are built; they are part of the selective construction of a culture, according to Breen and Corcoran. The mythology of the modern Olympics points up with pride parts of the actual Olympic history while suppressing other parts. The Nazi sympathies of some members of the International Olympic Committee (IOC) in 1936, including its president, Avery Brundage of the United States, are omitted from the mythology, while Jesse Owens's performance at the Berlin Games is foregrounded. The incredible privileges, bordering on bribes, available to the IOC White, male aristocracy as it junkets the world are minimized, while success stories of the underprivileged are emphasized, as in the case of Abebe Bikila of Ethiopia, who won the 1960 Olympic marathon running barefoot. The private fortunes made in connection with Olympic construction, contracts, training programs, endorsements, and so forth recede in Olympic mythology to make room for the achievements of athletes in pursuit of the Olympic motto: "Citius, altius, fortius" (faster, higher, stronger). Olympic mythology turns a blind eye to commercial exploitation of victory, preferring instead to stress the idealistic words of de Coubertin (quoted in Henry, 1984, p. 1):

> The important thing in the Olympic Games is not to win but to take part, the important thing in life is not the triumph but the struggle. The essential thing is not to have conquered but to have fought well. To spread these precepts is to build a stronger and more valiant and, above all, more scrupulous and more generous humanity.

Mythic analysis of Olympic media is especially valuable in raising for conscious consideration the underlying attitudes and practices that are widely accepted but seldom examined. Our contrived histories become "natural" and taken for granted. One culture's "common sense" becomes for its members the universal laws of nature. Ethnocentrism makes the resulting mythology invisible to members of the culture. This is where ideology and hegemony can most easily manipulate people and social forces. Mythic analysis can identify the ideological forms within which we think and act but of which we are largely unaware because they are taken to be "natural." Ideology, world view, and a sense of what is real and true arise increasingly from our media experience.

The scale and penetration of the Olympics around the world make it imperative that we explicitly comprehend what they contain and propose as cultural expressions. The Olympics are a global application of the task assigned by Breen & Corcoran (pp. 135–136) to mythic analysis: "The responsibility of the scholar is founded on the belief that analysis of the mythical dimension of telemediated messages allows us to more fully appreciate how we are shaped into what our culture considers to be moral creatures by both the form and content of television programming."

Idealism and Internationalism in the Modern Olympics

What does global Olympic media coverage mean, specifically in reference to *international understanding?* This question is of paramount importance today in a world capable of blowing itself up many times over. Tiny incidents of international misunderstanding can at any moment mushroom into an Armageddon. Countering these dangers, the modern Olympic Games *are said* to contribute to increased international cooperation. Similarly, the press and broadcasting *are said* to be the healthy fibers in the nervous system of the international body politic. The combination of these two institutions, the Olympics and super media, can play a major role in either enlightening the world or intensifying dark antagonisms of global tension. Which do the Olympics accomplish?

The modern Olympic Games were born and nourished with idealism. In planning the first modern Olympics, Baron Pierre de Coubertin wrote: "The revival of the Olympic games on a basis conforming to the conditions of modern life would bring together every four years the representatives of the nations of the world, and we can well believe that these courteous and peaceful contests would constitute the highest of international activities" (Henry, 1984, p. 23). De Coubertin's successor as president of the International Olympic Committee, Count Henri de Baillet Latour, wrote in 1936: "May the young athletes of the whole world come, through the Olympiad . . . to make an end of hate, to eliminate misunderstanding, and to contribute in association with all men of good will to the restoration of harmony among the peoples" (Henry, 1984, p. 174).

The difficulty of achieving those ideals became apparent when, following the 1936 Nazi-hosted Olympics, the 1940 and 1944 Olympics were prevented by World War II. Controversy haunts the modern Olympics in many forms, including nationalism, terrorism, commercialism, boycotts, politicization, and drugs. Viewing the Olympics from Great Britain, Garry Whannel (1984, p. 30) calls the Olympics "the ultimate media festival." To Whannel the Olympics both are a source of popular pleasure and "reproduce a series of ideological themes concerning competitive individualism, attitudes to gender-roles and capabilities, and nationalism and racial stereotypes." What emerges from a close look at central features of the Olympics as they are transmitted by media and received around the world?

Olympic Television: Economics, Technology, and Interpretations

Television and the Olympics have developed a symbiotic relationship in which each benefits profoundly from the other. The Olympics provide television with some of its most popular programming, programming that is popular in many countries among widely varied audiences. Television provides the Olympic movement with by far its largest single source of income, income that helps pay the bills for hosting the Olympics, running the International Olympic Committee, and operating the international sports federations that regulate and stage the competitions. Historically, in fact, television income in the second half of the 20th century has seemed almost to take over the Olympic movement.

A comparison of the dollar costs of staging the Summer Olympic Games with the dollar income from Olympic television revenues reveals the fundamental economic importance of television to the Olympics. Table 8.1 summarizes the trend in that direction.

Economically, in the quarter century between Rome and Los Angeles, television grew from an insignificant spectator to a central participant in the Olympic movement. In Rome in 1960, television provided only 1 of every 400 dollars of the cost of hosting the Olympics. In 1972, 1 of every 50 dollars was from television. In Moscow in 1980, 1 dollar of every 15 came from television revenues. By 1984 television provided more than half the income necessary to host the Summer Games.

Television's economic clout turned the 1988 Seoul Summer Olympics into the "Breakfast Games," with almost half the final events held before 2 P.M. for the benefit of North American prime-time viewing, in return for an NBC payment to Seoul of $300 million. The saying "He who pays the piper calls the tune" implies that Olympic television will inevitably influence the nature of future Olympics as well. Even the smaller Winter Games have become part of the television-Olympics symbiosis. ABC's payment of $309 million to Calgary in 1988 covered more than one third of the host city's expenses and led to extending the games from 12 to 16 days and the inclusion of three, rather than two, weekends. As a result, despite the poor showing of American athletes and the clutter of incessant advertisements, ABC-TV won the February network ratings sweep for the first time in four years. NBC did not fare as well with the Seoul Summer Games in September, as its ratings were low, and NBC had to return $30 million dollars in make-good advertising credit to sponsors. The large Olympic television rights fees

TABLE 8.1 Olympic Expenses and Television Rights Fees (in $1,000,000 U.S.)

Rome, 1960	$$$$$$$$	400
	.	1
Munich, 1972	$$$$$$$$$$$$$	650
	X	13
Moscow, 1980	$$$$$$$$$$$$$$$$$$$$$$$$$$$$$$	1,400
	XX	95
Los Angeles, 1984	$$$$$$$$$$	500
	XXXXX	275
Seoul, 1988	$$$$$$$$$$$$$$$$$$$$$ . . . $$$$$$$$$$$	3,100
	XXXXXXXX	400

NOTE: $ = cost of staging Games; X = television revenues.

remain a major portion of Olympic finance. CBS paid $243,000,000 for rights to the 1992 Winter Olympics in Albertville, France. NBC paid $401,000,000 for American rights to the 1992 Summer Games in Barcelona.

What countries pay the highest price for and telecast the most hours from the Olympic Games? As Table 8.2 shows, the United States in particular and the advanced capitalist countries in general pay the lion's share of fees and consequently have the greatest influence in tailoring the Games to television. The 1988 Seoul rights fees were similarly proportioned, although Japan's price increased. The United States paid $300 million, Japan $52 million, the European Broadcasting Union (EBU) $28 million, and Australia $7 million, as the largest investors in Olympic television.

A comparison of rights payments (in the middle column) and television hours (in the right column) by country and region reveals interesting differences. Australia paid a hefty $1.91 per TV set and transmitted a full 310 hours of Olympic television coverage. The United States paid the second-highest rate, $1.67 per TV set, and used only 187 hours of the 1,400 hours of events covered by ABC as host broadcaster. In contrast, the EBU, which covers most of Western Europe, paid only $.17 per TV set, and the OIRT of Eastern Europe bought the rights for only $.05 per set. In quantity of coverage, six other broadcast groups provided more hours of Olympic coverage than ABC did to its domestic U.S. audience, despite ABC's role as host broadcaster.

TABLE 8.2 1984 Summer Olympics Television Coverage

Broadcaster	Rights Payments (in $1,000,000 U.S.)	Total Hours Transmitted
ABC—USA	225.0	187
EBU—Europe	19.8	380+
Japan	18.5	235
Australia	10.6	310
Canada	3.0	220
OIRT—Warsaw Pact	3.0	0[a]
OTI—Latin America	2.1	200+
New Zealand	.5	210
Philippines	.4	100
UNRTA—Africa	.2	N.A.

[a]Transmission was canceled following Soviet boycott.

While television subsidizes the Olympics and the Olympics meet television's programming needs, these economic realities are complemented by an unmatched technological feat in television's actual transmission of the games.

Olympic coverage through television and other media is a near-miracle of sophisticated technology and complex organization. The 237 sports represented at the Seoul Summer Games were available in hundreds of countries in versions customized to meet the preferences of viewers in each country. The host broadcaster, the Korean Broadcasting System, provided an audio-video "world feed" from each venue. National television services received this feed at the World Broadcasting Center, where they could tape it or transmit it back to their country via satellite. That, in turn, could be telecast live or taped and edited for later replay. Announcer play-by-play or commentary could be added at any point. In addition, a national television service could add its own "unilateral" coverage by placing additional cameras and commentators at a venue, as NBC did for many events in Seoul. The resulting Olympics received in any one country might be completely different from the televised Games as seen in another country or region.

Extensive arrangements are necessary for any one country to transmit Olympic coverage from the host city back to the home country

(Morohoshi, in UNESCO, 1986). As an NHK producer, Morohoshi saw from the inside the complexity of negotiations for broadcast rights, agreements with the host broadcaster, signal transmission routes, an innovative "split-screening" technique, accreditation, visas, accommodations, transportation, daily briefings, program production, and the myriad other details behind the scenes of bringing Olympic coverage to distant audiences. Olympic television coverage is a technological and logistic challenge of the first order. Japan, with its 36 million television homes and long involvement in the Olympics, had paid $18.5 million for rights to carry 235 hours of coverage of the 1984 Summer Games. The resulting coverage was viewed by 90 percent of the Japanese public; two thirds watched the Olympics five days a week or more. Japan's commitment to Olympic television was even more tangible in 1988 when Japan paid almost three times as much, $52 million, for Olympic television rights for the nearby Seoul Summer Games.

How do viewers read and interpret the Olympic television text? Gunter and Wober (in UNESCO, 1986) surveyed the Olympic television audience in Great Britain. First, they found that 65 percent of British viewers reported watching the Olympics, the same percentage as had viewed Wimbledon tennis, England's major international sports event. The quantity of coverage seemed adequate. Of 1,076 survey respondents, 57 percent judged the amount of television coverage to be about right, 22 percent said there was too much, and 6 percent said there was too little. In regard to international understanding, more than half (53%) agreed that "having sports competition between nations has, up to now, generally helped countries to get on together better"; *but* 20 percent disagreed and 28 percent were not sure. In other words, almost half (48%) of the British respondents were not convinced of the positive international contribution of the Olympics. Asked whether Olympic scheduling should be dictated by needs of athletes or of television, 49 percent favored athletes, 16 percent thought they should be equal, and only 2 percent thought that television networks should dictate Olympic timing. Overall, British viewers liked the amount of coverage, favored the Olympics as a sporting event rather than a television show, and by a slight margin saw positive internationalist results.

In Australia more than *85 percent* of the urban population reported watching the Summer Games, a good response for the country that paid the highest rate per TV set for Olympic rights. The most common criticisms by Australian viewers charged that there were too many commercials and that the coverage was biased toward the United States and Australia.

Many Third World countries receive only limited Olympic television coverage and do not feel deeply involved (see Reyes Matta, in UNESCO, 1986; Ugbuoajah, in UNESCO, 1986), while others, such as India, have rapidly increased Olympic television viewing. In India, Khurana (in UNESCO, 1986) examined Olympic television audience viewing and preferences in 1984. A survey of 2,700 viewers in five major cities found the 58 hours of Olympic coverage were avidly followed. For example, *89 percent* of the television sets were tuned to the opening ceremony for the Summer Games in July. Of course, since the second channel in India did not begin transmitting until September 1984—after the Olympics were concluded—the only alternative was to watch tapes or turn off the set. Moreover, the 89 percent who viewed were from among those Indians with television sets, at present a minority of the Indian population. But, like increasing numbers of Third World countries, India made its population eyewitnesses to the making of sports history through the magic of television.

Broadcast and press reporting in the Mediterranean country of Cyprus reflects the marginal feeling that less powerful countries have toward the super media Olympics. Television and newspaper debate in Cyprus in 1984 emphasized the issues of the Olympic boycott and commercialism. The acrimony of the boycott, the absence of reporting on arts and countries instead of just athletic competition, and the minimal coverage of Cypriot athletes all tended to prevent the Olympics from being a significant instrument of international understanding in Cyprus (Avraamides, Constantinedes, & Nicolaou, in UNESCO, 1986). In contrast to the Eurovision Song Contest, for example, where each country receives equal media exposure, Cyprus in Olympic media coverage found itself "a minor participant on the sidelines," watching star athletes competing in a big city in the developed world. Cypriots also regretted the absence of media coverage of the fine arts connected with the Olympics, art in the form of painting, sculpture, music, and literature having been an official area of Olympic competition from 1912 to 1948.

International Press Reporting of the Olympics

Newspapers, magazines, radio, and other media report on the Olympics in addition to television's dominant coverage. Close examination of newspaper coverage raises numerous issues and concerns.

The content of newspaper coverage in Spain, for example, presented conflicting positions on issues of Olympic commercialism, nationalism, politicization, and gender and on the image, frequently negative, of Los Angeles and North American culture (Moragas Spa, in UNESCO, 1986). With Barcelona then a candidate city to host the 1992 Summer Games, the Spanish press gave special scrutiny to the role of the host city. The charges that the Los Angeles Games were too commercialized and too nationalistic were widely discussed. A high level of Olympic interest was evident in Spanish coverage, not surprising considering that Barcelona was a candidate city and that the president of the International Olympic Committee, Juan Antonio Samaranch, was from Barcelona.

What points of view and values are stressed in Olympic reporting? A study (Splichal, in UNESCO, 1986) from the host country of the 1984 Winter Games, Yugoslavia, examined the representation of "Olympic values" in four daily and four weekly Yugoslavian publications. Who were cited as sources of Olympic information and what themes were prevalent? Most evaluative assertions in the press were by Yugoslavs rather than others, more evidence of the nationalism common to Olympic reporting throughout the world. The assertions were also more commonly by journalists rather than sports figures. Thematically the assertions were similar for the Winter and Summer Games, except that coverage of the Winter Games in Yugoslavia was understandably more positive. Winter Games coverage emphasized confidence in the Olympic ideal and Sarajevo's hosting, while Summer Games coverage centered on the Soviet boycott and the commercialization of the Games.

Newspaper reporting in three countries in East Asia—China, Korea, and Japan—found slightly different national motives for Olympic participation in each country but a high level of interest throughout (May and Suzuki, in UNESCO, 1986). For the Chinese, Olympic sports symbolize the nation's move toward modernization. For the Koreans, Olympic performance states their readiness to assume a major role in the international community and in the Olympic movement. For the Japanese, Olympic success reflects their international role, despite the absence of an Olympic superstar to match their status as an economic superpower. Like many other parts of the world, newspapers in the three East Asian countries wrote of world peace and international friendship in their editorials but in their sports news focused instead on the triumphs of the nation's own athletes.

Less developed countries in Latin America and Africa remind us that the Olympic feast is not shared equally by all nations and peoples.

Newspaper coverage in six countries in Latin America gave less space to the Olympics than did other parts of the world (Reyes Matta, in UNESCO, 1986). This seemed to reflect the slight participation and success of Latin American Olympians. Latin America won only 3.6 percent of the medals in Los Angeles. Among Latin American countries, Brazil and Mexico were the only ones to win more than three medals, and those two countries also gave the Olympics far more press coverage than did other countries. For Latin American tastes, *fútbol* (soccer) was too little emphasized in Los Angeles. Fernando Reyes Matta concluded that Latin American Olympic coverage portrayed "a spectacle where one could only look at the richness of the North from the impoverishment of the South."

African interest in and access to the Olympics parallel those of Latin America, despite the famous Olympic victories of African distance runners. From a close examination of Nigerian Olympic media coverage, Frank Ugbuoajah (in UNESCO, 1986) estimates that not much more than 10 percent of the population of the largest Black nation in the world were exposed to the Los Angeles Games. Economics, the scarcity of electrical power, and illiteracy prevent most Nigerians from following the Games. Neither electronic nor print coverage is readily accessible to most Nigerians. The Summer Games were well reported in the Nigerian press, although Ugbuoajah found that photographs were underused and the coverage was "overwhelmingly male-oriented." Roughly equal attention was given to national and international Olympic activities. Like politicians in many countries, the Nigerian head of state capitalized on the publicity value of Olympic success by publicly identifying himself with the Nigerian medal winners; on their return he donated the equivalent of 1 million naira ($1.2 million U.S.) to the Nigerian Olympic committee. Still, the Olympics in Nigeria were available for the most part only to an urban English-speaking elite.

These specifics of Olympic media coverage take on a larger significance when we recall that the Olympics at present are the leading expression of an emerging form of "global culture" that crosses traditional cultural boundaries. International media events play dominant roles in semiotically expressing and structuring this global culture. There are pervasive long-term effects of these Olympic Games, royal weddings, May Day parades, a Live Aid concert, papal visits, funerals of heads of state, hijackings and hostages, assassinations, and other events widely covered by international media. The Olympics, World Cup football, and other media events constitute the "high holidays" of world culture, as Elihu Katz suggests.

The mass-mediated Olympics reveal a great deal about our world today, much as the major feast of any culture symbolizes numerous dimensions of that culture and its people. Ideology, world view, and a sense of what is real and true are all rooted in mythic structures of which we are largely unaware and which arise increasingly today from our media experience. Careful analysis can lay bare these myths.

Nationalism in Olympic Media Coverage

What countries most emphasize the Olympics as indicated by the amount of newspaper coverage devoted to the Games? From an international sampling of newspapers, the poorer countries of Latin America provided the least coverage, and those with special interests in hosting the Olympics provided the most. The United States gave about 6.5 percent of newspaper space to the Games, a middle to low-middle percentage (see Table 8.3).

Given the variety of newspaper types and emphases around the world, the variety in Table 8.3 is not surprising. The differences do not appear to correlate with the size or ideology of a country, nor do they correlate with region of the world or stage of development. The more important point concerns the aggregate statistics—namely, that developed countries appear to devote from 6 to 15 percent of their total newspaper copy to concurrent coverage of this single super media event.

Which countries appear to be most self-centered in their Olympic coverage? Table 8.4 is an approximation of an "index of nationalism" in media coverage. What percentage of each country's coverage was devoted to reporting that country's own athletes and teams?

Countries with higher percentages, toward the bottom of Table 8.4, had the least "internationalist" content in their 1984 Summer Olympics press coverage. Again the findings do not correlate with size, ideology, stage of development, or regional loyalties. The two East Asian powers,

TABLE 8.3 Percentage of Newspaper Space Devoted to Olympics

Country	0%	5%	10%	15%	20%	
Uruguay	XXX					1.4
Brazil	XXXXX					2.6
Ecuador	XXXXXX					3.4
Mexico	XXXXXX					3.4
Chile	XXXXXX					3.7
United States	XXXXXXXXXXX					6.5
China	XXXXXXXXXXXXX					7.3
Japan	XXXXXXXXXXXXXXX					8.5
Nigeria	XXXXXXXXXXXXXXXXXX					11.0
Cyprus	XXXXXXXXXXXXXXXXXXXX					12.5
Yugoslavia	XXXXXXXXXXXXXXXXXXXX					12.5
Spain	XXXXXXXXXXXXXXXXXXXXXXXXX					15.0
Korea	XXXXXXXXXXXXXXXXXXXXXXXXXXXX . . . XXXXXX					34.3

TABLE 8.4 Percentage of Own Country's Athletes in Olympic Coverage

Country	0%	20%	40%	60%	
Mexico	XXXXXXXXX				17.1
Yugoslavia	XXXXXXXXXXXXX				25.5
Japan	XXXXXXXXXXXXXXXX				31.3
Spain	XXXXXXXXXXXXXXXX				31.4
Chile	XXXXXXXXXXXXXXXXX				33.5
Australia	XXXXXXXXXXXXXXXXXXXXXX				44.0
Brazil	XXXXXXXXXXXXXXXXXXXXXXXXX				49.6
Nigeria	XXXXXXXXXXXXXXXXXXXXXXXXXX				52.2
China	XXXXXXXXXXXXXXXXXXXXXXXXXXXXXX				60.0
Korea	XXXXXXXXXXXXXXXXXXXXXXXXXXXXXXXXXXXXX				76.0
United States	XXXXXXXXXXXXXXXXXXXXXXXXXXXXXXXXXXXXXXXX				79.0

China and Korea, scored high in nationalism, but neighboring Japan scored very moderately.

Unfortunately, many charges about narrow American nationalism and self-centeredness appear confirmed by these findings. In measuring nationalistic emphasis, content analysis of a selected sample of U.S. papers found that 79 percent of coverage concerned Americans, the highest percentage of any of the countries studied. The sample included five random days during the Summer Games as reported by the *New York Times,* the *Chicago Tribune,* and the *San Francisco Examiner.* Of course, the United States in 1984 was the host country for the Summer Games, the United States entered large Olympic teams, and American athletes won by far the most medals. These special circumstances might be the cause of self-centered U.S. press coverage. However, even the less thoroughly Americanized Winter Games in 1984 found 73 percent of the reporting in American newspapers concerned with American athletes. The United States did not dominate the medal tally in those games, held in faraway Sarajevo. Yet, the "nationalism" of United States press coverage was only 6 percent less than for the Los Angeles Summer Games. Only once did any of the American newspapers on any of the sample dates in 1984 devote less than 50 percent of its coverage to American athletes. On that one date, the *New York Times,* likely the most international of major American newspapers, devoted a mere 37 percent of its Olympic coverage to Americans. That proved to be the exception, not the rule, in the United States press.

Critics of the United States have charged that America is not sufficiently sensitive to the different circumstances and preferences in other countries, a myopia that allows the United States to slip into an "ugly American" foreign policy of self-righteous dominance. American Olympic newspaper coverage reveals a comparatively narrow self-centeredness in the United States. Cultural studies might suggest that there is a direct connection in the "structure of feeling" in American culture between the nationalistic Olympic coverage and political insensitivity on the international level. The internationalism of American power would seem to call for a press system that was also internationalistic and reflective of the world, rather than a self-centered focus on only American interests and concerns.

Mexico was the least nationalistic of the sampled countries and Yugoslavia next lowest. Spain proved less nationalistic than many. It is difficult to discern patterns in these results. A qualification on interpreting these data is the fact that unfortunately, in this study, neither Soviet nor Eastern bloc countries were sampled, nor were Arab nations as such.

Olympic Media Contributions to International Understanding

What can we say then, pro and con, of the contributions of Olympic media coverage to international understanding and cooperation? The Olympics do perform positive functions. Functionalist theories of medium, message, and audience lead to generalizations about the ability of the Olympic media coverage to contribute to social integration at an international level. From the information available on Olympic media coverage around the world, we find three positive social functions performed by such super media.

First is the *communal* function: *Olympic media coverage provides a single event in which seemingly everyone in the world can share. The super media Olympics is the international tribal fire around which we gather to celebrate shared events and values.*

Countries all over the world, in varying degrees, give evidence of substantial media coverage and public interest in the Olympics. The Olympics, through the media, bring humans together communally in a unique and uniquely human tribal ritual. In most countries of the world, people gather around the glow of television screens, with sports pages and other media within easy reach, and celebrate collective values, dreams, and achievements. Anthropological explanations of ritual behavior and mythic power in Olympic media-related behavior tell us much (MacAloon, 1984). An almost mystic global oneness is achieved during special precious moments of Olympic media magic.

The Olympic special moments are sometimes expected, but at other times they delight by surprise as well. The intense beauty of the much anticipated gold medal performance by British skaters Jayne Torvill and Christopher Dean in 1984 provides a different experience than does sharing the overwhelming excitement of watching and hearing a tense Yugoslavian crowd await its first-ever Winter medal winner. In the 1984 Sarajevo Winter Games, young Yugoslavian skier Jure Franko comes on screen as one of two Yugoslav giant-slalom entrants with a chance of winning Yugoslavia's first Olympic skiing medal ever. Franko's second and final run is magnificent and vaults him into first place as his countrymen, lined along the ski run by the thousands, roar him on. Then, all are forced to wait tensely as favorite Andreas Wenzel takes his turn but fails to beat Franko! The camera catches Franko's joyous smile and anxious tears as the wait continues. Finally, previous Olympic winner Max Julen bests Franko's time. Immediately Franko steps over to hug and congratulate Julen, despite knowing, in the words of ABC's Frank Gifford, that "his gold just turned to silver." Still, the Yugoslavian medal creates palpable joy and fulfillment for the happy Franko and his ecstatic fans visible to the world. Afterward, the event takes on an exalted, mythic beauty as highlights, sometimes in slow motion and with musical soundtrack, recall that Camelot moment of Franko's along with those of Torvill and Dean and the other Winter Olympic victors. In this and other ways, Olympic media are capable of creating amounts of shared international communion.

Olympic athletes and spectators from all over the world convene in one spot in each Olympics, visually symbolizing the billions around the world convened technologically by Olympic coverage in television, radio, newspapers, magazines, and other media. If 100,000 people are present in an Olympic stadium, it would take 20,000 of these stadiums to represent the 2 billion television viewers. Spectators in the Olympic stadium at an opening or closing ceremony are sometimes organized as a vast card section, forming national flags from all over the world and symbolizing both the diversity *and* unity of the mediated Olympic experience. Flags of the world fly around the Olympic stadium while a television crane hovers above as a kind of Almighty Holy Spirit validating and sanctifying all that is below. The Olympics via media are communal.

Second is the *informative* function: *The Olympics tell us about each other. Olympic media coverage exposes audience members to other peoples and countries, providing direct access to information and personal representatives of usually remote human groupings from other countries and continents.*

In the midst of the immense amount of information concerned specifically with sports, Olympic media coverage contributes directly to international understanding by providing actual data and portrayals from distant peoples and countries, countries that may otherwise be reported on only because of disasters, conflicts, or wars. In the United States, for example, ABC for the opening ceremonies at times presents a map and actual political information about each country as its Olympic team marches in, information presented by ABC's news anchor rather than a sports announcer. In most instances, only a tragic earthquake or coup would occasion for that country such a prominent news report.

As a more vivid and specific example, the breathtaking performance of Nadia Comaneci in 1976 made "Rumania" a personal reality for persons around the world who otherwise might never hear of or meet someone from that small country. When the United States and the People's Republic of China were establishing new relations in the early 1970s, an effective instrument was "Ping-Pong diplomacy," which brought sports teams from each country to the other for competitions. Spectators, live or via media, and players can get to know each other in the pools and stadiums, on the tracks and playing fields, away from the distorting stereotypes of ideological, ethnic, and political antagonisms. In international sports competitions, viewers, listeners, and readers encounter the achievements of another people and are usually exposed to something of the other's appearance, language, dress, and style. Olympic media provide international information.

Third is the *interactive* function: *The Olympics literally bring us together. Olympic events and media require interaction between nations and cooperation between different peoples.*

Organizing Olympic athletic competitions and media coverage requires extensive real physical interaction and collaboration among widely scattered persons. International sports federations, national broadcasters and sportswriters, Olympic officials, cities bidding for the Olympics, ministries of state—all these and many more are forced to collaborate in the staging and transmitting of the Olympics and similar world-class competitions. This interaction is indirectly shared by audiences who follow the Olympics through press and broadcast reporting. In this organizing unity, there is tension, but the demands of presenting the events force organizers to set aside differences and collaborate. Olympic audience surveys find public awareness of the Olympics as a kind of surrogate warfare, but they also find public comfort in the fact that it is surrogate, and not actual, warfare.

The variety of national costumes in the Olympic ceremonies and the diversity of athletes on the field represent the complexity and success of Olympic interaction. The Picasso drawing used on the cover of the program for the opening ceremony of the 1984 Summer Games shows human figures dancing around the dove of peace, an image reminiscent of the rhetoric of Pierre de Coubertin and other founders of the modern Olympic Games. The Olympics and Olympic media coverage create healthy interaction on many levels.

Inequality and Hegemony in the Olympic Media Contribution

What of the negative side of Olympic media and international understanding? The perspectives of critical theory, political economy, and cultural studies raise questions about Olympic media. If Olympics and media exist within specific institutional contexts and represent specific ideological content, then what are some of the limitations and disadvantages that Olympic media coverage presents for international understanding? If super media carry an ideological message and if they exercise hegemonistic pressure, what is the deep structure of the perspective and value system being presented?

The first negative aspect is *unequal participation: Access to Olympic media coverage is not equal in all parts of the world. Technologically rich and literate countries receive abundant coverage while poor countries receive little.*

The research reports from Africa, Latin America, and other Third World regions (UNESCO, 1986) remind us of the disparities in access to the Olympics. Citizens of Nigeria, one of the richest countries in Africa, have only about a 1 in 10 chance for direct access to the Olympics through readily available media. Latin Americans see, hear, and read little of the Olympic Games. Cypriots, living near the seat of the ancient Games, Olympia, have some delayed television coverage but generally appear to feel relatively removed from the modern super media Olympic Games. However, countries and urban elites rich in communication technology, electricity, and literacy have access to the Games in abundance, just as their athletes have greater access to sophisticated training systems and support structures.

This disparity is not the fault of the Olympics so much as it is a reflection of more general imbalances in developmental stages in countries and regions. But, because Olympic media coverage depends on the given infrastructures of distribution, even Olympic promoters must admit that the Olympic feast is not equally shared by all. A high proportion of those with access to television in Third World countries actually watched the Games, but what of the still larger numbers of people in those countries who have no access to television? The Olympic torch does not burn for those without television, computers, satellites, high-speed presses, and the affluence to support them.

An expanded role for private enterprise in the Olympics does not aim at solving this problem and may increase it. Increased revenues from television and from commercial sponsorship of Olympic Games and teams may make the Games self-supporting but even less equally available to poorer countries and people. The IOC and Olympic host cities sell television coverage to countries for whatever the market will bear. They have shown an impressive willingness to provide a television feed for little more than a token fee to African, Latin American, and some Asian broadcasters. But as the commercializing drive reaches more deeply into the Olympic movement, those who cannot pay large sums and support large technical organizations at the Olympics may receive less attention. Pay cable and other commercializing ventures may remove segments of the public from access to parts of the Games.

Another question of inequality arises in regard to gender representation in the Olympics. The 56 hours of coverage of the 1984 Winter Olympics by ABC-TV in the United States gave 77 percent of the time to men's events and only 23 percent to women's events, a clear imbalance (Jacobs & Real, in UNESCO, 1986). However, when male-only sports such as ice hockey are eliminated and only equivalent men's and women's events are compared, the disparity in airtime in favor of men's events is only 56 percent to 44 percent. This means that the Olympic events are more gender-imbalanced than the television coverage. Given the powerful role modeling and perception shaping that Olympic media can perform, the question of how much coverage is given to the female half of the human race is significant. The Olympics are generally, in fact, the best of major television sporting events in terms of gender balance, but even the Olympics are far from parity in this regard.

A second negative is *nationalistic media gatekeeping: Selective national coverage and nationalistic commentaries interfere with the internationalism of the Olympic ideal.*

Audience surveys from various countries (UNESCO, 1986) report evidence of chauvinistic nationalism in the selection of Olympic coverage by media gatekeepers. The Olympics are not so much a single event transmitted to the world as a smorgasbord of many events, from which countries select their own partial version of "the Olympics." Technological sophistication now makes it possible to so individually tailor coverage for a given country that studies find some audience members (for example, in Australia, Japan, and the United States) specifically request that coverage not be so confined to only that country's participation in the Olympics. The "index of nationalism" used in Table 8.4 indicates how this factor can be measured and where this tendency may be most problematic.

In addition, ethnocentric and jingoistic reporter comments (in, for example, India and the United States) were on occasion found to exacerbate this problem of nationalistic gatekeeping. Broadcast announcers capture the zeal fans feel for their own athletes and sometimes extend this to more fanatic lengths of "us against the world." Announcer complaints about judges and scoring, as one example, can feed into a feeling of nationalistic grudges that can carry over into persecution-aggression complexes in other international affairs. In some countries, reporting of such confrontations as that between middle-distance runners Mary Decker and Zola Budd follows the international allegiances and ideologies of the reporting nation more than the facts of a case. Antagonisms are often already there. But with the increased power of super media in the Olympics, extreme care must be taken that Olympic coverage not be the occasion for stereotyping and exaggerated animosity toward other sovereign nations, athletes, and citizens.

Olympic ideals do not exclude patriotism, but they oppose any extreme patriotic fervor, which slips into chauvinism and ethnocentrism. Team uniforms, national anthems, and flags all symbolize the national identities of Olympic athletes. Are there equally powerful symbols of internationalism? National identities and symbols add impact to the competition and drama of the Games. Selective national coverage and announcer commentaries, together with written reports, create an invigorating national focus in each country as it follows the Games. If such coverage ignores the traditional values of fair play, sportsmanship, and respect for opponents, it cheapens the Olympics and becomes a disservice to that country and all others.

Further complicating the issue of nationalism, politicians around the world have discovered the self-promotional role of the Olympics in the age of super media. When the Olympics were still a minor newspaper event in Los Angeles in 1932, the president of the United States did not attend, instead sending his vice-president to officially open the Games. After the expansion of Olympic media coverage into a major global ritual, in Los Angeles in 1984 the president of the United States not only attended and opened the Games, he also argued for more television time to make a longer statement but was refused. Given the scale and drama of Olympic event coverage, nationalism and partisanship are always waiting to creep into Olympic media coverage.

The third negative aspect is that *sporting competition separates people: Olympic sports divide winners from losers instead of unifying the participants as other rituals might.*

This problem is a structural one, related to the issue of nationalistic zeal discussed above. Claude Levi-Strauss (1966) has pointed out that rituals have the "conjunctive" effect of taking subjects previously separate and unifying them, while games have the "disjunctive" effect of taking initially equal individuals or groups and separating them into winners and losers. The Olympics contain both games and ritual and so do both, but is the proportion correct? Similarly to Levi-Strauss, Johann Galtung (1982) questions the value of Olympic competition because of its conflict-based deep structure; he fears that Olympism imposes on multicultural world participants a set of Western structures of space, time, knowledge, nature, and relationships.

A major portion of sports' ability to generate drama and excitement comes from "the thrill of victory, the agony of defeat." The victory of one must be at the expense of the defeat of another. Participants have antagonistic goals that are structurally opposed to each other in sporting competition. There is no win/win alternative but only the win/lose outcome. All collaboration and friendship in sports must transcend this negative tension. When it does not, sport becomes counterproductive to human relationships, both between the immediate competitors and among fans, possibly spilling over into nonsport activities.

The world's most popular sport, soccer, provides abundant examples of tragic outcomes. In the 1967 "Soccer War" between Honduras and El Salvador, the countries' armies tried to settle what their *fútbol* players could not. In 1985, 40 died in the charge of Liverpool soccer fans against Italian fans. In 1964, 264 died following an Argentina-Peru match. The Olympics have been spared such sport-generated fatalities, although deaths of Israeli athletes in 1972 and Mexican students in 1968 illustrate the dangers of the Olympic occasion. Audience surveys in the United Kingdom and the United States, among others, found that Olympic fans get into an "us against the world" spirit of competition as well as into international friendship.

In contrast to sports, other ritual activities take previously separate persons or groups and attempt to unite them symbolically. Ritual initiations and religious ceremonies typically unite participants within a community. In the context of super media ritual, when an international treaty is signed, as in the case of the 1975 Helsinki accords, media attention can focus on the cooperation intended to achieve benefits, or "victory," for all participants. Commentaries may point to negative and competitive aspects, but the structure of the event lacks the internal conflict base present in sports.

In sporting events, conjunctive ritual activities are necessary, surrounding the disjunctive competition. Competitors shake hands before fighting, stand during a national anthem, and together observe the referee's decisions; and gracious victors congratulate losers. In many world-class competitions, it is customary to exchange small gifts between team members—a medallion, a flag, a pin—before the game and to line up for mutual handshaking after the game. When international competitors also share activities off the field, as happens even with Soviet and American team members at times, the full potential for friendship and understanding is realized but only by ritually rising above the formal sporting competition.

The Olympics live and breathe ritual, but it is possible for Olympic media coverage to slight the ritual and underscore the competition. A brief biography (called an "Up Close and Personal" segment by ABC) of a foreign athlete at home accomplishes what off-the-field shared activities do for competitors, but such segments can be expensive and difficult to produce, so they appear relatively seldom. The Olympic host city also hosts an Olympic arts festival, but how much of that celebration of nonsporting excellence receives significant media coverage and promotion? The Cyprus UNESCO study in particular noted that Olympic arts and culture festivals receive little major media attention.

A massive United States opinion survey by the Annenberg School of Communications at the University of Southern California found profound audience satisfaction in Olympic rituals and pageants. Fortunately, the magnificent and widely viewed opening and closing ceremonies celebrate international peace, understanding, cooperation, and friendship. Less fortunately, most other Olympic rituals during the Games—medal ceremonies, flags, uniforms, and anthems—tend to be nationalistic rather than international in character.

Conjunctive ritual and disjunctive sport must be properly mixed, not only in the Olympics themselves, but also in the super media version of the Olympics that is received in every corner of the world.

This leads to a modest *suggestion* from the UNESCO report (1986) to Olympic and media officials: *In addition to the opening and closing ceremonies, identify or create more international ritual activities for universal Olympic media coverage.*

The opening ceremony and closing ceremony are now almost the exclusive Olympic occasions for expressions of *inter*nationalism. The days of competition in between lack such expressions. In addition, the

different selection of events coverage by different countries elimi-
nates even a common frame of reference among Olympic media audiences. The inherent structure of sport separates people into victors and
vanquished. These negatives can be countered. Additional universal
coverage of certain rituals, as well as universal coverage of certain
appropriately international competitions, can move the mass-mediated
Olympics closer to the international ideals of Baron Pierre de Coubertin
and the many other noble contributors to the modern Olympics.

With understanding and care, perhaps the magic moments of genuine
internationalism in Olympic media coverage can be increased. Live by
satellite, Chinese children in front of the Great Wall of China and
Egyptian children in front of the Great Pyramid were shown joining all
the Olympic athletes and 90,000 people in the stands in Los Angeles at
the opening ceremony to sing together:

> "Reach out and touch
> somebody's hand.
> Make the world a better place,
> if you can."

In this and other ways, Olympic media coverage can and does, despite
its shortcomings, help to fulfill the high calling of the United Nations
charter: "To develop friendly relations among nations based on respect
for the principles of equal rights and self-determination of peoples."
The Olympics create McLuhan's "global village," however briefly and
however superficially. The text of the super media Olympics is a rich
one, the interpretations many, and the ideology complex. But even as
we point out its imperfections, we must be profoundly grateful for its
international global potential for the human family.

> On the high Himalayan plain, the Baktoos cheer the Indian team and
> mutter curses against the opponents. They want victory for Indian pride.
> They want a cause for celebration.
> Next they turn to other events. They watch an African runner, an East
> Asian gymnast, a West European swimmer, a Soviet volleyball team, an
> American cyclist. Their minds fill with foreign names and countries. They
> are moved by the grace and achievement of these strangers.
> The coverage ends. They turn their attention back to the immediate
> village, their day-to-day chores.
> But their consciousness will never be quite the same. They have seen
> more. They have met new people. They have traveled far away vicariously.

They know and share their world in a new sense.

The global ritual of super media Olympics has entered their lives and will return.

Questions

1. Why are certain Olympic memories so vividly etched in our individual and collective memories?

2. What mythic functions do the Olympics perform for global culture?

3. How important is television, technologically and economically, to the worldwide Olympic movement?

4. How large an audience do the Olympics reach in various countries, and what different responses result?

5. Which countries spend the most money on Olympic television, and which countries provide the largest proportion of Olympic newspaper coverage?

6. Which countries devote the largest percentage of their newspaper coverage to their own athletes and teams and the smallest to the athletes and teams of other countries?

7. How do the super media Olympics contribute to international understanding and cooperation?

8. What inequalities and negatives are present in the super media Olympics?

9. Can the super media Olympics be said to be reflecting and creating a new world culture?

9

Conclusions:
Super Media—the Clouded Mirror

In his somber classic on the gradual descent into the mystical madness of schizophrenia, Ingmar Bergman exposes the complexity of digging beneath the surface of life. Surrounded in the film by a seemingly loving but remote husband, a fragile younger brother, and a philosopher father, the central character, Karin, searches their isolated island and relationships for anchors of normality but moves further and further into her own world of sounds, voices, and images. In the climactic scene, the noisy helicopter descends in the background to remove her to a hospital, as she describes with terror her sensation of a repulsive black spider coming toward her and climbing up the front of her body. The spider bears subtle resemblances to her clinically distant husband, a doctor. But no one explanation of her problem or its interpretation does justice to the potential meanings evoked by Bergman's moving images. Bergman calls this film *Through a Glass Darkly*, basing it on St. Paul's words (1 Corinthians 13), "We see now through a glass darkly but then face to face. Now I know in part; then I shall understand fully."

In our understanding of super media, there can be no doubt that we see them now only "through a glass darkly." Our window onto media is yet blurred and smudgy, but we do see the outlines and some details of what is there. It is difficult for human understanding to do better than this in any form of complex or profound knowledge. We use our theories and research as a lens through which to comprehend and direct external reality. What understanding we can manage in this way of biology, history, life, and meaning, we must treasure and make the most of.

"Through a glass darkly" also describes the vision that media provide us of the world. It is epistemologically and metaphysically impossible for media of communication, no matter how sophisticated, to present a complete picture of the world; only the world itself does that. When we use language, science, myth, or any other symbolic system to represent and manipulate reality, we can accomplish great things, but we never ultimately symbolize through these glasses better than "darkly." Claims that super media provide objective, undistorted access to reality and the world are patent nonsense.

Media themselves are often referred to as a "mirror of society," a similar and problematic analogy. In fact, the more accurate contemporary translation of Paul's phrase is "we see in a mirror dimly" (Revised Standard Version). The "glass" of the King James translation referred to the filmy mirrors of former times, not to windows at all. The implications of *window* and *mirror* are similar, but in our emphasis on "our media, ourselves," the value of a mirror for self-knowledge has special importance. This mirror, of course, is clouded, giving us less-than-perfect reflections of our human selves, individually and collectively.

But several problems in this metaphor go beyond the cloudiness of the mirror. First, the metaphor tends to absolve media creators, managers, and audiences of responsibility by implying that, whatever media do, they "simply reflect" the world. This ignores the centuries-old tradition of expecting leadership and social responsibility from our media: the mirror should not reflect only the worst or only what is but also what could be. Second, as Tony Bennett (1982, p. 287) points out, the mirror analogy implies a dividing line between reality or society, on one hand, and the world of representation, on the other. It implies that media exist above society and passively mirror it rather than forming an active and integral part of it.

It is this last point, perhaps as much as any, that sets cultural studies apart from the media theory and research traditions that contrast with it. The pluralist and behavioral effects tradition tends to isolate media as a variable and to separate off specific media behavior from other behavior. It removes from context certain aspects of reality for controlled observation and measurement, free of confounding variables. In the larger view, which cultural studies insists on, it is precisely the "confounding variables" that demand attention. The institutional context of production, the latent messages in a text, the group identities of the audience, the history and cultural context in which each discrete communication act takes place—these constitute the larger importance of how super media and society interact.

The clouded mirror of super media provides at one and the same time an immediate experience of existence in itself—in the darkened theater, from the printed page, through the small screen, or however—and a second-hand experience of other existence: the information or story and characters in the electronic or printed text. Whatever is loved or hated in the larger reality of the world passes through into this text and makes the immediate experience itself the dialectic conflict of love and hate as well. Different analyses emphasize different aspects of this complex experience of our media, ourselves.

Critical, Structural, and Ritual Characteristics of Super Media

There are characteristics within super media, as well as within contending analyses of them, that trigger our complex love-hate reaction to them. These general characteristics emerge from particular case studies of super media based on empirical, structural, critical, and ritual analyses. We may not see yet all the finer details of super media and the world they represent in our clouded mirror, but general shapes and contours emerge along with some specific points.

Specifics of the case studies contain the positives and the negatives of super media. Presidential assassinations and the other cases indicate the variety of problematics worthy of examination. The Academy Awards illustrate the promotional thrust behind super media, the industrial style of production with its dispersion of accountability, and the mixture of anticipation and cynicism with which viewers await the awards. The telling differences between popular films directed by men and women indicate how ideological distortions become embedded in dominant discourses that serve a historically advantaged group. Likewise, Bill Cosby's recoding of ethnicity indicates the scale of need for ideological correction and the limitations of correction possible through dominant industrially structured media systems. The way the Cold War creeps in to bias the representations of popular Hollywood films, of televised hearings, and of superpower Olympic boycotts illustrates the distorting potential of ideological forces and special interests in the overall portrayal of social reality. In these cases, as well as in the global ritual of the Olympics, massive institutions and networks interact to produce the event, varied texts are transmitted with multiple levels of meaning, audiences decode these texts with unique interpretive frames, and particular interests are served or submerged.

The broader general contours of our media, ourselves, appear notably in four characteristics of super media.

Characteristic One: Super Media Pervade Human Culture

Key concepts from empirical media-centered research clarify the role and influence of media in modern society. Super media "diffuse information" and bring about the "adoption of innovations," whether in agriculture, medicine, family planning, or other areas of human social life. Even more commonly than acting as agents of social change, however, the media of communication serve to "reinforce the status quo." Media give to cultural oddities—guns and social violence, greed and personal instability—the aura of common sense. With this cultural tool, media professionals act as "gatekeepers," reducing the impossible mass of daily information to that simple set of stories and facts available to us each day as "news" or "information" or "entertainment." The resulting media agenda of reported and emphasized news, in turn, "sets the agenda" for the public and for individuals: media tell us what to think about. They "confer status" and "enforce social norms."

Empirical research also reveals that super media function indirectly as well as directly. Media reach "opinion leaders" who, in turn, influence the "less active segments" of the population in the classic "two-step flow" of media through personal influence. Media "cultivate values" among the population: heavy television viewers differ from light viewers on a number of attitudinal items, especially in their perception of the "mean-world syndrome" of crime, violence, police, and victimization. Super media "gratify audience needs" by offering an abundance of cultural products to choose from, an abundance but not necessarily a true diversity. In the age of super media, a member of the public may choose her television program, her movie, her music, her fashion, all for her own unique reasons but always within the given mass-mediated culture.

Only a genuine hermit can avoid super media today. One can ignore, but not be spared, the billboards along the highway or the Musak in the elevator. Empirical behaviorism became immobilized on the false question of "powerful" versus "limited" media effects. The question is a methodological and theoretical trap. As "cultural norms" theory argues, media today provide a near-total environment in which we live rather than specific stimuli causing or not causing only specific behaviors. Super media are pervasive today as cultural factors.

Characteristic Two: Super Media Structure Human Experience

The study of language and other sign systems has revealed the profound extent to which human understanding is not a given but is a construction. From chaotic experience, we construct meaning and purpose. *Structuralism* shows how, along with language and other sign systems, super media are sources of the structure of meaning that is our lives.

The texts of super media are tools with which we express our lives. They teach us language through which we express our existence. The texts are "polysemic" and speak to different people in different ways. The acting that inspired DeNiro's Oscar also inspired Hinckley's attempt on Reagan's life. Texts are multilayered and complex in how they enable us to structure our lives. Super media provide us with "popular genres" and "consensus narratives" to identify in our own lives the central plot structure, the primary characters and their development, the context and complications, the expectations, the heroes and villains, the peaks and valleys. With such structures, we construct meaning in our life and in all life.

The semiotics of "advertising and consumerism" in super media also construct our culture, creating commodity fetishes and false consciousness unimaginable even to Marx himself. In a bad mood? Go shopping. Want status? Upgrade your wardrobe, your car, your house, and if necessary, your mate. The once-dreaded Seven Deadly Sins have become the motivational deep structure of a culture of commercialism and consumption. Greed, lust, gluttony, envy, and all the once-presumed "lower" urges have been reclaimed from Hieronymus Bosch and made all-gorgeous through the cleverness of Madison Avenue, Wall Street, and their advertising. The classic Beatitudes—blessed are the meek, the humble, the peacemakers—have no place in this promotional culture of super media narcissism and consumption.

Super media provide a vehicle for constructing our interpretations of existence and social reality also with regard to gender and ethnicity. Fortunately, Remus, Rastus, and Sambo have been largely replaced by Bill Cosby, Whitney Houston, and Michael Jordan in our "recoded ethnicity," but the range of Black roles is still restricted primarily to comedy, music, and sports. Similarly, the narrowness of females' confinement to hearth and home, to being wife and mother, is changing dramatically in life and media, but males remain dominant in ownership and management, as well as in portrayals and interpretations in super media. Media offer opportunity and new structures, but they also offer stereotypes and "symbolic annihilation" of subordinate populations such as nonmales and non-Whites.

Structuralism and semiotics account for the mechanisms through which we construct our human experience. They raise our consciousness of our expressive abilities through signs and symbols, and they raise troubling questions about the power and adequacy of media-constructed representations and signifying practices today.

Characteristic Three: Super Media Express Social Power

Critical research reveals to us the extent to which super media can "concentrate social power" in fewer hands. In such circumstances, media become self-serving industries "colonizing the mind" in the service of narrow and exploitive political-economic interests. Media express, not just individual creativity, but also institutional priorities, and restrictive management shrivels up the expressiveness and diversity of super media. Not human justice and growth broadly and humanely conceived, but economic profit and control come to dictate the structures and practices of oligopolistic super media decision making.

The *contraction of ownership* of super media within capitalism may be the counterpart to oppressive party control of super media within socialism. By 1986, 25 companies controlled 60 percent of daily newspaper circulation in the United States. The percentage of group-owned television stations rose steadily from 35 percent in 1954 to 73.3 percent in 1983. In television production during the 1970s, the leading 20 firms increased their audience share from 59 to 74 percent in prime-time programming and from 97 to 100 percent in network daytime programming. Between 1981 and 1986 the number of corporations controlling most of the business in newspapers, magazines, television, books, and motion pictures was reduced from 46 to 29 (Sterling, 1984, p. 66; and Gudorf, 1988).

Not only is contraction in media ownership continuing, but ownership is "demographically narrow," not at all reflective of the general population. Only 1.7 percent of television stations in the United States are owned by minorities or minority companies, and only 1.9 percent of radio stations are (Sterling, 1984, p. 56). Minority-owned stations are seldom large stations. Small women's presses are sometimes shut out by bookstore chains owned increasingly by publishing giants. Ownership contraction means that "the chief means of information and consciousness formation in our society are controlled by a smaller and smaller number of powerful wealthy white men" (Gudorf, 1988). The self-interest of this group is opposed to any major shift in gender, ethnic, or other arrangements in society.

The resulting ideology expressed through super media favors, for example, economic profit over social commitment, abstract corporations over actual workers, anticommunism over internationalism, opportunism over principle. As Ted Koppel (1987) says, television would have Moses come down from the mountain with "The Ten Suggestions." The media foster a relativism that is less that of situational ethics than that of commercial exploitation. A child may be failing in school but learning the lessons of private-enterprise super media: brand names, celebrity endorsements, commercial jingles, and corporate logos.

Critical analysis examines how "hegemony" of the dominant over the subordinate is maintained through super media. It is engineered not through coercion but through a more sophisticated mechanism, consent. The public seeks at the altar of super media its daily bread and learns to accept willingly burnt toast. The hegemony of super media restricts the voices heard through media and removes from consciousness multiple alternatives for social growth and development.

Yet, the media are not someone else's cultural instruments; they are ours. Critical research seeks to empower individuals to criticize and resist all that is inadequate in media and yet to do so without losing the ability to appreciate, express, and celebrate through media.

Characteristic Four: Super Media Celebrate Human Solidarity

Despite their imperfection and shortcomings, or perhaps because of them, super media remain in essence us, the people. Media are truly the "expressive face of culture," warts and all. Collectively we express ourselves, our political-economic institutions, our ideology, our fears and anxieties, our hopes and dreams.

Our place and time in history, our myths and memories past and future, are raised by super media to a higher level for us to see, hear, read, and feel anew. "Ritual analysis" shows how the media provide us access to and participation in our collectively shared symbols and acts. These media celebrations reflect and reinforce many of our most cherished moments and values—in the signing of an arms control agreement, in the launching of a space flight, in the selection of a new president.

Ritual analysis also shows us the paraliturgical role of super media as sources of "liminal transcendence." Just as preliterate ritual marked a passage to a higher state, so super media offer opportunities for life, death, and resurrection, esthetically, emotionally, and culturally. Super media can be vehicles of transcendence, sources of the "esthetic experience" sought by artists and visionaries of all stripes. Maturely understood and critically appreciated, the media can take us beyond a threshold—the liminal—and return us more whole and human, more gentle and redeemed.

Additional characteristics of super media operate at levels other than the four above. For example, super media are *technological*. The technologies and techniques of electronic and print media make possible the phenomenon of super media and are determining of its central characteristics. But technologies are means only, whereas the characteristics above are both means and end—structuring, expressing, celebrating. Super media today are also more *institutional* than individual. The achievements of Spielberg, Coppola, Bochko, Cosby, or Disney are collective endeavors in ways that those of Dostoevsky or Shakespeare were not. But that institutional characteristic is not uniformly present in super media and is subsumed under the characteristic of super media as expressing social power. Super media also have the characteristic of being *ideological* instruments as well as information conveyers, but that too is a subset of the social-power characteristic. The four characteristics of super media outlined above parallel again the structure of Chapter Two and this book as a whole: super media examined through the lens of cultural studies, which draws in turn from empiricism, structuralism, criticism, and ritual analysis.

The Struggle for Mastery of Super Media

The clouded mirror of super media can transfix victims as if they were watching only the shadows on the wall in Plato's cave. But super media have liberating potential as well. Understood, appreciated, and acted upon, the media and their contents can be made to serve human ends and not merely their own technological, economic, or other purposes. The challenges are similar in North America and the United Kingdom, in Australia and New Zealand and throughout the English-speaking world, in India and Japan and Western Europe, and, in varying ways, in socialist and in Third World countries. To achieve "mastery" of super media, persons and groups must take action.

1. *Share and control* the experience by developing and using a *reference group* or interpretive community that offers reliable points of departure for interpreting and utilizing super media. Parents are now

taught to watch television *with* their children to help interpret the experience and moderate its influence (Lickona, 1985). Satisfied film-goers select movies to attend under the recommendations of trusted film critics with articulated standards and serious judgments. News readers debate their interpretations of current affairs with informed and thoughtful acquaintances, columnists, and intellectuals, wherever these may be found. The lone individual facing super media without a refer-ence group becomes immensely more susceptible to misrepresenta-tions, fads, and superficiality. Against this, a consciously selected interpretive community can be consulted as a "significant other" guid-ing super media selection, evaluation, and implementation.

2. *Take responsibility* and *grow* through exposure to stimulating super media experiences. There is a time and place for passivity and even stupidity in super media if these are kept within limits and in perspec-tive. *The Rocky Horror Picture Show,* "Monty Python," televised wres-tling, and schizoid drive-time radio all have a place in human life if balanced with less trivial pursuits. But it is absolutely imperative in a healthy super media diet to *include experiences that enlighten, inform, and provide knowledge,* as well as those that simply entertain. Mental and emotional health requires attention, care, and discipline just as physical health does. It is likewise imperative to seek out super media experiences that *confront social problems* and create discomfort, as well as those that comfort us and reinforce the status quo. Super media should afflict the comfortable as much as they should comfort the afflicted.

3. *Think critically* and *conduct research* on super media. Massive subsidized research and rationalization serve entrenched interests in super media, but only idealistic initiative is available to gather infor-mation and use insights to serve higher interests. Cultural studies encourages us to think seriously and systematically about strengths and inadequacies in super media texts, contexts, institutions, and influ-ences. Whose interests are being served? How? Why? "Imagination" takes on special importance because of the ability of super media to "naturalize" ideologically as necessary and permanent what is little more than accidental and temporary. Without questioning, criticism, and imagination, super media can make arbitrary social arrangements and perceptions into an expectation of what all society and common sense should be. If we cannot question and imagine, we cannot appre-ciate or improve.

4. Act to *democratize super media* and empower people to use and influence media and express themselves through media. This requires an effort to find or create alternative media, to organize for positive change, to influence super media policies, regulations, and practices. From making programming for local cable access to lobbying regulators, one must produce as well as consume, act as well as react, if our super media are to become what they might be. Media leaders are trained with technical skills more than public ideals and easily conform to commercial imperatives and constraints that undershoot the proclaimed goal of serving "the public interest, convenience, and necessity," in the idealistic phrasing of the 1934 Federal Communications Act. Different super media practices and public policies might more responsibly serve the interests of varied groups that constitute the public. What are they and how can they be implemented without destroying other benefits? How can we collectively improve or replace the cracked and smudgy mirror in which we now, sometimes enthusiastically and sometimes despairingly, see ourselves?

5. *Appreciate and enjoy* the experience of super media alongside the other joys and satisfactions that life has to offer. Super media are not only a challenge but also an opportunity. Together with the experience of existence itself, super media are not so much a problem to be solved as a mystery to be lived. Through super media we can discover insight, meaning, and transcendence, but only to the extent that we are determined to use them for those ends. Like a peak experience in any field of human endeavor, a well-selected, appreciated, and acted-upon super media experience has everything to commend it. The availability of easy distractions and cheap thrills through super media does not invalidate the greater achievements possible through it.

To take responsibility for super media is not a requirement for only the academic or policy specialist, the public official, or the media professional. It is an expectation of any educated adult in the same way that appreciation of music, art, literature, architecture, and other cultural expressions is expected. To train mere technocrats, without cultural self-consciousness, is impermissible at any level of education, as traditional curricula for elementary, secondary, and postsecondary education have always contended. To prepare knowledgeable and conscious participants in super media and cultural expression of all kinds requires experience of ideas, criticism, and questioning that are classical components of the self-actualized adult and mature citizen.

The democratization of culture, together with the power of self-determination of peoples, remains an overt goal for many who identify themselves within the tradition of cultural studies. The democratization of culture requires that the public not be reduced to audiences of passive receptors but be elevated to active participants who responsibly play a part in creating and expressing culture. The democratization of culture requires that each citizen have an equal voice in the varied creations and disseminations of culture, that wealth and privilege not be allowed to narrow the range available to subordinate groups or dictate which expressions shall thrive and which shall be suppressed, that the democratic tradition of "one person, one vote" not be lost to the commercial substitute of "one dollar, one vote." The democratization of culture also requires that each citizen reach maturity with a developed sense of personal and public welfare, nurtured by family, school, and work experience, so that the majority will not be tyrannical, the self-selected culture not be brutal. The democratization of culture does not stand in opposition to standards of quality and excellence; rather, it calls for more direct attention to those standards in service to all peoples.

The case studies developed in these pages indicate how far we have to go in creating a balanced, democratic culture *and* how far we have come in creating extensive media instruments and varied cultural expressions. The cup of super media is both half full and half empty. At this point in history, super media, with their central role in facilitating or inhibiting the self-determination of conscious people, have accomplished much, but they are decisively short of any goal state of ideal performance.

This clouded mirror of super media, which has made such qualitative as well as quantitative differences in the way we interact and advance, can serve our needs or can be reduced to serving its own insatiable appetite for profit, sensation, and expansion. Super media change the way we perceive distance, time, and identity. Super media direct our consciousness and our group memberships. Super media carry us into the future or shackle us in the past. In the words of Cassius, "The fault, dear Brutus, is not in our stars, but in ourselves." A rich super media culture requires neither isolation nor relativism. As Mahatma Gandhi reflected: "I do not want my house to be walled on all sides and the windows stuffed. I want the cultures of all lands to be blown about my house as freely as possible, but I refuse to be blown off my feet by any one of them" (Hamelink, 1983a, p. 37).

The hundreds of sources cited in these pages and thousands more unnamed place us on the shoulders of giants as we move forward. Whether we creatively and effectively take advantage of this powerful position is the critical choice that cultural studies and super media offer us. The accumulated knowledge of 70 years of super media research tells us how, through this glass darkly, we live and breathe and have our being.

In the clouded mirror, we find our best selves and our worst selves. We have reason to love super media for what they bring to our human lives as information or art, as diversion or inspiration. We also have reason to hate super media for the inhumanity and destruction. The same vehicles that bring us Hemingway and Faulkner, Milos Forman and Ingrid Bergman, Garrison Keillor and Florence Griffith Joyner, also bring us slasher movies, Morton Downey, Jr., and *Hustler.* Great art, captivating music, engrossing sports, useful data, and challenging political information share airtime and copy space with ecological disintegration, a demographic explosion, political oppression, and economic disequilibrium. The task, personally and collectively, is to appreciate the best, change the worst, and struggle to recognize the difference. If these pages aid in the effort to improve our super mediated vision, to wipe away dirt from this glass, then they will have served a worthwhile purpose: to make our media and ourselves more human, in our own time and place, within an awareness of all times and places.

Questions

1. What are advantages and disadvantages of conceiving of super media as a mirror of society, as the glass through which we see darkly?
2. How do empiricism, structuralism, criticism, and ritual analysis lead to four generalizations about the character of super media today?
3. What are the goals of the democratization of culture?
4. What actions, taken from cultural studies, assist in achieving mastery of super media?
5. Why understand our super media as ourselves?

References

Abercrombie, N., Hill, S., & Turner, B. S. (1980). *The dominant ideology thesis*. London: Allen & Unwin.

Alexander, J. (1986). The "form" of substance: The Senate Watergate hearings as ritual. In S. Ball-Rokeach & M. Cantor (Eds.), *Media, audience, and social structure* (pp. 243–251). Newbury Park, CA: Sage.

Altheide, D. (1976). *Creating reality: How TV news distorts events*. Newbury Park, CA: Sage.

Arlen, M. (1979, April 30). The air: The big parade. *New Yorker*, pp. 122–124.

Arnheim, R. (1933). *Film* (L. M. Sieveking & F. D. Morrow, Trans.). London: Faber and Faber.

Attwood, W. (1987). *The twilight struggle: Tales of the Cold War*. New York: Harper & Row.

Atwood, R., & McAnany, E. (Eds.). (1986). *Communication and Latin American society*. Madison: University of Wisconsin Press.

Bach, S. (1985). *Final cut*. New York: New American Library.

Bakhtin, M. (1981). *The dialogic imagination: Four essays* (C. Emerson & M. Holquist, Trans.). Austin: University of Texas Press.

Balazs, B. (1952). *Theory of the film: Character and growth of a new art* (E. Bone, Trans.). London: Dobson.

Ball-Rokeach, S., & Cantor, M. (Eds.). (1986). *Media, audience, and social structure*. Newbury Park, CA: Sage.

Barnouw, E. (1975). *Tube of plenty: The evolution of American television*. New York: Oxford University Press.

Barnouw, E. (1975). *The sponsor: Notes on a modern potentate*. New York: Oxford University Press.

Barthes, R. (1972). *Mythologies* (A. Lavers, Trans.). New York: Hill & Wang.

Barton, L. (1982). Coverage of the 1980 Olympic boycott: A cross-network comparison. In W. Adams (Ed.), *Television coverage of international affairs*. Norwood, NJ: Ablex.

Barton, L. (1983). *The Olympic boycott of 1980: The amalgam of diplomacy and propaganda in influencing public opinion*. Unpublished doctoral dissertation, Boston University.

Bazin, A. (1967). *What is cinema?* (H. Gray, Trans.). Berkeley: University of California Press.

Beck, M. (1984). *Secret contenders: The myth of Cold War counterintelligence*. New York: Sheridan Square.

Becker, S. L. (1985, Fall). Critical studies: A multidimensional movement. *Feedback*, pp. 24–27.

Bell, D. (1961). *The end of ideology*. New York: Basic Books.

Bell, D. (1976). *The cultural contradictions of capitalism.* New York: Basic Books.

Bennett, L., & Edelman, M. (1985). Toward a new political narrative. *Journal of Communication, 35*(4), 156–171.

Bennett, T. (1982). Media, "reality," signification. In M. Gurevitch, T. Bennett, J. Curran, & J. Woollacott (Eds.), *Culture, society and the media* (pp. 287–308). London: Methuen.

Bennett, T. (1986). Gramscian ideology and popular culture. In T. Bennett, C. Mercer, & J. Woollacott (Eds.), *Popular culture and social relations.* Milton Keynes, England: Open University Press.

Bennett, T., Mercer, C., & Woollacott, J. (Eds.). (1986). *Popular culture and social relations.* Milton Keynes, England: Open University Press.

Bennett, T., & Woollacott, J. (1986). *Bond and beyond: The political career of a popular hero.* London: Macmillan.

Berger, J. (1980). *Ways of seeing.* New York: Penguin.

Berlo, D. (1960). *The process of communication.* New York: Holt, Rinehart and Winston.

Bigsby, C. W. (Ed.). (1975). *Superculture: American popular culture and Europe.* Bowling Green, OH: Bowling Green University Popular Press.

Biskind, P. (1983). *Seeing is believing: How Hollywood taught us to stop worrying and love the fifties.* New York: Pantheon Books.

Bloom, A. (1987). *The closing of the American mind.* New York: Simon & Schuster.

Bordenave, J. D. (1988). An answer, and more. *Journal of Communication, 38*(2), 144–146.

Bottome, E. (1986). *The balance of terror: Nuclear weapons and the illusion of security, 1945–1985.* Boston: Beacon Press.

Braestrup, P. (1983). *Big story.* New Haven, CT: Yale University Press.

Breed, W. (1952). Social control in the newsroom. In W. Schramm (Ed.), *Mass communication* (pp. 178–194). Urbana: University of Illinois Press.

Breen, M., & Corcoran, F. (1982, June). Myth in the television discourse. *Communication Monographs, 49,* 128–140.

Breen, M., & Corcoran, F. (1986). Myth, drama, fantasy theme, and ideology in mass media studies. In B. Dervin & M. Voigt (Eds.), *Progress in communication sciences* (Vol. 7, pp. 195–224). Norwood, NJ: Ablex.

Brockriede, W. (1970). *Moments in the rhetoric of the Cold War.* New York: Random House.

Browne, N. (1984, Summer). The political economy of the television (super) text. *Quarterly Journal of Film Studies,* pp. 174–182.

Cantor, M. (1971). *The Hollywood TV producer: His work and his audience.* New York: Basic Books.

Cantor, M. (1980). *Prime-time television: Content and control.* Newbury Park, CA: Sage.

Cantril, H. (1940). *The invasion from Mars.* Princeton, NJ: Princeton University Press.

Carey, J. (1968). Harold Adams Innis and Marshall McLuhan. In R. Rosenthal (Ed.), *McLuhan: Pro and con* (pp. 270–308). New York: Funk and Wagnalls.

Carey, J. (1975a). Communication and culture. *Communication Research, 2,* 173–191.

Carey, J. (1975b). Canadian communication theory: Extensions and interpretations of Harold Innis. In G. Robinson & D. Theall (Eds.), *Studies in Canadian communications* (pp. 27–59). Toronto: McGill University.

Carey, J. (1979a). Mass communication research and cultural studies: An American view. In J. Curran, M. Gurevitch, & J. Woollacott (Eds.), *Mass communication and society* (pp. 409–425). Newbury Park, CA: Sage.

Carey, J. (1979b). *The roots of modern media analysis: Lewis Mumford and Marshall McLuhan.* Paper presented at the meeting of the Association for Education in Journalism, Houston, TX.

Carey, J. (1981a). Graduate education in mass communication. *Communication Education, 28*, 282–293.

Carey, J. (1981b). *Foundations of modern communication research.* Address to the International Communication Association, Minneapolis.

Carey, J. (1985). Overcoming resistance to cultural studies. In M. Gurevitch & M. Levy (Eds.), *Mass communication review yearbook* (Vol. 5, pp. 27–40). Newbury Park, CA: Sage.

Carey, J. (Ed.). (1988). *Media, myths, and narratives: Television and the press.* Newbury Park, CA: Sage.

Carey, J., & Christians, C. (1981). The logic and aims of qualitative research. In G. Stempel & B. Westley (Eds.), *Research methods in mass communication.* Englewood Cliffs, NJ: Prentice-Hall.

Carey, J., & Kreiling, A. (1974). Popular culture and uses and gratifications: Notes toward an accommodation. In E. Katz & J. Blumler (Eds.), *The uses of mass communication* (pp. 225–248). Newbury Park, CA: Sage.

Carpenter, E., & McLuhan, M. (Eds.). (1960). *Explorations in communication: An anthology.* Boston: Beacon Press.

Cassirer, E. (1944). *An essay on man.* New Haven, CT: Yale University Press.

Cassirer, E. (1946). *The myth of the state.* New Haven, CT: Yale University Press.

Castro, J. (1988, January). Women in television: An uphill battle. *Channels*, pp. 43–52.

Cawelti, J. (1976). *Adventure, mystery, and romance.* Chicago: University of Chicago Press.

Cervantes, M. (1937). *Don Quixote of the Mancha* (T. Shelton, Trans.). New York: Collier. (Original work published 1605)

Chomsky, N. (1982). *Towards a new Cold War.* New York: Pantheon Books.

Chomsky, N. (1983). *Modular approaches to the study of the mind.* San Diego, CA: San Diego State University Press.

Chomsky, N. (1987, Winter). Propaganda systems: Orwell's and ours. *Propaganda Review*, pp. 14–18.

Chorbajian, L., & Mosco, V. (1981). 1976 and 1980 Olympic boycott media coverage: All the news that fits. *Arena Review: The Institute for Sports and Social Analysis, 5*, 3–28.

Cirino, R. (1972). *Don't blame the people.* New York: Random House/Vintage Books.

Cirlin, A. (1983, October). Superpower rhetorical confrontation over KAL incident. *Exetasis*, pp. 3–34.

Cockburn, A. (1987). *Corruptions of empire.* New York: Methuen.

Collins, R., Curran, J., Garnham, N., Scannell, P., Schlesinger, P., & Sparks, C. (Eds.). (1986). *Media, culture and society: A critical reader.* Newbury Park, CA: Sage.

The compact edition of the Oxford English dictionary (2 vols.). (1971). Glasgow: Oxford University Press.

Comstock, G., Chaffee, S., Katzman, N., McCombs, M., & Roberts, D. (1978). *Television and human behavior.* New York: Columbia University Press.

Contreras Arellano, J. A. (1987). *Influncia de la televisión en la formación del hombre latinoamericano*. Caracas: Universidad Central de Venezuela, Ediciones de la Biblioteca.

Cook, P. (1979). Approaching the work of Dorothy Arzner. In P. Erens (Ed.), *Sexual stratagems: The world of women in film*. New York: Horizon.

Cosby, W. (1973). *The wit and wisdom of Fat Albert*. New York: Windmill Books.

Cosby, W. (1975). *Fat Albert's survival kit*. New York: Windmill Books.

Cosby, W. (1986). *Fatherhood*. New York: Doubleday.

Cripps, T. (1983). "Amos 'n' Andy" and the debate over American racial integration. In J. O'Connor (Ed.), *American history/American television: Interpreting the video past*. New York: Ungar.

Curran, J., Gurevitch, M., & Woollacott, J. (1982). The study of the media: Theoretical approaches. In M. Gurevitch, T. Bennett, J. Curran, & J. Woollacott (Eds.), *Culture, society and the media*. London: Methuen.

Curran, J., & Seaton, J. (1981). *Power without responsibility: The press and broadcasting in Britain*. Glasgow: Fontana Books.

Curran, J., Smith, A., & Wingate, P. (Eds.). (1987). *Impacts and influences: Essays on media power in the twentieth century*. London: Methuen.

Current Digest of the Soviet Press. (1980, April–August).

Current Digest of the Soviet Press. (1984, April–August).

Czitrom, D. J. (1982). *Media and the American mind: From Morse to McLuhan*. Chapel Hill: University of North Carolina Press.

Davis, G. (1985). "Trusting the culture": A commentary on the translation of African-American cultural systems to media imaging technology. In B. Reagon (Ed.), *Black American culture and scholarship: Contemporary issues* (pp. 99–105). Washington, DC: Smithsonian Institution.

DeFleur, M. (1966). *Theories of mass communication*. New York: McKay.

DeFleur, M., & Ball-Rokeach, S. (1982). *Theories of mass communication* (4th ed.). New York: Longman.

Delia, J. (1987). Communication research: A history. In C. Berger & S. Chaffee (Eds.), *Handbook of communication science* (pp. 20–98). Newbury Park, CA: Sage.

Denby, D. (1987, August 3). Ollie North, the movie. *New Republic*, pp. 59–60.

Dickey, D. W. (1978). *The Kennedy corridos: A study of the ballads of a Mexican American hero*. Austin: University of Texas Press.

Doane, M. A., Mellencamp, P., & Williams, L. (Eds.). (1984). *Re-vision: Essays on feminist film criticism*. Frederick, MD: University Publications of America.

Dorman, W. (1988). Mass media and international conflict. In T. Govier (Ed.), *Selected issues in logic and communication* (pp. 65–72). Belmont, CA: Wadsworth.

Eco, U. (1983). *The name of the rose* (W. Weaver, Trans.). San Diego, CA: Harcourt Brace Jovanovich.

Eco, U. (1986). *Travels in hyperreality: Essays*. San Diego, CA: Harcourt Brace Jovanovich.

Efron, E. (1971). *The news twisters*. Los Angeles: Nash.

Eisenstein, E. (1979). *The printing press as an agent of change: Communications and cultural transformations in early modern Europe*. New York: Cambridge University Press.

Eisenstein, E. (1983). *The printing revolution in early modern Europe*. New York: Cambridge University Press.

Eisenstein, S. (1942). *The film sense* (J. Leyda, Ed. and Trans.). San Diego, CA: Harcourt Brace Jovanovich.

Eliade, M. (1959). *The sacred and the profane: The nature of religion.* San Diego, CA: Harcourt Brace Jovanovich.

Elliot, P. (1986). Intellectuals, the "information society" and the disappearance of the public sphere. In R. Collins, J. Curran, N. Garnham, P. Scannell, P. Schlesinger, & C. Sparks (Eds.), *Media, culture and society: A critical reader.* Newbury Park, CA: Sage.

Elliot, P., Murdock, G., & Schlesinger, P. (1986). "Terrorism" and the state: A case study of the discourses of television. In R. Collins, J. Curran, N. Garnham, P. Scannell, P. Schlesinger, & C. Sparks (Eds.), *Media, culture and society: A critical reader.* Newbury Park, CA: Sage.

Ellul, J. (1986). *Propaganda: The formation of men's attitudes* (K. Kellen & J. Lerner, Trans.). New York: Knopf.

Enzensberger, H. (1974). *The consciousness industry.* New York: Seabury Press.

Epstein, J. (1974). *News from nowhere: Television and the news.* New York: Random House.

Ewen, S. (1983). The implications of empiricism. *Journal of Communication, 33*(3), 220–231.

Eysenck, H., & Nias, D. (1978). *Sex, violence and the media.* London: Temple Smith.

Farber, J. (1982). *A field guide to the aesthetic experience.* Los Angeles: Foreworks.

Fejes, F. (1984). Critical mass communication research and media effects: The problem of the disappearing audience. *Media, Culture, and Society, 6,* 219–232.

Fishbein, L. (1983). *Roots:* Docudrama and the interpretation of history. In J. O'Connor (Ed.), *American history/American television* (pp. 279–305). New York: Ungar.

Fishwick, M. (1970). Entrance. In M. Fishwick & R. Browne (Eds.), *Icons of popular culture.* Bowling Green, OH: Bowling Green State University Popular Press.

Fishwick, M. (1978). Icons of America. In R. Browne & M. Fishwick (Eds.), *Icons of America.* Bowling Green, OH: Bowling Green State University Popular Press.

Fiske, J. (1982). *Introduction to communication studies.* New York: Methuen.

Fiske, J. (1986). Television: Polysemy and popularity. *Critical Studies in Mass Communication, 3*(4), 391–405.

Fiske, J. (1987). *Television culture.* London: Methuen.

Fiske, J., & Hartley, J. (1978). *Reading television.* New York: Methuen.

Frey, J. (1984, March). *The United States and Great Britain: Responses to the 1980 boycott of the Olympic Games.* Paper presented at the meeting of the Sport Sociology Academy, AAHPERD, Anaheim, CA.

Fullerton, D. (1984). *Current issues in United Nations Decade on Women.* Occasional paper, UNESCO Publishing, Paris.

Galtung, J. (1982). Sport as carrier of deep culture and structure. *Current Research on Peace and Violence, 5,* 2–13.

Galtung, J., & Ruge, M. (1965). The structure of foreign news. *Journal of Peace Research, 1,* 64–90.

Gans, H. (1974). *Popular culture and high culture.* New York: Basic Books.

Gans, H. (1980). *Deciding what's news.* New York: Random House.

Geertz, C. (1973). *The interpretation of cultures.* New York: Basic Books.

Geist, C., & Nachbar, J. (Eds.). (1983). *The popular culture reader* (3rd ed.). Bowling Green, OH: Bowling Green State University Popular Press.

Gentile, M. C. (1985). *Film feminisms.* Westport, CT: Greenwood Press.

Gerbner, G. (1967). Mass media and human communication theory. In F. Dance (Ed.), *Human communication theory* (pp. 40–57). New York: Holt, Rinehart and Winston. Also in D. McQuail (Ed.), (1972), *Sociology of mass communications.* Harmondsworth, England: Penguin.

Gerbner, G. (1972). Violence in television drama: Trends and symbolic functions. In G. Comstock & E. Rubinstein (Eds.), *Media content and control: Television and social behavior* (Vol. 1). Washington, DC: U.S. Government Printing Office.

Gerbner, G. (1978). The dynamics of cultural resistance. In G. Tuchman, A. Daniels, & J. Benet (Eds.), *Hearth and home: Images of women in the mass media* (pp. 46–50). New York: Oxford University Press.

Gerbner G., & Siefert, M. (Eds.). (1983). Ferment in the field [Special issue]. *Journal of Communication, 33*(3).

Gerbner, G., & Signorielli, N. (1979). *Aging with television: Images of television drama and conceptions of social reality* (preview report to HEW). Philadelphia: University of Pennsylvania, Annenberg School of Communication.

Giddens, A. (1979). *Central problems in social theory.* London: Macmillan.

Gitlin, T. (1978). Media sociology: The dominant paradigm. *Theory & Society, 6*(2), 205–253.

Gitlin, T. (1983). *Inside prime time.* New York: Pantheon Books.

Gitlin, T. (Ed.). (1986). *Watching television.* New York: Pantheon Books.

Glasgow University Media Group. (1976). *Bad news.* London: Routledge & Kegan Paul.

Glasgow University Media Group. (1981). *More bad news.* London: Routledge & Kegan Paul.

Gledhill, C. (1980). *Klute* 1: A contemporary film noir and feminist criticism. In A. Kaplan (Ed.), *Women in film noir.* London: British Film Institute.

Goethals, G. (1981). *The TV ritual: Worship at the video altar.* Boston: Beacon Press.

Golding, P. (1977). Media professionalism in the Third World: The transfer of an ideology. In J. Curran, M. Gurevitch, & J. Woollacott (Eds.), *Mass communication and society.* London: Edward Arnold. Republished (1979, pp. 291–308), Newbury Park, CA: Sage.

Golding, P., & Murdock, G. (1979). Ideology and the mass media: The question of determination. In M. Barrett, P. Corrigan, A. Kuhn, & J. Wolff (Eds.), *Ideology and cultural production.* London: Croom Helm.

Goldman, W. (1983). *Adventures in the screen trade: A personal view of Hollywood and screenwriting.* New York: Warner Books.

Gottlieb, R., & Wolt, I. (1977). *Thinking big: The story of the* Los Angeles Times, *its publishers, and their influence on Southern California.* New York: Putnam.

Green, M., & MacColl, G. (1987). *Reagan's reign of error.* New York: Pantheon Books.

Greenberg, B., & Parker, E. (Eds.). (1965). *The Kennedy assassination and the American public.* Stanford, CA: Stanford University Press.

Guback, T. (1969). *The international film industry: Western Europe and America since 1945.* Bloomington: Indiana University Press.

Guback, T. (1974, Winter). Film as international business. *Journal of Communication,* pp. 90–101.

Guback, T. (1979). Theatrical film. In B. Compaine (Ed.), *Who owns the media?* (pp. 179–249). White Plains, NY: Knowledge Industries.

Gudorf, C. (1988, October). *Negotiating gender: Personal and social identity in a mass-mediated world.* Paper presented at Conference on Moral Imagination, Media, and the Shape of Public Culture, Marquette University, Milwaukee.

Gumpert, G., & Cathcart, R. (Eds.). (1986). *Inter-media: Interpersonal communications in a media world* (3rd ed.). New York: Oxford University Press.

Halberstam, D. (1979). *The powers that be.* New York: Knopf.

Hall, S. (1973). *Encoding and decoding in the television discourse.* Occasional paper, Centre for Contemporary Cultural Studies, University of Birmingham, England.

Hall, S. (1980). Cultural studies: Two paradigms. *Media, Culture and Society, 2*(2), 57–72. Also in R. Collins, J. Curran, N. Garnham, P. Scannell, P. Schlesinger, & C. Sparks (Eds.), (1986), *Media, culture and society: A critical reader* (pp. 33–48). Newbury Park, CA: Sage.

Hall, S. (1982). The rediscovery of 'ideology': Return of the repressed in media studies. In M. Gurevitch, T. Bennett, J. Curran, & J. Woollacott (Eds.), *Culture, society and the media* (pp. 56–90). London: Methuen.

Hall, S. (1986). Popular culture and the state. In T. Bennett, C. Mercer, & J. Woollacott (Eds.), *Popular culture and social relations.* Milton Keynes, England: Open University Press.

Hall, S., Chritcher, C., Jefferson, T., Clarke, J., & Roberts, B. (1978). *Policing the crisis: Mugging, the state, and law and order.* New York: Holmes & Meier.

Hallin, D. (1986). We keep America on top of the world. In T. Gitlin (Ed.), *Watching television* (pp. 9–41). New York: Pantheon Books.

Hamelink, C. (1983a). *Cultural autonomy in global communications: Planning national information policy.* New York: Longman.

Hamelink, C. (1983b). *Finance and information: A study of converging interests.* Norwood, NJ: Ablex.

Hartley, J. (1984). Encouraging signs: Television and the power of dirt, speech and scandalous categories. In W. Rowland & B. Watkins (Eds.), *Interpreting television: Current research perspectives* (pp. 119–141). Newbury Park, CA: Sage.

Haskell, M. (1979). Madame de: A musical passage. In P. Erens (Ed.), *Sexual stratagems: The world of women in film.* New York: Horizon.

Havelock, E. (1963). *Preface to Plato.* Cambridge, MA: Harvard University Press.

Hazan, B. (1982). *Olympic sports and propaganda games: Moscow 1980.* New Brunswick, NJ: Transaction Books.

Heath, S. (1981). *Jaws,* ideology, and film theory. In T. Bennett, S. Boyd-Bowman, C. Mercer, & J. Woollacott (Eds.), *Popular television and film.* London: British Film Institute.

Henry, B. (1984). *An approved history of the Olympic Games.* Sherman Oaks, CA: Alfred.

Himmelstein, H. (1984). *Television myth and American mind.* New York: Praeger.

Hinds, H. (1988). Popularity: The *sine qua non* of popular culture. In R. Browne & M. Fishwick (Eds.), *Symbiosis: Popular culture and other fields* (pp. 207–216). Bowling Green, OH: Bowling Green State University Popular Press.

Hirsch, E. D. (1987). *Cultural literacy: What every American needs to know.* New York: Random House.

Hirsch, P. (1977). Occupational, organizational, and institutional models in mass communication. In P. Hirsch, P. Miller, & F. Kline (Eds.), *Strategies for communication research* (pp. 13–42). Newbury Park, CA: Sage.

Hofstetter, C. R. (1976). *Bias in the news.* Columbus: Ohio State University Press.

Hoggart, R. (1957). *The uses of literacy: Aspects of working class life with special reference to publications and entertainments.* London: Essential Books. Also available in paper (1970), New York: Oxford University Press.

Holsti, O. R. (1969). Content analysis. In R. North, O. Holsti, M. Zaninovich, & D. Zinnes (Eds.), *Content analysis: A handbook with applications for the study of international crisis* (2nd ed.). Evanston, IL: Northwestern University Press..

Hovland, C., Janis, I., & Kelley, H. (1953). *Communication and persuasion.* New Haven, CT: Yale University Press.

Hovland, C., Lumsdaine, A., & Sheffield, F. (1949). *Experiments on mass communication.* Princeton, NJ: Princeton University Press.

Illinois State Museum. (1987). *The Lincoln image: Selections from the Vroegindewey-Wright Collection* [Exhibition]. Springfield, IL.

Innis, H. (1950). *Empire and communication.* Toronto: Clarendon Press.

Innis, H. (1951). *The bias of communication.* Toronto: University of Toronto Press.

Johnson, N. (1970). *How to talk back to your television set.* Boston: Atlantic/Little, Brown.

Jowett, G. (in press). *Mass culture and American media: The communication of culture.* Boston: Allen & Unwin.

Kaplan, E. A. (1983). *Women and film: Both sides of the camera.* New York: Methuen.

Katz, E. (1980). Media events: The sense of occasion. *Studies in Visual Communication, 6*(3), 84–89.

Katz, E., Blumler, J., & Gurevitch, M. (1973–74). Uses and gratifications research. *Public Opinion Quarterly, 37,* 509–523.

Keely, J. (1971). *The left-leaning antenna: Political bias in television.* New Rochelle, NY: Arlington House.

Kellner, D. (1979, May–June). TV, ideology, and emancipatory popular culture. *Socialist Review,* pp. 13–53.

Kellner, D. (1980). Television images, codes and messages. *Televisions, 7,* 1–19.

Kellner, D. (1981). Network television and American society: Introduction to a critical theory of television. *Theory & Society, 10,* 31–62. Also in E. Wartella & C. Whitney (Eds.), (1982), *Mass communication review yearbook* (pp. 411–442). Newbury Park, CA: Sage.

Kellner, D. (1982). Television, mythology and ritual. *Praxis, 6,* 133–155.

Kellner, D. (1984). *Herbert Marcuse and the crisis of Marxism.* London: Macmillan.

Kellner, D. (1988). Postmodernism as social theory: Some challenges and problems. *Theory, Culture and Society, 5,* 2–3.

Kennan, G. (1983). *The nuclear delusion: Soviet-American relations in the atomic age.* New York: Pantheon Books.

Klapp, O. (1963). *Heroes, villains, and fools: The changing American character.* Englewood Cliffs, NJ: Prentice-Hall.

Klapper, J. (1960). *The effects of mass communication.* New York: Free Press.

Koppel, T. (1987, July–August). The last word [Commencement address at Duke University, May]. *AGB Reports,* pp. 45–48.

Kracauer, S. (1947). *From Caligari to Hitler: A psychological history of the German film.* Princeton, NJ: Princeton University Press.

Kroker, A., & Cook, D. (1986). *The postmodern scene: Excremental culture and hyper-aesthetics.* New York: St. Martin's Press.

Kwitney, J. (1986). *Endless enemies: The making of an unfriendly world.* New York: Penguin.

LaFeber, W. (1971). *The origins of the Cold War, 1941–47: A historical problem with interpretations and documents.* New York: Oxford University Press.

La Fee, S. (1988, November 13). Most believe Oswald part of a conspiracy: San Diego poll results. *San Diego Union,* pp. D1, D7.

Lasch, C. (1978). *The culture of narcissism.* New York: Norton.

Lasswell, H. (1960). The structure and function of communication in society. In W. Schramm (Ed.), *Mass communication.* Urbana: University of Illinois Press. (Original work published 1948)

Lazarsfeld, P. (1941). Remarks on administrative and critical communication research. *Studies in Philosophy and Social Science, 9,* 2–16.

Lazarsfeld, P., Berelson, B., & Gaudet, H. (1944). *The people's choice.* New York: Harper & Row.

Lazarsfeld, P., & Merton, R. (1957). Mass communication, popular taste, and organized social action. In B. Rosenberg & D. M. White (Eds.), *Mass culture: The popular arts in America.* New York: Van Nostrand Reinhold. (Original work published 1948)

Lazere, D. (Ed.). *American media and mass culture: Left perspectives.* Berkeley: University of California Press.

Lefever, E. (1974). *TV and national defense.* Chicago: Institute for American Strategy.

Lenihan, J. (1985). *Showdown: Confronting modern America in the western film.* Urbana: University of Illinois Press.

Lenne, G. (1979). Monster and victim: Women in the horror film. In P. Erens (Ed.), *Sexual stratagems: The world of women in film* (pp. 31–40). New York: Horizon.

Lesage, J. (1979). Feminist film criticism: Theory and practice. In P. Erens (Ed.), *Sexual stratagems: The world of women in film* (pp. 41–51). New York: Horizon.

Malinowski, B. (1961). *Sex, culture and myth.* San Diego, CA: Harcourt Brace Jovanovich.

Levi-Strauss, C. (1966). *The savage mind.* Chicago: University of Chicago Press.

Levy, E. (1987). *And the winner is . . . : The history and politics of the Oscar awards.* New York: Ungar.

Lewis, P. (1987). Joke and anti-joke: Three Jews and a blindfold. *Journal of Popular Culture, 21*(1), 63–74.

Lichter, R., & Rothman, S. (1981, October–November). Media and business elites. *Public Opinion,* pp. 42–46, 59–60.

Lickona, T. (1985). *Raising good children.* New York: Bantam Books.

Lippmann, W. (1922). *Public opinion.* New York: Free Press.

Lodziak, C. (1986). *The power of television: A critical appraisal.* London: Frances Pinter.

Lowery, S., & DeFleur, M. D. (1983). *Milestones in mass communication research: Media effects.* New York: Longman.

Lull, J. (Ed.). (1987). *Popular Music and Communication.* Newbury Park, CA: Sage.

MacAloon, J. (Ed.). (1984). *Rite, drama, festival, spectacle: Rehearsals toward a theory of cultural performance.* Philadelphia: Institute for the Study of Human Issues.

MacDonald, D. (1983). *Against the American grain: Essays on the effects of mass culture.* New York: Da Capo.

Macdonald, J. F. (1985). *Television and the Red menace: The video road to Vietnam.* New York: Praeger.

Mander, J. (1978). *Four arguments for the elimination of television.* New York: Morrow Quill Paperbacks.

Mander, M. (1983). *Communications in transition: Issues and debates in current research.* New York: Praeger.

Marc, D. (1984). *Demographic vistas: Television in American culture.* Philadelphia: University of Pennsylvania Press.

Martin-Barbero, J. (1987). *De los medios a las mediaciones: Communicación, cultura y hegemonia.* Mexico and Barcelona: Ediciones Gustavo Gili.

Marx, K., & Engels, F. (1970). *The German ideology* (C. Arthur, ed.). New York: International Publishing.

Masterman, L. (Ed.). (1984). *Television mythologies: Stars, shows, and signs.* London: Comedia Publishing Group/MK Media Press.

McAnany, E. (1986). Cultural industries in international perspective: Convergence or conflict? In B. Dervin & M. Voigt (Eds.), *Progress in communication sciences* (Vol. 7). Norwood, NJ: Ablex.

McCombs, M., & Shaw, D. (1972). The agenda-setting function of mass media. *Public Opinion Quarterly, 36,* 176–187.

McGuire, W. (1986). The myth of massive impact: Savagings and salvagings. In G. Comstock (Ed.), *Public communication and behavior* (Vol. 1, pp. 173–257), Orlando, FL: Academic Press.

McLuhan, M. (1964). *Understanding media: The extensions of man.* New York: McGraw-Hill.

McNeil, J. C. (1975). Feminism, femininity, and the television series. *Journal of Broadcasting, 19*(3), 259–271.

McQuail, D. (1987). *Mass communication theory: An introduction* (2nd ed.). Newbury Park, CA: Sage.

McQuail, D., & Windahl, S. (1981). *Communication models for the study of mass communications.* New York: Longman.

Melody, W., & Mansell, R. (1983). The debate over critical administrative research: Circularity or challenge. *Journal of Communication, 33*(3), 103–116.

Metz, C. (1974). *Film language: A semiotics of the cinema* (M. Taylor, Trans.). New York: Oxford University Press.

Meyrowitz, J. (1985). *No sense of place: The impact of electronic media on social behavior.* New York: Oxford University Press.

Mills, C. W. (1956). *The Power Elite.* New York: Oxford University Press.

Montgomery, K. (1981). Gay activists and the networks. *Journal of Communication, 31,* 49–57.

Mosco, V. (1983). Critical research and the role of labor. *Journal of Communication, 33*(3), 237–248.

Mosco, V., & Wasko, J. (1985). *The critical communications review: Vol. 3. Popular culture and media events.* Norwood, NJ: Ablex.

Munsterberg, H. (1970). *The film: A psychological study.* New York: Dover. (Original work published 1916)

Murdock, G. (1982). Misrepresenting media sociology: A reply to Anderson and Sharrock. In D. Whitney, E. Wartella, & S. Windahl (Eds.), *Mass communication review yearbook* (Vol. 3, pp. 755–766). Newbury Park, CA: Sage.

Nachbar, J. (Ed.). (1978). *The popular culture reader.* Bowling Green, OH: Bowling Green State University Popular Press.

Newcomb, H. (1974). *TV: The most popular art.* New York: Anchor Books.

Newcomb, H. (1987). *Television: The critical view* (4th ed.). New York: Oxford University Press.

Newcomb, H. (1988). One night of prime time: An analysis of television's multiple voices. In J. Carey (Ed.), *Media, myths, and narratives: Television and the press* (pp. 88–112). Newbury Park, CA: Sage.

Newcomb, H., & Alley, R. (1983). *The producer's medium: Conversations with America's leading television producers.* New York: Oxford University Press.

Newcomb, H., & Hirsch, P. (1985). Television as a cultural forum: Implications for research. In M. Gurevitch & M. Levy (Eds.), *Mass communication review yearbook (Vol. 5,* pp. 275–280). Newbury Park, CA: Sage.

Nichols, B. (1981). *Ideology and the image: Social representation in the cinema and other media.* Bloomington: Indiana University Press.

Noelle-Neumann, E. (1973). Return to the concept of powerful mass media. *Studies in Broadcasting* [Tokyo: NHK], *9,* 67–112. Excerpted in E. Dennis, A. Ismach, & D. Gillmor (Eds.), (1978), *Enduring issues in mass communication.* St. Paul: West.

North's story (1987, July 27). *Los Angeles Times,* pp. 1, 3.

O'Connor, J. E. (Ed.). (1983). *American history/American television.* New York: Ungar.

Ong, W. (1967). *The presence of the word.* New Haven, CT: Yale University Press.

Ong, W. (1982). *Orality and literacy: The technologizing of the word.* New York: Methuen.

Ortega y Gasset, J. (1932). *Revolt of the masses.* New York: Norton.

Parenti, M. (1986). *Inventing reality: The politics of the mass media.* New York: St. Martin's Press.

Parkin, F. (1972). *Class inequality and political order.* London: Paladin.

Paull, P. (1987). What Reagan reads. *Propaganda Review, 1*(1), 30–31.

Paulsen, P. (1987, Summer/Fall). Sit-com sermons preach loving lessons. *Media and Values,* pp. 26–27.

Peterson, R. (Ed.). (1976). *The production of culture.* Newbury Park, CA: Sage.

Phelan, J. (1980). *Disenchantment: Meaning and morality in the media.* New York: Hastings.

Pious, R. (1979). *The American presidency.* New York: Basic Books.

Porter, W. (1976). *Assault on the media: The Nixon years.* Ann Arbor: University of Michigan Press.

Postman, N. (1985). *Amusing ourselves to death: Pubic discourse in the age of show business.* New York: Viking Press.

Radway, J. (1984). *Reading the romance: Feminism and the representation of women in popular culture.* Chapel Hill: University of North Carolina Press.

Ranney, A. (1983). *Channels of power: The impact of television on American politics.* New York: Basic Books/American Enterprise Institute.

Real, M. (1977). *Mass-mediated culture.* Englewood Cliffs, NJ: Prentice-Hall.

Real, M. (1980). Media theory: Contributions to an understanding of American mass communications. *American Quarterly, 32*(3), 238–258.

Real, M. (1984, Autumn). The debate on critical theory and the study of communication. *Journal of Communication,* pp. 72–80.

Real, M. (1985). Understanding Oscar: The Academy Awards telecast as international media event. In V. Mosco & J. Wasko (Eds.), *The critical communication review: Vol. 3 Popular culture and media events* (pp. 152–178). Norwood, NJ: Ablex.

Real, M. (1986, December). Demythologizing media: Recent writings in critical and institutional theory. *Critical Studies in Mass Communication,* pp. 459–486.

Real, M., & Christians, C. (1979, Winter). Jacques Ellul's contribution to critical media theory. *Journal of Communication,* pp. 83–93.

Real, M., & Hassett, C. (1981, May). Audience perceptions of the Academy Awards telecast. Paper presented at the meeting of the International Communication Association, Minneapolis.

Riordan, J. (1982). Great Britain and the Olympics: Victory for Olympism. *Current Research on Peace and Violence, 5,* 2–3, 144–158.

Rollins, P. (1983). Nightmare in red: A Cold War view of the Communist revolution. In J. E. O'Connor (Ed.), *American history/American television* (pp. 134–158). New York: Ungar.

Rosenberg, B., & White, D. M. (Eds.). (1957). *Mass culture: The popular arts in America.* New York: Free Press.

Rowland, W. (1983). *The politics of TV violence: Policy uses of communication research.* Newbury Park, CA: Sage.

Rusher, W. (1988). *The coming battle for the media: Curbing the power of the media elite.* New York: Morrow.

Ryan, M., & Kellner, D. (1987). *Camera politica: The politics and ideology of contemporary Hollywood films.* Bloomington: University of Indiana Press.

Sarris, A. (1966). *Cahiers du Cinema in English.* (Beginning in 1966 the journal *Cahiers,* published in New York, made Bazin and other French film critics available in English)

Schell, J. (1982). *The fate of the earth.* New York: Discus/Avon.

Schiller, H. (1981). *Who knows: Information in the age of the Fortune 500.* Norwood, NJ: Ablex.

Schiller, H. (1984). *Information and the crisis economy.* Norwood, NJ: Ablex.

Schramm, W., & Porter, W. (1982). *Men, women, messages, and media: A look at human communication* (2nd ed.). New York: Harper & Row.

Schudson, M. (1982, Fall). The politics of narrative form: The emergence of news conventions in print and television. *Daedalus,* pp. 97–111.

Schwartz, T. (1984). *Media: The second god.* New York: Doubleday.

Servan-Schreiber, J., with Crecine, B. (1986). *The knowledge revolution: New American challenge.* Pittsburgh: Carnegie Mellon Press.

Shannon, C., & Weaver, W. (1949). *The mathematical theory of communication.* Urbana: University of Illinois Press.

Shils, E. (1963). Mass society and its culture. *Daedalus, 89*(2). Reprinted in B. Rosenberg & D. M. White (Eds.), (1971), *Mass culture revisited* (pp. 61–84). New York: Van Nostrand Reinhold.

Siebert, F., Peterson, T., & Schramm, W. (1956). *Four theories of the press.* Urbana: University of Illinois Press.

Silverstone, R. (1981). *The message of television: Myth and narrative in contemporary culture.* London: Heinemann Educational Books.

Slack, J. (1984). *Communication technologies and society: Conceptions of causality and the politics of technological intervention.* Norwood, NJ: Ablex.

Slack, J., & Allor, M. (1983). The political and epistemological constituents of critical communication research. *Journal of Communication, 33*(3), 208–218.

Smythe, D. (1981). *Dependency road: Communications, capitalism, consciousness, and Canada.* Norwood, NJ: Ablex.

Smythe, D., & Van Dinh, T. (1983). On critical and administrative research: A new critical analysis. *Journal of Communication, 33*(3), 117–127.

Smythe, D., & Wilson, H. (1968). Cold War mindedness and the mass media. In N. Houghton (Ed.), *Struggle against history: U.S. foreign policy in an age of revolution* (pp. 59–78). New York: Washington Square Press.

Snead, J. (1985, June 20). *Recoding Blackness: The visual rhetoric of Black independent film.* Speech given in "The New American Filmmakers Series: Exhibitions of Independent Film and Video," No. 23, Whitney Museum of American Art, New York.

Snow, C. P. (1963). *The two cultures—and a second look.* New York: Mentor Books.

Stein, B. (1979). *The view from Sunset Boulevard: America as brought to you by the people who make television.* New York: Basic Books.

Sterling, C. (1984). *Electronic media: A guide to trends in broadcasting and newer technologies, 1920–1983.* New York: Praeger.

Taking the stand: The testimony of Lieutenant Colonel Oliver L. North. (1987). New York: Pocket Books.

Tan, A. (1985). *Mass communication theories and research* (2nd ed.). New York: Wiley.

Tedesco, N. (1974, Spring). Patterns in prime time. *Journal of Communication,* p. 120.

Thompson, E. P. (1963). *The making of the English working class.* London: Merlin.

Thorburn, D. (1988). Television as an aesthetic medium. In J. Carey (Ed.), *Media, myths, and narratives: Television and the press.* Newbury Park, CA: Sage.

Tocqueville, A. de. (1944). *Democracy in America* (2 vols.; B. Phillips, Ed.). New York: Knopf. (Original work published 1835, 1840)

Toffler, A. (1970). *Future shock.* New York: Random House.

Tuchman, G. (1978). *Making news: A study in the construction of reality.* New York: Free Press.

Tuchman, G., Daniels, A., & Benet, J. (Eds.). (1978). *Hearth and home: Images of women in the mass media.* New York: Oxford University Press.

Turner, V. (1977). *The ritual process: Structure and anti-structure.* Ithaca, NY: Cornell Paperbacks.

UNESCO (1986). *Global ritual: Olympic media coverage and international understanding* (M. Real, Ed.). San Diego, CA: San Diego State University, Department of Telecommunications and Film.

U.S. Civil Rights Commission. (1977). *Window dressing on the set: Women and minorities in television.* Washington, DC: U.S. Government Printing Office.

Wartella, E., & Reeves, B. (1985). Historical trends in research on children and the media: 1900–1960. *Journal of Communication, 35,* 118–133.

Wasko, J. (1982). *Movies and money: Financing the American film industry.* Norwood, NJ: Ablex.

Weibel, K. (1978). *Mirror, mirror: The image of women in two hundred years of American popular culture.* New York: Doubleday.

Westley, B., & MacLean, D. (1957). A conceptual model for mass communication research. *Journalism Quarterly, 34,* 31–38.

Whannel, G. (1984). The television spectacular. In A. Tomlinson & G. Whannel (Eds.), *Five ring circus: Money, power and politics at the Olympic Games.* London: Pluto Press.

Whelan, J., & Dixon, M. (1986). *The Soviet Union in the Third World: Threat to world peace?* Washington, DC: Pergamon-Brassey International Defense Publishers.

White, A. (1985, October). Telling it on the mountain. *Film Comment,* pp. 39–41.

White, D. M. (1950). The "gatekeeper": A case study in the selection of news. *Journalism Quarterly, 27,* 383–390.

White, D. M. (1957). Mass culture in America: Another point of view. In B. Rosenberg & D. M. White (Eds.), *Mass culture: The popular arts in America.* New York: Free Press.

White, D. M. (1971). Mass culture revisited II. In B. Rosenberg & D. M. White (Eds.), *Mass culture revisited.* New York: Van Nostrand Reinhold.

White, R. (1983). Mass communication and culture: Transition to a new paradigm. *Journal of Communication, 33*(3), 279–301.

Williams, R. (1958). *Culture and society: 1780–1950.* New York: Columbia University Press.

Williams, R. (1962). *The long revolution.* New York: Columbia University Press.

Williams, R. (1977). *Marxism and literature.* New York: Oxford University Press.

Williams, R. (1981). *The sociology of culture.* New York: Schocken Books.

Winn, M. (1975). *The plug-in drug.* New York: Viking.

Wollen, P. (1973). *Signs and meaning in the cinema.* Bloomington: Indiana University Press.

Woodruff, J., with Maxa, K. (1982). *This is Judy Woodruff at the White House.* Reading, MA: Addison-Wesley.

Woodward, R. (1987). *Veil: The secret wars of the CIA, 1981–1987.* New York: Simon & Schuster.

Wright, C. (1959). *Mass communication: A sociological perspective.* New York: Random House.

Wright, C. (1986). Mass communication rediscovered: Its past and future in American sociology. In S. Ball-Rokeach & M. Cantor (Eds.), *Media, audience, and social structure* (pp. 22–33). Newbury Park, CA: Sage.

Index

About the Author

MICHAEL R. REAL is Professor and Chair of Telecommunications and Film at San Diego State University. He is the author of *Mass-Mediated Culture* (1977) and numerous studies of mass media and contemporary culture in *Journal of Communication, Journal of Popular Culture, Media Development, Journalism Quarterly, American Quarterly, Newsday,* and other journals and popular media. He has also produced television series on problems of science and technology and issues of aging.

NOTES

NOTES

NOTES

NOTES

NOTES